MULTICULTURAL EDUCATION SERIES
James A. Banks, Series Editor

Teaching Democracy:
Unity and Diversity in Public Life
WALTER C. PARKER

The Making – *and Remaking* – of a Multiculturalist
CARLOS E. CORTÉS

Transforming the Multicultural Education of Teachers:
Theory, Research, and Practice
MICHAEL VAVRUS

Learning to Teach for Social Justice
LINDA DARLING-HAMMOND, JENNIFER FRENCH, AND
SILVIA PALOMA GARCIA-LOPEZ, EDITORS

Culture, Difference, and Power
CHRISTINE E. SLEETER

Learning and Not Learning English:
Latino Students in American Schools
GUADALUPE VALDÉS

Culturally Responsive Teaching:
Theory, Research, and Practice
GENEVA GAY

The Children Are Watching:
How the Media Teach About Diversity
CARLOS E. CORTÉS

Race and Culture in the Classroom:
Teaching and Learning Through Multicultural Education
MARY DILG

The Light in Their Eyes:
Creating Multicultural Learning Communities
SONIA NIETO

Reducing Prejudice and Stereotyping in Schools
WALTER STEPHAN

We Can't Teach What We Don't Know:
White Teachers, Multiracial Schools
GARY R. HOWARD

Educating Citizens in a Multicultural Society
JAMES A. BANKS

teaching democracy

Unity and Diversity in Public Life

WALTER C. PARKER

TEACHERS
COLLEGE
PRESS

Teachers College, Columbia University
New York and London

370.115
A244t
2003

Published by Teachers College Press, 1234 Amsterdam Avenue, New York, NY 10027

Copyright © 2003 by Teachers College, Columbia University

Library of Congress Cataloging-in-Publication Data

Parker, Walter.
    Teaching democracy : unity and diversity in public life / Walter C. Parker.
       p. cm.
    Includes bibliographical references and index.
    ISBN 0-8077-4272-4 (paper : alk. paper) — ISBN 0-8077-4273-2 (cloth : alk. paper)
    1. Citizenship—Study and teaching—United States. 2. Democracy—Study and teaching—United States. 3. Civics—Study and teaching—United States. 4. Education—Aims and objectives—United States. I. Title.
LC1091 .P37   2002
370.11'5—dc21   2002075236

ISBN 0-8077-4272-4 (paper)
ISBN 0-8077-4273-2 (cloth)

Printed on acid-free paper
Manufactured in the United States of America

10   09   08   07   06   05   04   03   8   7   6   5   4   3   2   1

for my teachers in the public schools of Englewood, Colorado

Contents

Series Foreword

The nation's deepening ethnic texture, interracial tension and conflict, and the increasing percentage of students who speak a first language other than English make multicultural education imperative in the 21st century. The U.S. Census Bureau estimated that people of color made up 28% of the nation's population in 2000 (U.S. Census Bureau, 1998). The Census predicted that they would make up 38% of the nation's population in 2025 and 47% in 2050.

American classrooms are experiencing the largest influx of immigrant students since the beginning of the 20th century. About a million immigrants are making the United States their home each year (Martin & Midgley, 1999). More than seven and one-half million legal immigrants settled in the United States between 1991 and 1998, most of whom came from nations in Latin America and Asia (Riche, 2000). A large but undetermined number of undocumented immigrants also enter the United States each year. The influence of an increasingly ethnically diverse population on the nation's schools, colleges, and universities is, and will continue to be, enormous.

In 1998, 34.9% of the students enrolled in U.S. public schools were students of color; this percentage is increasing each year, primarily because of the growth in the percentage of Latino students (Martinez & Curry, 1999). In some of the nation's largest cities and metropolitan areas, such as Chicago, Los Angeles, Washington, D.C., New York, Seattle, and San Francisco, half or more of the public school students are students of color. During the 1998–1999 school year, students of color made up 63.1% of the student population in the public schools of California, the nation's most populous state (California State Department of Education, 2000).

Language and religious diversity is also increasing among the nation's student population. Sixteen percent of school-age youth lived in homes in which English was not the first language in 1990 (U.S. Census Bureau, 1998). Harvard professor Diana L. Eck (2001) calls the United States the "most religiously diverse nation on earth" (p. 4). Most teachers now in the classroom and in teacher education programs are likely to have students from diverse ethnic, racial, language, and religious groups in their classrooms during their careers. This is true for both inner-city and suburban teachers.

An important goal of multicultural education is to improve race relations and to help all students acquire the knowledge, attitudes, and skills needed to participate in cross-cultural interactions and in personal, social, and civic action that will help make our nation more democratic and just. Multicultural education is consequently as important for middle-class White suburban students as it is for students of color who live in the inner-city. Multicultural education fosters the public good and the overarching goals of the commonwealth.

The major purpose of the *Multicultural Education Series* is to provide preservice educators, practicing educators, graduate students, scholars, and policy makers with an interrelated and comprehensive set of books that summarizes and analyzes important research, theory, and practice related to the education of ethnic, racial, cultural, and language groups in the United States and the education of mainstream students about diversity. The books in the Series provide research, theoretical, and practical knowledge about the behaviors and learning characteristics of students of color, language minority students, and low-income students. They also provide knowledge about ways to improve academic achievement and race relations in educational settings.

The definition of multicultural education in the *Handbook of Research on Multicultural Education* (Banks & Banks, 2001) is used in the Series: "multicultural education is a field of study designed to increase educational equity for all students that incorporates, for this purpose, content, concepts, principles, theories, and paradigms from history, the social and behavioral sciences, and particularly from ethnic studies and women studies" (p. xii). In the Series, as in the Handbook, multicultural education is considered a "metadiscipline."

The dimensions of multicultural education, developed by Banks (2001) and described in the *Handbook of Research on Multicultural Education,* provide the conceptual framework for the development of the books in the Series. They are: *content integration, the knowledge construction process, prejudice reduction, an equity pedagogy,* and *an empowering school culture and social structure.* To implement multicultural education effectively, teachers and administrators must attend to each of the five dimensions of multicultural education. They should use content from diverse groups when teaching concepts and skills, help students to understand how knowledge in the various disciplines is constructed, help students to develop positive intergroup attitudes and behaviors, and modify their teaching strategies so that students from different racial, cultural, language, and social-class groups will experience equal educational opportunities. The total environment and culture of the school must also be transformed so that students from diverse groups will experience equal status in the culture and life of the school.

Although the five dimensions of multicultural education are highly interrelated, each requires deliberate attention and focus. Each book in the series focuses on one or more of the dimensions, although each book deals with all of them to some extent because of the highly interrelated characteristics of the dimensions.

As the ethnic, racial, language, cultural, and religious texture of the United States continues to deepen and become more complex, the challenge of constructing a democratic and just society increases. However, democracy and diversity within the United States have existed in tension and contradiction since the nation's founding. The gradual institutionalization of slavery in the 17th century posed a tremendous challenge to the ideals of democracy, freedom, and justice that are codified in the Declaration of Independence, the Constitution, and the Bill of Rights (Berry, 1995). At the nation's founding, these ideals were restricted to White males with property. The three-fifths clause in the Constitution, which stipulated that three-fifths of a state's slaves were to be counted for congressional representation, was an attempt by the Founding Fathers to embrace two contradictory ideals—democracy and slavery.

Throughout its history, the United States has attempted to reconcile the idea of freedom with institutionalized racism and inequality. Indian removal in the 1830s, the interment of Japanese Americans during World War II, and apartheid in the South from the post-Reconstruction period to the 1950s are examples of historical events that contradicted American democratic ideals. Pak (2002) describes how Japanese American schoolchildren in Seattle were interned while they were being taught lessons about freedom and democracy in America.

Although democracy and freedom are frequently contradicted in practice in U. S. society, they are powerful American ideals which are sources of hope and possibility. Myrdal (1944) believed that American creed values such as justice, equality, and freedom had the potential to foster social and humane change because most Americans have internalized these values even though their behavior frequently contradicts them. The discrepancy between ideals and behavior, Myrdal believed, creates an American dilemma that contains the seeds for change. The civil rights movement of the 1960s and 1970s, in several important ways, exemplifies Myrdal's analysis.

Walter Parker, the author of this timely, engaging, and significant book, advances a theory and a teaching strategy—deliberation—for deepening democracy in our schools and society, for enhancing citizen participation, and for extending democracy to cultural, ethnic, racial, and language communities. Parker describes why a political democracy must embrace cultural democracy. Diverse democratic nation-states must legitimize diversity and allow individuals and groups to maintain aspects of their cultural, ethnic, language, and religious identities. In the multicultural nation-state that Parker envisions, citizens with cultural identities freely participate in the nation's civic community, share power within it, and influence state and national policy. Unity and diversity coexist in a delicate and complex balance.

Parker's position belies the critics of multicultural education who view it as a divisive force within the commonwealth (Schlesinger, 1991). He convincingly argues that multicultural education and citizenship education are "not two things but two aspects of the same thing." Parker's vision is consistent with Will Kymlicka's (1995) idea of multicultural citizenship as well as with the needs of a diverse democratic nation-state such as the United States.

Parker's book is not only theoretically strong and well argued; it is also highly practical and readable. Parker's ability to link sound theory with powerful teaching ideas and strategies derives from his years as an astute public school social studies teacher, a gifted teacher of methods courses at the university level, and his wide and thoughtful reading of the social science literature. This book will enrich the conversation about democracy, diversity, and deliberation in the schools, and will hopefully contribute to closing the gap between the nation's democratic ideals and practices.

James A. Banks
Series Editor

REFERENCES

Banks, J. A. (2001). Multicultural education: Historical development, dimensions, and practice. In J. A. Banks & C. A. M. Banks (Eds.), *Handbook of research on multicultural education* (pp. 3–24). San Francisco: Jossey-Bass.

Banks, J. A., & Banks, C. A. M. (Eds.). (2001). *Handbook of research on multicultural education*. San Francisco: Jossey-Bass.

Berry, M. F. (1995). Slavery, the Constitution, and the founding fathers. In J. H. Franklin & G. R. McNeil (Eds.), *African Americans and the living Constitution* (pp. 11–32). Washington, DC : Smithsonian Institution Press.

California State Department of Education (2000). On-line; available: http://data1.cde.ca.gov/dataquest

Eck, D. L. (2001). *A new religious America: How a "Christian country" has become the world's most religiously diverse nation*. New York: HarperCollins.

Kymlicka, W. (1995). *Multicultural citizenship: A liberal theory of minority rights*. New York: Oxford University Press.

Martin, P., & Midgley, E. (1999). Immigration to the United States. *Population Bulletin, 54* (2), 1–44. Washington, DC: Population Reference Bureau.

Martinez, G. M., & Curry A. E. (1999, September). *Current population reports: School enrollment-social and economic characteristics of students* (update). Washington, DC: U.S. Census Bureau.

Myrdal, G., with Sterner, R., & Rose, A. (1944). *An American dilemma: The Negro problem and modern democracy.* New York: Harper & Brothers.

Pak, Y. K. (2002). *Wherever I go, I will always be a loyal American: Schooling Seattle's Japanese-Americans during World War II.* New York: Routledge.

Riche, M. F. (2000). America's diversity and growth: Signposts for the 21st century. *Population Bulletin, 55* (2), 1–43. Washington, DC: Population Reference Bureau.

Schlesinger, A. M. Jr. (1991). *The disuniting of America: Reflections on a multicultural society.* Knoxville, TN: Whittle Direct Books.

United States Census Bureau (1998). *Statistical abstract of the United States* (118th edition). Washington, DC: U.S. Government Printing Office.

Preface

Idiot (*idiotes*) was a term of reproach in ancient Greece reserved for persons who paid no attention to public affairs and engaged only in self-interested or private pursuits, never mind the public interest—the civic space and the common good. This book is about the role schools can play in the contemporary struggle against idiocy, that is, the quest for a just democracy in a diverse society. It is at once a book about citizenship education and multicultural education. Democratic character development (moral education) is central to both of these because neither democratic living nor justice appears magically out of the blue. Both are hard-won cognitive, moral, and social achievements; none of us wanders into them accidentally, easily, or alone. Access to such an education is a central topic, too, because it does not now widely exist nor can it ever be assumed in a society where educational opportunity is so unequally allocated, school funding so inadequate and wildly uneven, and where economic motives for education so often overtake liberal (mind-expanding) and public (community-building) purposes.

Acknowledgments. Over the last few years, as this book has come together, I have been fortunate to have colleagues in several nations—educators and social scientists alike—who are deeply concerned about inequality and discrimination in societies that are trying to educate for justice and democracy. I am grateful for their camaraderie. Closer to home, I want to acknowledge James A. Banks, whose passion for equity, social justice, history, and the social sciences is transforming curriculum and instruction in the United States. I could not have a dearer or more stimulating colleague.

Let me thank my editor at Teachers College Press, Brian Ellerbeck, for his enthusiasm for the manuscript and for seeing it through to publication. I want to thank also the blind reviewers of the initial book proposal who were most encouraging generally and welcomed especially the revival of the concept *idiotes*. Of course, all errors of fact or judgment here remain my own.

I want to acknowledge the friendship and wise counsel of Carole Hahn, Patricia Avery, Lynn Nelson, Nathaniel Jackson, Patricia Wasley, Anna Ochoa, Nancy Beadie, Gene Edgar, Joe Jenkins, Steve Kerr, Diana Hess,

Jonathan Miller-Lane, Yih-Sheue Lin, John King, Wendy Ewbank, and, as always, Lynn Parker and Sheila Valencia.

A number of the ideas in this book have been worked out in papers I have written over the past few years. Chapter 2 is based on "Advanced Ideas about Democracy: Toward a Pluralist Conception of Citizen Education," published in *Teachers College Record 98* (1), 1996. It is adapted here with permission of Blackwell Publishing. Chapter 3 is a version of a chapter by the same name that was published in W. B. Stanley (Ed.), *Critical Issues in Social Studies Research* (Greenwich, CT: Information Age, 2001), and is adapted here with permission of the publisher. Chapter 4 is based on "Justice, Social Studies, and the Subjectivity/Structure Problem," published in 1986 in *Theory and Research in Social Education, 24* (4), by the College and University Faculty Assembly of the National Council for the Social Studies, and is adapted here with permission of the publisher. Chapter 6 is a version of an article that also appeared in that journal. That version was coauthored with my colleague from the Evans School of Public Affairs here at the University of Washington, Bill Zumeta. Its title was "Toward An Aristocracy of Everyone: Policy Study in the High School Curriculum" (vol. 27, no. 1, 1999). It is adapted with permission of the publisher. Finally, Chapter 7 appeared in a somewhat different form as a chapter in J. J. Patrick and R. S. Leming (Eds.), *Principles and Practices of Democracy in the Education of Social Studies Teachers: Civic Learning in Teacher Education*, Vol. 1 (Bloomington, IN: ERIC Clearinghouse for Social Studies/Social Science Education, 2001).

W.C.P.
Seattle, Washington

Introduction

Democratic living is not given in nature, like gold or water. It is a social construct, like a skyscraper, school playground, or new idea. Accordingly, there can be no democracy without its builders, caretakers, and change agents: democratic citizens. These citizens are constructs, too. Who "builds" and cares for them? Parents, peers, educators, corporations, media, social forces, and structures—all these are responsible, but among them educators are the primary stewards of democracy. They must do what no one else in society has to do: intentionally specify the democratic ideal sufficiently to make it a reasonably distinct curriculum target, one that will justify selecting from the universe of possibilities a manageable set of subject matters, materials, instructional methods, modes of classroom interaction, and school experiences. Do they aim toward a democracy that fears diversity and tries to assimilate it? Do they envision citizens who mainly vote and pay taxes? Or are they imagining a stronger democracy than this?

Stronger forms of democratic life converge on the moral conviction that the democratic project can and must be deepened and extended. Stronger forms challenge the notion that citizens need only to elect representatives occasionally and then return to "private life." Also challenged are the racism, religious intolerance, sexism, classism, and other prejudices and social conditions that restrict access to democracy and its creation. Democracy's defining attribute is popular sovereignty (i.e., self-government), but this idea needs to be fleshed out if it is to serve as a curriculum goal. For example, does democracy pervade social life—in schools, neighborhoods, and workplaces? Are cultural groups free to express their interests in the political process and use their language? Is there free and open public discussion? Is there liberty and privacy? Is there equality of opportunity and freedom from exploitation? Are ordinary citizens expected to know justice and injustice when they see them?

I suggest in this book that cultural pluralism and equality are best served by nurturing the kind of democratic political community that in turn protects and nurtures cultural pluralism and equality, which in turn protect and nurture a democratic political community. And, I propose practical tools with which educators can draw children creatively and productively into this way of life, this civic culture. These rest on five assertions. First, democratic education is not a neutral project, but one that tries to predispose citizens to principled reasoning and just ways of being with one another. Second, educators need simultaneously to engage in multicultural education and citizenship education. These are not two things but two aspects of the same thing. Third, the diversity that schools contain makes extraordinarily fertile soil for democratic education. Schooling is the first sustained *public* experience for children, and it affords a rich opportunity to nurture public virtue—for example, kindness and tolerance and the disposition and skills to dialogue across difference. Fourth, this dialogue plays an essential and vital role in democratic education, moral development, and public policy. In a diverse society, dialogue is the avenue of choice to enlightened action. Fifth, the access/inclusion problem that we (still) face today is one of extending democratic education to students who typically are not afforded it. This includes most students, I believe. Some are members of historically oppressed groups, and some are members of the mainstream culture and affluent groups whose democratic education is superficial and trivial. Not only should tools of power be shared with those who now don't have them; those who do have them must be educated to use them fairly and compassionately. Democratic education is for everyone, and this certainly includes those who (for now) have the most power, for they are in a position to do the most harm when they lack virtue. Just as multicultural education is not only for "others," neither is citizenship education.

Several concepts carry the book: democracy, diversity, and deliberation along with idiocy (selfishness) and its opposite, citizenship (public engagement). As well, justice (fairness) and interbeing (mutuality) are central concepts, for they guide, challenge, and realize the effort to shape public life in general and schools in particular. Social position (group circumstance) and individual moral development (character education) are core concepts, too, and the relationship between these two is one of the most engaging and challenging puzzles that students of any age can confront.

My overall aim cannot be said better than did John Dewey in 1916: "Instead of reproducing current habits, better habits shall be formed, and thus the future adult society be an improvement of their own" (1916/1985a, p. 85). Dewey understood how far we were from creating democratic education:

> [W]e are doubtless far from realizing the potential efficacy of education as a constructive agency of improving society, from realizing that it represents not only a development of children and youth but also of the future society of which they will be the constituents. (p. 85)

Chapter 1 sets the stage by specifying the curriculum target, citizenship, and its opposite, "idiocy." Both are defined against the standard set by the likes of Martin Luther King Jr., whose reasoning about justice and democracy is clearly on display in his actions, speeches, and writing. I feature his "Letter from Birmingham Jail" (1963a) but also the speeches *Beyond Vietnam* (1967a), *Where Do We Go From Here?* (1967b), and others not only in Chapter 1 but throughout the book. They are treated as exemplars of the non-idiotic life. By itself, the "Letter" has only a handful of peers in the democratic canon, mainly the one he admired and cited: the U.S. Constitution.

A word is needed about choosing King. I understand that some people on both sides of the racial divide have become tired of King, concluding that King the Legend prevents a genuine hearing, let alone scrutiny, of his conduct and the ideas and values that shaped it. Others believe that the world doesn't need another White author, like me, taking refuge in what they think is a "safe" figure like King. Michael Eric Dyson (2001) worries that Blacks and Whites alike revere him too much, drowning his humanity and his radicalism in a chorus of half-hearted, iconic "I Have a Dream" ceremonies, then returning to business as usual. I believe there are enormously good reasons for choosing King: his extraordinary moral wisdom and its availability to us in several media; his unembarrassed advocacy of love and his fearless nonviolent direct action; his wide appeal to people not only in this nation but throughout the world; and the fact that he has already gotten a great deal of attention, which means that most readers already have some knowledge of his work on which we can build here.

King's work should not be jettisoned; to the contrary, our comprehension of it should be deepened and challenged. That way, we will see that King was no mere "dreamer," as any serious reading of his thinking and action makes entirely clear (e.g., Johnson, 1998). Andrew Young (2001) writes that King's "voice was more than the communication of intellectual ideals and spiritual vision. It was a call for action. . . ." (p. vii). This was not action that he asked of others but spared himself. He personally led much of it—on his feet, in jail, under surveillance, sleepless, in countless planning meetings, and at the podium—for 14 years until his assassination in Memphis on April 4, 1968, at the young age of 38 years. "For Martin," Young continues, "social justice would not 'roll in on the wings of inevitability,' but would come through struggle and sacrifice" (p. x).

In Chapter 2, "Democracy and Difference," I try to understand the unity-diversity confusion that can be found in popular media as well as in multicultural- and citizenship-education initiatives, which undermines the coherence and effectiveness of each. I show how *unum* and *pluribus* are interdependent aspects of a vibrant democratic life in a diverse society. Three ideas—three building blocks for a stronger conception of democratic citizenship and, therefore, a better target for curriculum planning—are put forward. One involves the tension between engagement in public life and spectatorship or, worse, idiotic withdrawal. The second concerns the tension between viewing democracy as an accomplishment needing only protection and viewing it as a way of life—a path that people try to walk together. The third deals with the tension between pluralism and assimilation. At issue here is the relationship of diversity to a democratic political community. I argue that the two are interdependent and that the ideal relationship of *unum* and *pluribus* is this: a unity of individuals alongside a plurality of groups, a singular citizen identity alongside a buzzing array of cultural identities. This relationship can be called multicultural citizenship (Kymlicka, 1995) or, when properly understood, simply *democratic citizenship*.

In Chapter 3, "Toward Enlightened Political Engagement," I specify the mission of democratic education as enlightened political engagement. The term "political engagement" refers to the action domain of citizenship, from voting to nonviolent civil disobedience. "Democratic enlightenment" refers to the knowledge and commitments that direct this engagement: knowledge of the ideals of democratic living, including the ability to discern just from unjust action and the commitment to recognize difference and fight prejudice. Without democratic enlightenment, participation cannot be trusted: the freedom marchers of the Civil Rights movement "participated," but so did Hitler's thugs and so did (and does) the Ku Klux Klan. Participation without democratic enlightenment can be worse than apathy.

Schooling has long been associated with enlightened political engagement. School attendance, in fact, is its most powerful predictor. Curriculum battles have raged for decades over how best to increase this "school effect" (e.g., from requiring particular texts to banning them; from integrating schools to creating separate "academies" for girls and African American boys). Meanwhile, much goes on outside school that is powerfully educative, too—membership in voluntary and involuntary associations especially. Whether an adolescent is active in 4-H or a religious group on the voluntary side, or born into poverty or affluence on the involuntary side, her ability to learn about and influence the political system is affected, as is her ability to cope with and appreciate diversity.

Chapter 4, "Justice: Two Views," addresses the question of what we mean when we say "justice," and it asks whether schools should teach children to respect justice even when it contradicts conventional ways of doing things. *Enlightened* political engagement is, if anything, just. It may not be caring; one may not much care for one's political opponents or persons whose beliefs and customs are revolting to one's own sensibilities. The monogamist may not much care for the polygamist, the matriarch for the patriarch, the cultural nationalist for the cultural pluralist, the orthodox Muslim for the orthodox Jew. Still, one's political engagement must be steered by something, and justice is the better compass. Otherwise, how will one determine which struggles to support? How can one know which parts of the legal system to defend and which parts to change? Without justice, cooperative living in a diverse society is impossible. Still, what *is* justice?

I proceed by looking through two lenses. One shows justice to be a particular kind of judgment and action that a morally principled individual is capable of rendering, such as when King and Socrates landed themselves in jail by breaking local statutes. The other reveals justice to be a particular social formation—a way of organizing society—such as when King argues in his penultimate speech, *Where Do We Go From Here?* (1967b), that American society needs to be "restructured." The first lens, drawing on cognitive-moral developmental theory, is placed alongside one that draws on sociological theory, generally, and historical materialism, particularly. Both theories are coherent and convincing in their own ways. A powerful tension arises between individualistic and socialistic conceptions of justice, and I suggest, with King, that it invites a "both/and" synthesis rather than an "either/or" choice.

In Chapter 5, "Can We Talk?", deliberative discussion is defined, and I explore its promise as the centerpiece of democratic education in schools. Deliberation is discussion with right action in mind. Its purpose is enlightened political engagement. *Deliberation achieves its democratic and moral legitimacy on the assumption that if diverse people are to exercise power well, then they must reason together about the power they are exercising.* Through the give and take of deliberation and the conflicts among beliefs and social perspectives that inevitably surface when there are diverse participants and when this diversity is seen and heard, people's understandings can be enlarged and enlightened, public policies can be subjected to scrutiny, and more just decisions can be encouraged. Clearly, this is an ideal. Oppression and discrimination are alive and well in many forms, both subtle and gross, and they often prevent this kind of free and inclusive deliberation. But this is no reason to abandon the struggle. It is all the more reason to pursue it wholeheartedly.

This chapter, the heart of the book and its longest chapter, shows how democratic educators can exploit the fact that schools are public places in which diverse populations of young people are congregated. Three keys are detailed: Increase the variety and frequency of interaction among students who are different from one another; orchestrate these contacts to foster deliberation about the problems that inevitably arise from the friction of that interaction; and strive to develop communicative competence, particularly the receptive practice of listening across social perspectives. Diversity, I will show, is a deliberative asset to be nurtured, not a problem to be overcome.

Chapter 6, "Making Publics, Finding Problems, Imagining Solutions," extends the work in Chapter 5 on building a deliberative curriculum for public schools, and the work in Chapter 4 on the quest for social justice. The field of study most relevant to this objective is the one known for centuries as *the practical* (James, 1958; Schwab, 1970). Its subject matter is shared problems and its methods are research and deliberation in tandem: identifying and framing problems, mapping the array of social perspectives on them, listening intently to these perspectives, deliberating through them, bringing every bit of relevant knowledge to bear, and imagining solutions (making decisions) that are revised and clarified in the course of working toward them.

I outline a high school course that engages students in this work while teaching them how. A public problem, one after another, is tackled. Strategic attention is paid to the problem and to those affected by it. A conceptual framework is deployed to enlighten collective work on the problem, spreading deliberators' attention across its multiple dimensions and across the multiple perspectives of those affected. It is a political and pluralistic model, so it presumes disagreement and struggle. It does not deny the social positions of stakeholders. While related instructional models are described elsewhere in the book (Just Community, Student Advisory Councils, Structured Academic Controversy), this one is treated in greater depth so as to display clearly the ideas, values, and procedures involved.

In Chapter 7, "Leading Discussions," I share methods my students and I have been exploring to help teachers and other educators lead productive face-to-face discussions about controversial issues and texts. Leading discussions, whether deliberations or discussions of other kinds, is difficult, as any one knows who has tried and is honest. Those who are demonstrably very good at it speak mainly of their deficiencies. It is worth the effort, however. Discussion is important to understand and do, regularly, in classrooms and other educational settings, as a means of deepening and widening one's understanding of the matter at hand, as an inclusive and democratic way of being together, and as a way of choosing better futures.

In this chapter, I distinguish between deliberation and a complementary mode of discussion, the seminar, and describe how I go about teaching both to beginning teachers. I have found the distinction to be a powerful one for classroom teachers because two basic purposes of discussion, each vitally important, are contrasted and clarified. While a deliberation is discussion aimed at making decisions about what action to take, a seminar is discussion aimed at enlarging participants' understandings of powerful issues, ideas, and values. One mode of dialogue without the other—understanding without action, action without understanding—is not desirable.

In the book's final chapter, "Access to a Non-Idiotic Education," the problem of winning admittance to a reasonably high-quality education for democracy is addressed directly. A central dilemma in any modern (diverse, industrialized) capitalist democracy is the disjuncture between the ideology of equal opportunity for vertical mobility and the limited number of actual opportunities in the upper reaches of organizational hierarchies. The American dream is promoted as if it could be granted to all even though, clearly, it cannot; situations of opportunity are also situations of denial. Racism and other forms of discrimination, combined with poverty, rig the competition for upward mobility in ways that benefit children from dominant groups, placing them disproportionately in the few spots at upper ends of the various hierarchies—board rooms, laboratories, and legislatures, for example. Even these advantaged children, however, are not necessarily getting a high-quality education for democracy, which is a problem of its own sort. After all, they will land in positions of considerable power with the means to do considerable harm or good. With high-quality education across the board, more persons are qualified for upward mobility, making competition for the top spots more fair, making barriers to fairness more transparent, and making everyone, regardless of position, better educated in the ends and means of democratic living.

From Idiocy to Citizenship

Somehow, in a time like our own, when the capacity for imagining
appears to be endangered, both by the technology of television and
by the poverty of public dreams, it seems especially crucial to
introduce our students to the meaning of such a question as "Is
America possible?"
                                            —Vincent Harding (1990, p. 178)

James A. Banks suggests that "multicultural education fosters the public
good and the overarching goals of the commonwealth" (Series Foreword,
this volume). I want to ask, how? How does multicultural education accomplish this? Banks suggests an answer: The central purpose of multicultural education is "to improve race relations and to help all students
acquire the knowledge, attitudes, and skills needed to participate in cross-
cultural interactions and in personal, social, and civic action that will help
make our nation more democratic and just."

Clearly, multicultural education is for *everyone*, for the middle and
upper classes as well as the poor, for suburbanites and city dwellers, for
White students as well as students of color, for teachers as well as students,
for parents as well as children, for "our children" as well as "other people's
children" (Delpit, 1995)—for everyone who will have neighbors and be a
neighbor, for everyone who will go to work, raise children, vote, argue over
common problems, and serve on juries. Multicultural education is integral
and indispensable to the education of *democratic citizens*: people who are
capable of democratic living, who want it, and who are determined to
achieve it—to work toward the fuller realization of democratic ideals.

The reverse is true as well. As multicultural education fosters the development of democratic citizens, so does democratic citizenship education foster pluralism—specifically, a culturally, racially, and politically
diverse society. Democratic citizenship education seeks to teach, among
other things, that diversity *is* a social fact, that it *is* a social good, *why* this
is so, and *how* diversity and democracy require one another. It seeks to do
this by educating young and old alike in the arts of democratic living, which
include, centrally, an understanding of both *pluribus* (the many) and *unum*
(the one), and an understanding that the two are, in fact, interdependent.

1

The very idea that *pluribus* and *unum* are interdependent—mutually dependent—is perplexing to many. It is perplexing to unity advocates who believe that diversity is a threat to democracy and needs, therefore, to be scrutinized, managed, and contained. This is the misunderstanding at the core of Arthur Schlesinger's defensive *The Disuniting of America* (1992). It is perplexing as well to those diversity advocates who believe that unity inherently threatens pluralism, that social organization and government authority inevitably squelch minority viewpoints and lifestyles or, worse, are cruelly oppressive. This is the misunderstanding at the core of cultural separatist movements, from Quebec to Serbia and from White supremacy movements to Black Nationalism in the United States.

The failure to grasp the interdependence of *pluribus* and *unum* in a healthy democratic society is mirrored, unfortunately, in the longstanding gap between multicultural education and citizenship education. These have remained, with some notable exceptions, largely distinct discourses, social movements, and professional communities. The gap is both bizarre and miseducative. Attending exclusively and defensively to the citizen identity while ignoring, denying, repressing, or trying to "melt" away cultural and racial identities avoids the fact that diversity is, as we shall see, essential to liberty; it *causes* liberty. Doing the opposite has the same effect: By attending exclusively and defensively to our diverse individual, cultural, and racial identities, we ignore the shared political identity and its context—the commonwealth—on which we rely to secure and nurture our diversity.

IDIOCY

The interdependencies of *pluribus* and *unum*, diversity and liberty, and multicultural education and citizenship education, are at the heart of this book. Another overarching idea is *idiocy*. "Idiotic" in its origin is not what it means to us today—stupid or mentally deficient. This recent meaning is entirely and deservedly out of usage by educators, but the original meaning needs to be reclaimed. It is an ancient Greek term that shares with "idiom" and "idiosyncratic" the root *idios*, which means private, separate, self-centered—selfish. This conception of idiocy achieves its force when contrasted with *polites* (political) or *public*. Here we have a powerful opposition: the private individual and the public citizen. Christopher Berry writes in *The Idea of a Democratic Community* (1989) that the force of this opposition and hence the appropriateness of the term is that "idiotic" was in the Greek context a term of reproach. Drawing on the Greek historian John Myers, Berry writes: "If a man's conduct and discourse ceased to be politic it became idiotic—self-centered, unregardful of his neighbour's need, inconsequent in itself, as in the case of a rudderless ship, and without consequence therefore in his neighbour's eyes" (p. 1).

The contrast between the self-centered individual (the "idiot") and the public actor (the "citizen") is helpful both analytically and rhetorically, a tool both for more carefully understanding social life and for steering it toward a fuller realization of what it could be. An idiot is one whose self-centeredness undermines his or her citizen identity, causing it to wither or, worse, never to take root in the first place. An idiot does not know that self-sufficiency is entirely dependent on the community. "Not being self-sufficient when they are isolated," Aristotle wrote, "individuals are so many parts all equally depending on the whole which alone can bring self-sufficiency" (1958, p. 6). Idiots do not take part in public life—do not *have* a public life. In this sense, the idiot is immature in the most fundamental way, his or her life fundamentally out of balance, ajar, untethered, and unrealized: The idiot has not yet met the challenge of "puberty," the transition to public life.

Idiocy, consequently, is an enormous threat to the struggle. By struggle I mean the continuous, hopeful quest for a fuller realization of democratic ideals. I follow Vincent Harding's meaning, as stated in the opening question of this chapter, "Is America possible?", and James Baldwin's meaning in his 1963 masterpiece, *The Fire Next Time*:

> If we—and now I mean the relatively conscious whites and the relatively conscious blacks, who must, like lovers, insist on, or create, the consciousness of the others—do not falter in our *duty* now, we may be able, handful that we are, to end the racial nightmare, and *achieve our country*, and change the history of the world. (p. 141, emphases added)

Our *duty*? Harding and Baldwin are patriotic—wanting this country to live up to itself—and at the same time realistic and idealistic. Their realism is indicated in the sobriety of their statements: Harding's "in a time like our own," and Baldwin's "we may be able, handful that we are." Their idealism is indicated in their appreciation that liberty and justice for all is a path and a project, not an accomplishment: "Is America possible?", Harding asks. We must "achieve our country," Baldwin implores. Recently, Cornel West (1999) echoed Harding and Baldwin. West acknowledges that it is now an open question whether that "handful" can still be found: "One of the fundamental questions of our day is whether the tradition of struggle can be preserved and expanded. I refer to the struggle for decency and dignity, the struggle for freedom and democracy" (1999, p. 5). Idiocy threatens this struggle because idiocy simply and devastatingly pays it no attention. Let me now clarify idiocy and its opposite: citizenship.

Transporting us from the ancient to the current context, the former mayor of Missoula, Montana, Daniel Kemmis, writes of the *idios/polites* opposition, though in different terms, in *The Good City*:

> People who customarily refer to themselves as *taxpayers* are not even remotely related to democratic citizens. Yet this is precisely the word that now regularly holds the place which in a true democracy would be occupied by "citizens." Taxpayers bear a dual relationship to government, neither half of which has anything at all to do with democracy. Taxpayers pay tribute to the government, and they receive services from it. So does every subject of a totalitarian regime. What taxpayers do not do, and what people who call themselves taxpayers have long since stopped even imagining themselves doing, is *governing*. In a democracy, by the very meaning of the word, the people govern. . . . (1995, p. 9)

Tocqueville (1848/1969), writing in *Democracy in America* 150 years before Mayor Kemmis, also describes idiocy. All democratic peoples face a "dangerous passage" in their history, he wrote, when they "are carried away and lose all self-restraint at the sight of the new possessions they are about to obtain" (p. 540). Tocqueville's principal concern was that getting "carried away" causes citizens to lose the very freedom they are wanting so much to enjoy: "These people think they are following the principle of self-interest," he continues, "but the idea they entertain of that principle is a very crude one; and the more they look after what they call their own business, they neglect their chief business, which is to remain their own masters." But how do people remain their own masters? By maintaining the kind of community that secures their liberty. Freedom and community are not opposing forces any more than pluribus and unum. We are free *so that* we can create a community life *so that*, in turn, we can be free. Tocqueville's singular contribution to our understanding of idiocy and citizenship is this notion that *idiots are idiotic precisely because they are indifferent to the conditions and contexts of their own freedom*. They fail to grasp the interdependence of liberty and community.

Similarly, Jane Addams argued in 1913 that if a woman was planning to "keep on with her old business of caring for her house and rearing her children," then it was necessary that she expand her consciousness to include "public affairs lying quite outside her immediate household." The individualistic consciousness was "no longer effective":

> Women who live in the country sweep their own dooryards and may either feed the refuse of the table to a flock of chickens or allow it innocently to decay in the open air and sunshine. In a crowded city quarter, however, if the

street is not cleaned by the city authorities, no amount of private sweeping will keep the tenement free from grime; if the garbage is not properly collected and destroyed a tenement house mother may see her children sicken and die of diseases from which she alone is powerless to shield them, although her tenderness and devotion are unbounded. (1913, p. 1)

Addams concluded that for women to tend only to their "own households" was, to use the Greek term, idiotic. For to do only that would, ironically, prevent one from doing that at all. One cannot maintain the familial nest without maintaining the public, shared space in which the familial nest is itself nested. "[A]s society grows more complicated," Addams wrote, "it is necessary that woman shall extend her sense of responsibility to many things outside of her own home if she would continue to preserve the home in its entirety" (p. 1). Here is a clear statement of the opposite of idiocy and of the relationship between privacy and publicity.

Let us explore two more extensions on the concept. We will go first to a small Italian village and then to the modern industrial world writ large. In both cases, we see idiocy played out on a societal scale. We shift from the notion of idiotic persons to idiotic social structures, making a necessary sociological turn.

Social scientist Edward Banfield found a village where no one displayed Addams's intelligence; that is, where no one extended their sense of obligation to the "many things outside" their home. Writing in *The Moral Basis of a Backward Society* (1958), Banfield thus extended the idea of idiocy from individuals to groups. Banfield found in southern Italy an impoverished village that fairly could be described as, in the Greek sense of the term, idiotic. There were virtually no associations. There was no organized action in the face of striking and pressingly real local problems, and these were *felt* problems. Locals complained bitterly about them but did nothing. There was no hospital, no newspaper, only five grades of school, no charities or welfare programs, no agricultural organizations. Even the two village churches played no part in the secular life of the community, carrying on no charitable activities and organizing no relief work or community-building programs. Granted, an order of nuns struggled to maintain an orphanage in the remains of an old monastery, but this was not a local undertaking. The villagers contributed nothing to its upkeep, although the children came from local families. Quoting Banfield (1958, p. 19):

The monastery is crumbling, but none of the many half-employed stone masons has ever given a day's work to its repair. There is not enough food for the children, but no peasant or landed proprietor has ever given a young pig to the orphanage.

The only "association," so to speak, was the nuclear family. Banfield concluded that the villagers' inability to improve their common life was best explained by their inability and unwillingness to conjoin—to associate and organize outside their families. They were unable "to act together for their common good or, indeed, for any end transcending the immediate, material interest of the nuclear family" (p. 10). Banfield called this kind of idiocy *amoral familism* and gave its ethos as "Maximize the material, short-run advantage of the nuclear family; assume that all others will do likewise" (1958, p. 83). Several hypotheses follow logically. In a society of amoral familists:

1. No one will further the interest of the group or community except as it is to his private advantage to do so. In other words, the hope of material gain in the short run will be the only motive for concern with public affairs.
2. Only officials will concern themselves with public affairs, for only they are paid to do so. For a private person to take a serious interest in public problems will be regarded as abnormal and even improper.
3. There will be few checks on officials, for checking on officials will be the business of other officials only.
4. Organization (i.e., deliberately concerted action) will be very difficult to achieve and maintain. (pp. 83–86)

Banfield ends his report on a cheerless note: Even if measures could be identified for improving the common lot of these villagers—the improvement of schools, for example, or better care for the children in the orphanage—still there is little likelihood that any such measures will be tried. Why? For the very reasons just enumerated. Read again the four statements and imagine yourself attempting to mount a school-improvement campaign, create a newspaper, or organize a health clinic, homeless shelter, or food bank.

In *Teaching the Commons* (1997), Paul Theobald stops us short of bemoaning this dysfunctional village as though it was Other—not me or my people or my world. He argues that its condition and ethos are not so different from our common lot. If we do not see this, it is because, as the adage has it, the last thing the fish sees is the water it is swimming in. Theobald argues that the very fabric of modern industrial life, both its yarn and its weave, is idiotic. His theme is that an individually oriented worldview, indeed an infatuation with the individual, has replaced a communally oriented worldview capable of seeing and acting on the common good.[1] The building blocks of this cataclysmic shift from community to individual include all the markers of "progress" since feudal times, most notably the rise of individually oriented liberalism (with its individual rights, choices, and privately owned property) in the Reformation, Renaissance, and Enlightenment. Greed and autonomy became a virtue, turning virtue upside down. Now, virtue was equated with success. Now, "one of the nicest things we can say about someone," Theobald observes, is that he or she is "successful."

> As we have embraced liberal tenets more tightly than ever in this society, that is, as we have more steadfastly clung to an individual orientation to life, as we have defined life plans as synonymous with competition in the race for material accumulation, and as we have elevated the status of the risk takers among us, the accolade "successful" has come to be a much better cultural "fit" than the accolade "virtuous." Virtue speaks of attention to shouldering one's obligations to others and is therefore more at home in a community-oriented worldview. Success, by contrast, confines itself to the level of the individual. (1997, p. 47)

What this radical individualism replaced is *intradependence. Inter-* dependence captures a sort of mutuality (it means mutual dependence or dependence among parts), but it does not in its common usage include the natural environment. By intradependence, Theobald means "to exist by virtue of necessary relations *within a place*" (1997, p. 7, emphasis in original).

> Throughout most of human history, people lived their lives in a given locality and were highly dependent on the place itself and on those others with whom the place was shared. It has only been since the seventeenth century or so that intradependence of this sort has eroded and people have begun to think of themselves as individuals unencumbered by the constraints of nature or community. (p. 7)

"Freedom" is the term we use to describe our unencumbered and unobligated lives. Freedom to be you and me, freedom to march to the beat of a different drummer, freedom to relocate and "start over," freedom to purchase one product over another, freedom from government intervention. Family obligations and "committed" relationships are celebrated, of course, at least some of the time in some situations. But to stop there, to draw the line of obligation so close to the nuclear family is tantamount to *amoral familism*. An example from popular culture should help: When modern suburbanites purchase passenger trucks ("sports utility vehicles"; "four-by-fours") and use them as commuter cars and soccer cars, and are criticized for widening the ozone hole and wasting nonrenewable resources, they often justify their purchases on the grounds of "freedom," "personal safety," and "family safety." What this rationalization recalls is the inability of those Italian villagers to combine for any purpose, not even to improve the schools their own children attend. It suggests a suicidal blindness to intradependence. As Lewis Lapham (2001) puts it, democracy cannot be "understood as a fancy Greek name for the American Express Card" (p. 10).

In each case, from Kemmis's taxpayers to Theobald's infatuation with the individual, idiocy means not paying attention to the public household—both natural and humanmade—*even at the expense of what are apparently one's own private interests*. It is one thing to say that liberty is dependent on diversity, which was my earlier point, and another to say that liberty is dependent on community, my present point.

CITIZENSHIP

Now, let me turn to the other pole in this opposition, *citizenship*. Among the most compelling of the many contemporary examples of the non-idotic life—the citizen's life—are the civil disobedience campaigns of Mohandas Gandhi and Martin Luther King Jr. Here are two examples where ordinary persons chose to uphold public life at the same time they fought to restructure it. They respected the law and, *therefore*, they broke it. They did so in the name of the "tradition of struggle" that Cornel West invokes—the struggle for decency and dignity, freedom and democracy. King, having read Gandhi (e.g., 1951), went to Birmingham in 1963 to lead a mass, nonviolent protest against lawful racial segregation in public facilities. Arrested and jailed, he wrote the now famous "Letter from Birmingham Jail." Begun on the margins of a newspaper given to him in his cell, this was his response to local clergy who had published a statement calling for an end to the demonstrations. In that letter, Reverend King followed Henry David Thoreau's lead who, when asked, "Henry, why are you in jail?", is said to have responded "Why are you not?"

First, King offers a moral defense for being an "outsider" (from Atlanta) in Birmingham. His defense: "Because injustice is here."

> Injustice anywhere is a threat to justice everywhere. We are caught in an inescapable network of mutuality, tied in a single garment of destiny. Whatever affects one directly, affects all indirectly. Never again can we afford to live with the narrow, provincial "outside agitator" idea. Anyone who lives inside the United States cannot be considered an outsider anywhere within its bounds. (1963a, p. 77)

This "inescapable network of mutuality"—intradependence—could well be a motto of the non-idiotic life.[2] Because of it, anyone's injustice is everyone's injustice. Because of it, "ethnic cleansing" is *self*-destructive, genocide is suicide, and generosity is *self*-serving. Thich Nhat Hanh, the Vietnamese Buddhist monk nominated by King for the Nobel Peace Prize in 1967, gives us a very clear notion of just what this network of mutuality includes. Like Theobald, he goes beyond interdependence to intradependence, then further:

> If you are a poet, you will see clearly that there is a cloud floating in this sheet of paper. Without a cloud, there will be no rain; without rain, the trees cannot grow; and without trees, we cannot make paper. The cloud is essential for the paper to exist. If the cloud is not here, the sheet of paper cannot be here either. So we can say that the cloud and the paper *inter-are*. "Interbeing" is a word that is not in the dictionary yet, but if we combine the prefix "inter-" with the verb "to be," we have a new verb, so we can say that the cloud and the sheet of paper *inter-are*. (1988, p. 3)

Hanh would have us look more deeply still into this sheet of paper, where we will see (if we are poets) the sunshine, too, without which the forest cannot grow, nor we or our children. The paper, the sunshine, and the reader inter-are. Looking further, we see the logger who fell the tree, the workers at the paper mill and their families, and the Western Spotted Owl threatened by the whole enterprise. "Your mind is in here and mine is also," Hanh notes, because all this is part of our perception. "So we can say that everything is in here with this sheet of paper. . . . Everything coexists with this sheet of paper" (1988, p. 4). To be, then, is to "inter-be." "You cannot just *be* by yourself alone. You have to inter-be with every other thing" (p. 4).[3]

We are caught in an inescapable network of inter-being, "tied in a single garment of destiny," as King (1963a, p. 77) says. This is clear. But why, then, King's *law breaking*? Law is part of that mutuality, after all, binding everyone together in an agreement—a social contract—that affirms and supports both liberty and community. (Was this not precisely Socrates' point when he refused to be sneaked out of jail by his friend, Crito, thereby escaping the hemlock?[4]) "You express a great deal of anxiety over our willingness to break laws" (1963a, p. 82), King writes to his fellow clergy. "This is certainly a legitimate concern," he concedes, aware that his own campaign obliges others to obey the law, referring now to the Supreme Court's 1954 decision on school desegregation in *Brown v. Board of Education*. Then he asks rhetorically, "How can you advocate breaking some laws and obeying others?"

> The answer lies in the fact that there are two types of laws: just and unjust. I would be the first to advocate obeying just laws. One has not only a legal but a moral responsibility to obey just laws. Conversely, one has a moral respon-

sibility to disobey unjust laws. . . . Thus it is I can urge men to obey the 1954 decision of the Supreme Court, for it is morally right; and I can urge them to disobey segregation ordinances, for they are morally wrong. (pp. 82–83)

The network of mutuality is nothing but social habits and customs—mere convention (or worse, an oppressive nightmare)—if not *just*. And so King the moral philosopher brings the Enlightenment tradition of fair play, accessed through reason, to bear on the apartheid conventions that had locked down the South since the Emancipation Proclamation. Meanwhile, King the prophetic minister brings a revolutionary and inclusive *love ethic* (Moses, 1997) to bear on the law breaking itself. He urges obedience to the law when it's right, and disobedience when the law does not square with justice. One is obliged to break the law when it is unjust. One is obliged also to do so publicly, appearing before others as a public citizen appealing to justice, and lovingly as one who understands that hate cannot and should not be fought with hate, or violence with violence. In this way, one expresses the highest respect for the law and for the basic goodness (however well hidden) of one's opponents. Again from the "Letter": "In no sense do I advocate evading or defying the law, as would the rabid segregationist. That would lead to anarchy. One who breaks an unjust law must do so openly, lovingly, and with a willingness to accept the penalty" (p. 83).

"Lovingly." He used the word, and he used it often (bell hooks [2000a] calls him "a prophet of love"). When he was accepting the Nobel Peace Prize in Oslo on December 10, 1964, King asked rhetorically why the prize had been awarded to a movement that had "not yet won the very peace and brotherhood which is the essence of the Nobel Prize." He answered that this award had been given to nonviolent struggle:

I conclude that this award, which I receive on behalf of that movement, is a profound recognition that nonviolence is the answer to the crucial political and moral questions of our time: the need for man to overcome oppression and violence without resorting to violence and oppression. . . . The foundation of such a method is love. (1964, p. 1)

The concept of love that he is invoking in the context of nonviolent struggle is the disinterested love that comprehends what Thich Nhat Hanh called "inter-being." This love "does not begin by discriminating between worthy and unworthy people" (1958, p. 104), King wrote years before Birmingham and the "Letter." Rather: "It begins by loving others for their own sakes. It is an entirely 'neighbor-regarding concern for others. . . .'" This kind of love makes no distinction between friend and enemy. Consequently, he taught, "the best way to assure oneself that Love is disinterested is to have love for the enemy-neighbor from whom you can expect no good in return, but only hostility and persecution" (p. 105).

A few years after Birmingham, the horrors of the Vietnam War and poverty weighed heavily on King's mind, and his popularity waned among Blacks as well as the White liberals who earlier had supported the cause of racial equality. It seems that war and poverty were less popular issues than segregation. King's compass, however, was unchanged: Pursue justice and do so publicly and lovingly. Consider this excerpt from the "Beyond Vietnam" speech delivered in New York on April 4, 1967, one year before he was murdered.

> As we counsel young men concerning military service we must clarify for them our nation's role in Vietnam and challenge them with the alternative of conscientious objection. I am pleased to say that this is a path now chosen by more than seventy students at my own alma mater, Morehouse College, and I recommend it to all who find the American course in Vietnam a dishonorable and unjust one. Moreover, I would encourage all ministers of draft age to give up their ministerial exemptions and seek status as conscientious objectors. These are the times for real choices and not false ones. . . . I am convinced that if we are to get on the right side of the world revolution, we as a nation must undergo a radical revolution of values. We must rapidly begin (applause), we must rapidly begin the shift from a thing-oriented society to a person-oriented society. When machines and computers, profit motives and property rights, are considered more important than people, the giant triplets of racism, materialism, and militarism are incapable of being conquered. (1967a, p. 8–9)

To lead a non-idiotic life is to lead the unavoidably connected and engaged life of the citizen, paying attention to and caring for the public household, the common good. Idiots come to the public square, when they do, to advance their own interests, to *get* something. More typically they fail to argue at all, letting others go to the public square to listen and talk and reason and decide with others—to deliberate. It is citizens who walk the paths to public squares and, by walking them, *create* them. There, struggling to absorb as well as express, to listen as well as to be heard, they strive to communicate across their differences, recognizing them and joining them with deliberation. This is how publics come to be. Citizens, then, balance the need to enjoy private liberties with the obligation to create a public realm, specifically to create policy decisions about how we will be with one another and what problems we will solve together and how.

Justice itself is served by deliberation. The reason is transparent. Justice is far more likely to be served by democratic citizens who reason together in search of mutually acceptable decisions than it is by people who have no public life or are interested in it only for the sake of power and getting what they want. "Even when deliberative citizens continue to disagree, as they often will," Amy Gutmann (1999) writes, "their effort to reach mutually justifiable decisions manifests mutual respect."

> Because ongoing disagreement among reasonable people of good will is inevitable in any free society, mutual respect is an important virtue. Deliberation manifests mutual respect since it demonstrates a good faith effort to find mutually acceptable terms of social cooperation, not merely terms that are acceptable only to the most powerful, or for that matter to the most articulate. (p. xiii)

To lead a non-idiotic life is to have both a private and a public life and to understand how the two support one another. Finding one's way out of idiocy into citizenship—a citizenship that embraces both *unum* and *pluribus*—is not easy. The pathways are not easily discerned. The continual tug from the warm nests of family and ethnic group of origin can cause any of us to lose sight of the public square altogether. The tug is often strong for the new immigrant, of course, who longs for solidarity and solace in the face of disorientation, discrimination, and alienation. It is strong, too, for members of cultural minorities who after generations still face oppression. Think of the cultural separatist who has resigned from the promise of a just public life and seeks comfort in homogeneity. Think of victims with old or fresh memories of virulent injustice at the hands of thugs who savaged the public square, using it as a staging ground for their own hatred—Hitler seizing Germany, or police chief Bull Conner turning loose the dogs in Birmingham. But the tug is strongest, perhaps, for members of the cultural majority—middle-class Whites in the United States—whose ethnic nest has become broadly and deeply institutionalized and, therefore, so pervasive in social life as to be, ironically, invisible to themselves. The culturally privileged come to believe they are "the inclusive kind of human . . . the norm and the ideal" (Greene, 1993, p. 215). They don't call their own ethnic group's food "ethnic food"; instead, they "go out" for ethnic food.

CONCLUSION

Going back to the public square again and again, re-creating it, keeping the dream alive, asserting "a hope in the unseen" (Suskind, 1998)—this is the public work of public citizens. This is the "struggle." And for King (1958), this is love:

Agape is a willingness to go to any length to restore the community. It doesn't stop at the first mile, but it goes the second mile to restore community. It is a willingness to forgive, not seven times, but seventy times seven to restore community. (p. 105)

King helps us clarify the "dream"—the aim—while at the same time allowing us closely to examine several crucial details: the slippery concept of justice itself, the revolutionary love ethic, the tension between the development of just individuals and the development of a just society, and the existential question all teachers must confront: Will I be a keeper of that dream or, through indifference, its killer (Smith, 1994)? Must my own teaching practice make the torch burn brighter, or may I retreat safely, with my dignity intact, from the public square?

Cultural pluralism and racial equity are best served by nurturing the kind of public life that, in turn, protects and nurtures cultural pluralism and racial equity. On this view, multicultural education and citizenship education are one thing, not two.

Democracy and Difference

We have come to cash this check.
—Martin Luther King Jr. (1963b, p. 1)

There is a democratic education problem in the United States. The young are not learning properly to care for the body politic and the body politic is not adequately caring for the young. If parents, citizens, and educators (distinct roles played sometimes by the same person) are to grapple with this problem successfully, it will be necessary, among other things, to take a fresh look at an old idea in American education—*democratic citizenship education*. My concern is that much is excluded by the conventional conception, two things especially: first, pluralism, or the social and cultural dimensions of citizenship; second, the central tension of modern social life—the tension between unity and diversity. After these exclusions, we are left with a feeble conception, one that mirrors the longstanding confusion in the United States over the meaning of one of its chief mottoes, the one on its coins: *e pluribus unum*.

Recall three recent events on the democratic landscape, each a poignant argument against democratic business as usual. The first, set in eastern Europe, portrays the submersion of democratic activist women in Poland following the collapse of the socialist dictatorship. Elzbieta Matynia, now at the New School University in New York, returned to her native and "already virtually 'post-Communist' Poland" after an 8-year absence. What struck her was the

> almost total absence of those capable women who had played such an active and essential role in the clandestine operations of the pro-democratic movements of the '70s and '80s. I knew many of them well and had been active along with them, but, like them, I had never defined the crucial problems in terms of gender. The primary objective of every social protest and movement then was to fight for the political rights of *all* members of society. All other issues seemed to be of secondary importance; it was felt that these problems could be dealt with after the final battle for democracy had been won. But now, watching the free-wheeling debates in the new Parliament and reading about those newly created democratic institutions, I found myself wondering where all the women were. (1994, pp. 351–352)

    Scene 2 brings us back to the North American continent, to Florida. Florida is one of 11 states in the United States that disenfranchise all felons for life. Thomas Johnson, an ex-felon and an African American man, is suing to restore ex-convict voting rights (Goldhaber, 2000). Disenfranchised ex-felons are 5% of the voting age population of Florida, and when one considers the Black community alone, 24% of Florida's Black males cannot vote. Supporters of the disenfranchisement of felons invoke social contract theory: Attorney Roger Clegg of the Center for Equal Opportunity in Washington, DC argued, "It is not too much to demand that those who would make the laws for others—who would participate in self-government—be willing to follow those laws themselves" (quoted in Goldhaber, p. 2). But Johnson argues that Jim Crow is to blame. In 1868 Florida's new postwar constitution gave Blacks the vote, but not felons—and this was at a time when felons were overwhelmingly Black.
    Scene 3 takes us to Asia and serves to summarize the first two. It is Tiananmen Square in the summer of 1989. Among many unforgettable moments was this one captured by Vincent Harding (1990).[1] A young Chinese woman, shortly before government troops crushed the uprising, told a Western television reporter that what Chinese students and intellectuals wanted from the United States was its "advanced technology." The reporter asked if the protesters were not interested also in any *ideas*, such as democracy. Her response came quickly: "Yes, but only if they are *advanced* ideas about democracy" (p. 33).
    Fused together, these scenes fashion a reflective mirror in which educators can ponder the meaning of American citizenship in general and citizenship education in particular. Common to these scenes is a problem that is relevant to existing and would-be democracies everywhere: the double failure of institutionalized democracy to address its own substantive shortcomings while at the same time believing itself to be a fully developed response to the puzzle of living together, or what Francis Fukuyama called the "end point of mankind's ideological evolution" (1992, p. xi). The Polish and American scenes concentrate on three shortcomings in particular—the marginalization of cultural minorities, racism, and the stifling routines of big-party politics—while the Chinese scene expresses the possibility that something better can be devised, that "advanced" versions can be concocted. The question is thus raised: Should citizenship education in the United States continue to roll along as it has for a century, relying on rituals and slogans that belie the double failure here at home? Can citizenship education, both as a curricular program and a school mission, continue to ignore yearnings for a kind of democratic citizenship that serious democrats could embrace?
    At issue is a conception of citizenship that has been remarkably helpful in the struggle to secure individual rights and to limit government

power. These are enormous, world-changing achievements, as anyone with a modicum of historical knowledge will appreciate. Before these achievements—before "rights" and "limited government" became taken-for-granted realities enjoyed by many people—those holding absolute power could do *whatever* they wanted with and to those under their power, whether slaveholders to slaves, conquistadors to the vanquished, men to women, or (as Foucault [1977] has shown so vividly) kings to their subjects. Still, this conception of citizenship remains narrow, defensive, and exclusive. It could be called "modern." Modern citizenship was constructed in a way that made the development of modern democracy possible, to be sure, but at the same time, paradoxically, an obstacle to its own possibilities—to what Chantal Mouffe (1992) calls a deepening and widening of the democratic revolution.

In this chapter, I will first portray the dominant conception of democratic citizenship education—both its traditional and progressive wings. Then I will delineate three "advanced" ideas, borrowing on the young woman's usage in Tiananmen Square. These three ideas, I argue, should be helpful to teachers and curriculum workers who are seeking a more satisfying conception of democratic citizenship and, in turn, democratic citizenship education.

THE DOMINANT CONCEPTION OF CITIZENSHIP EDUCATION: DIFFERENCE AS DISSOLUTION

In *The Federalist No. 2*, John Jay wrote that Americans were one ethnic group—"descended from the same ancestors, speaking the same language, professing the same religion, attached to the same principles of government, very similar in their manners and customs. . . ." (1787/1937, p. 9). They were, he said, a "band of brethren." The brethren faced a common danger, he wrote, which was their dissolution into "a number of unsocial, jealous, and alien sovereignties." Jay wrote these words on behalf of winning approval for a document that was aimed, as the Call for the Federal Constitutional Convention in February of 1787 put it, at overcoming "defects in the present Confederation (and) establishing in these states a firm national government. . . ."

Jay's assertion reveals something important: the United States's long-standing difficulty negotiating the tension between unity and diversity was present at the creation. The conflict between the one and the many goes all the way back. More central to my purpose than showing this tension to be an old one, however, is showing that its meaning is oblique. The tension between unity and difference or "oneness" and "manyness" (Walzer, 1992b,

p. 29) is not a straightforward one between a desire for enough community to satisfy common needs (e.g., safety, heat and lights, water purification, trade, defense, waste disposal) while otherwise leaving people free to flourish in their differences. Rather, it is skewed off to one side, the unity side, by a garrison mentality that fends off the other side, pluralism, fearing instability and, consequently, the fragile unity's collapse, and straining to narrow the range of allowable difference. On this conception of unity/difference, diversity of the *political* kind is sanctioned to a greater extent than diversity of the *social* and *cultural* kind. For example, differences of opinion on matters of common concern (i.e., public policy questions) receive some attention while differences of religion, language, race, ethnicity, and gender are moved off to the sidelines in the name of an official policy of "color blindness" and neutrality.

I will elaborate the neutrality premise later, but let me first pursue a bit further the narrow conception of unity/difference. Recall that European American men without property, along with all women, were disenfranchised at the time of the creation of the United States, and that African American men and women generally were regarded as chattel. Native peoples were simply a scourge to be contained or, perhaps, assimilated, or simply eliminated or killed off outright. The "brethren's" response to these "Others" makes it clear that the working conception of difference at the creation attended more or less exclusively to just one kind of difference: difference of *opinion* among insiders on matters of mutual concern (e.g., taxation, representation, property law). A more inclusive conception of difference, one that might include gender or even race, was not necessary at the top of the status hierarchy, in the realm of governance, for these differences were not to be found there.

The narrow conception is revealed as well in James Madison's (1787/1937) argument in *The Federalist No. 10*. The chief advantage of a "well-constructed Union," Madison wrote, is its ability to "break and control the violence of faction" (p. 53). By faction, he meant "a number of citizens, whether amounting to a majority or minority of the whole, who are united and actuated by some common impulse of passion, or of interest, adverse to the rights of other citizens, or to the permanent and aggregate interests of the community" (p. 54). This was man-to-man talk, insider to insider.

The narrow conception holds today. It pervades citizenship education and explains at least some of the failure of both citizenship education and multicultural education to be taken seriously in many school settings (Sleeter, 1992). It is a conception that seeks to control and contain the expression of political diversity, holding it at bay, while ignoring or opposing the vigorous expression of social and cultural diversity. If the conception had a motto, it might read: *Contain political diversity; constrain social and cultural diversity.*

Ironically, this is the meaning of the actual motto, *e pluribus unum*. This phrase is interpreted generally to mean "from manyness, oneness." Not *alongside* manyness, but *from* manyness. This means transcending difference, conquering and overcoming it. Perhaps difference should be tolerated, yes, and tolerance might be valued as a civic virtue. But there is a withholding, reluctant quality to tolerance. The reluctance can be seen not only in Jay's "brethren" discourse but, to some degree, in the recent communitarian calls for homogeneous, organic community (e.g., Bellah et al., 1985; Etzioni, 1993).[2] Both the Federalist and communitarian views shy away from social heterogeneity, regarding it a danger. Both avoid to some degree a conception of the relationship of unity to difference that would allow political oneness to exist *with* (alongside) social and cultural diversity. On this broader conception, diversity does not need to be conquered or colonized, and not even transcended. It can be fostered.

Citizenship Education

But it is the narrower conception that undergirds the citizenship education literature in the United States. This is true on both its traditional and progressive wings. I turn to these now.

The traditional wing consists of the familiar values-knowledge-skills theme advanced by R. Freeman Butts (1980) and others. Citizenship education, he wrote, "embraces the fundamental values of the political community, a realistic and scholarly knowledge of the working of political institutions and processes, and the skills of political behavior required for effective participation in a democracy" (p. 122). Emphasized mainly is teaching the young to hold the "office of citizen," meaning one who votes, develops opinions on matters of public concern, holds dear commitments to liberty and justice, and has a deep understanding of the mechanics of democratic government, from its three branches to its protection of individual rights. Harry Boyte (1994) calls this "mainstream civics," and criticizes the recent *Civitas* curriculum framework (Bahmueller, 1991) for not reaching beyond it. That 600–page text expresses the traditional wing's bias that politics is what politicians and government officials do while citizens mainly vote for them and then watch, or cynically ignore, what they do.

Scholars of the progressive wing, at least those who are careful, do not denigrate this knowledge base in particular nor wish generally to dismiss knowledge bases. They do not regard disciplinary knowledge as a problem or an outmoded tool. They are not generally fixated on "processes" and "skills" and integrated education, as their traditionalist detractors like to claim (e.g., Ravitch, 2000). Scholars on the progressive wing spend a good deal of time specifying the knowledge base, but they work also on developing the "intellectual framework (that) will be used to guide the teacher and, in turn, the student in handling these materials" (Oliver & Shaver, 1974; see also Oliver, 1957; Stanley & Nelson, 1994). Perhaps the fact that any serious attention at all is paid to an "intellectual framework" for interpreting and using data distinguishes this wing. A more sharply distinguishing characteristic, however, is that progressives want a more participatory, direct form of citizenship. Direct democracy emphasizes the many ways people can behave in the citizen role other than by voting, campaigning for a representative, or running for elected office. Emphasized is the development of "public agency—people's capacities to act with effect and with public spirit" (Boyte, 1994, p. 417)—and rehabilitating citizens' capacity for practical reasoning. In the arena of curriculum and instruction, here is Fred Newmann's citizen action curriculum (1975), Shirley Engle's decision-making model (1960), Paul Hanna's *Youth Serves the Community* (1936), the 1916 commission's "Problems of Democracy" course, Oliver and Shaver's jurisprudential framework (1974), Kohlberg's "just community" approach (Power, Higgins, & Kohlberg, 1989), Stanley and Whitson's practical competence curriculum (1992), and Vivian Paley's remarkable model for moral discourse in kindergarten classrooms (1992).

At the heart of the progressive critique of traditional citizenship education is disappointment with orthodox liberalism. Liberal democracy celebrates the civil and political rights of individuals and representative/republican government. Meanwhile, the political economy of liberal democracy renders participatory citizenship superfluous and creates what Anne Phillips calls "liberal democratic minimalism" (1993, p. 109). Made into spectators rather than citizens, adults are left to preoccupy themselves with their rights. Consequently, civic discourse degenerates to "rights talk" (Glendon, 1991).

Traditionalists want more study, progressives want more practice. Traditionalists concentrate on knowledge of constitutional democracy, progressives on this *plus* deliberation on public issues, problem-solving/community action that brings together people of various identities, and other forms of direct and deliberate participation in state matters as well as in the middle sector or "civil society" (Walzer, 1992a), that is, the public space between government and private interests. Progressives, then, are more exacting in their interpretation of popular sovereignty. Democracy, for them, is "the form of politics that brings people together as citizens" (Dietz, 1992, p. 75). Progressives oppose limiting citizenship activity to voting for representatives who, in turn, are the only people who think and behave like citizens. "People who simply drop scraps of paper in a box or pull a lever," writes community organizer Karl Hess (1979)," are not acting like citizens; they are acting like consumers, picking between prepackaged political items" (p. 10). Traditionalists, on the other hand, are content with this scheme, for it is integral to the faction-controlling, dissolution-fearing vision articulated by Jay.

Despite the progressive wing's expectation that citizens act like citizens, still this wing minimizes social and cultural heterogeneity. Both wings believe that what matters most are the civil and political relations among the brethren—those citizens who are secured within the *unum* and whose differences, therefore, are disagreements on matters of common concern. By distancing matters of race, gender, and ethnicity from the central concerns of governmental and direct democracy, the progressives, like the traditionalists, are limited in their ability to advance contemporary thinking about the unity/difference tension or what is arguably the central citizenship question of our time: *How can we live together justly, in ways that are mutually satisfying, and which leave our differences, both individual and group, intact and our multiple identities recognized?*

Thus, the two wings share the narrow conception of unity and difference. This conception has only one viable approach to the unity/difference tension, only one tool at its disposal, and that is assimilation. Assimilation is thus built into the common sense of citizenship education as one of its bearing walls. Whether one elaborates the construct in progressive or traditional ways, still a "band of brethren" vision dominates the citizenship construction site. Social and cultural diversity, having been driven away from this site, had to find attention in what, remarkably, became an altogether different literature: multicultural education.

"ADVANCED" IDEAS ABOUT DEMOCRACY

A more fully articulated conception of citizenship education would need to incorporate the ideals of public agency, citizen action, and practical politics—that is, direct democracy, which the progressive wing has done quite well. But this alone would not widen the conception sufficiently to include social and cultural difference or what has been called "the new cultural politics of difference" (West, 1993a) and the "politics of recognition" (Taylor, 1994). This is precisely what an "advanced" (to borrow the Tiananmen Square usage) concept of citizenship education must incorporate. To accomplish this, it should be helpful now to bring two additional ideas forward. Both are tensions really, one concerning the ends of democratic participation, the other the contest between pluralism and assimilation.

Path/Accomplishment

Tied to the participatory idea is a view of democracy as a path or journey.[3] Dewey (1927; 1985a) called this *creative democracy*, by which he meant that democracy is a way of living with others, a way of being. It has no end other than the path itself. Ends arise on the path, "*right within* the process of problem solving, not prior to it" (Lee, 1965, p. 129). It follows on this view that there is "no period, either in the past or the present, that serves as a model for democracy" (Phillips, 1993, p. 2). Viewed as a creative, constructive process, democracy is not already accomplished, in which case citizens today need only to celebrate and protect it, but a trek that citizens in a pluralist society make together. It is a political path, a *tradition* of sorts, that unites them, not a culture, language, or religion. The ratification of the Constitution and the several democratic struggles that followed (ending slavery, extending the franchise to women, and dismantling Jim Crow, for example) hardly closed the book on democracy in the United States; they hardly dispensed with its possibilities. The work called "democracy" is not now finished. The need for this work arises anew, within itself, continually.

To be able to think about the democratic path as a tradition, which at first glance seems contradictory, we must reject the false opposition between tradition, which has us looking back, and creativity, which has us looking forward (see Gadamer, 1984). This opposition denies the role of creativity in the cultivation and affirmation of traditions just as it ignores the traditions within which people do their creating. "Politics," writes Michael Oakeshott, "springs neither from instant desires, nor from general principles, but from the existing traditions of behavior themselves" (1967, p. 123). "The form it [politics] takes," he continues, "because it can take no other, is the amendment of existing arrangements by exploring and pursuing what is intimated in them." Thus, Martin Luther King Jr. demands in his 1963 march on Washington address the *fulfillment* of a tradition, a *re*invention, not something new:

> [W]e have come to our nation's capital to cash a check. When the architects of our republic wrote the magnificent words of the Constitution and the Declaration of Independence, they were signing a promissory note to which every American was to fall heir. . . . We have come to cash this check, a check that will give us upon demand the riches of freedom and the security of justice." (1963b, p. 1)

In this sense, the purpose of the Civil Rights Movement was not to alter the American dream, nor to revise it, but to realize it. "Now is the time to make real the promises of democracy," King then said. "Now is the time to lift our nation from the quicksands of racial injustice to the solid rock of brotherhood" (p. 1).

In this same vein Gary Okihiro (1994) writes in *From Margins to Mainstream* that "the core values and ideals of the nation" are animated not by those already secured within the mainstream, not by those privileged already, but by those *not* secured and *not* privileged, by those living at the margins—today by African Americans, Latinos, American Indians, and gays and lesbians. "In their struggles for equality," he writes, these groups have helped preserve and advance the principles and ideals of democracy." Similarly, Richard Rorty (1999) express his wish that children be taught to consider themselves heirs to a dynamic tradition that sponsors a continual deepening of democracy and a continual rethinking of its tenets. He calls this a tradition "of increasing liberty and rising hope," arguing that children should think of themselves

> as proud and loyal citizens of a country that, slowly and painfully, threw off a foreign yoke, freed its slaves, enfranchised its women, restrained its robber barons and licensed its trade unions, liberalized its religious practices and broadened its religious and moral tolerance, and built colleges in which 50 percent of its population could enroll—a country that numbered Ralph Waldo Emerson, Eugene V. Debs, Susan B. Anthony, and James Baldwin among its citizens. (p. 121)

This does not mean that democratic citizens do not pursue specific social and economic ends. Of course they do, for this is what politics is. The path is not without clamor, rancor, and direct action (disagreement, boycotts, civil disobedience, etc.). Self-governance is inherently disagreeable, if it is honest. The democratic path is no way out of this; rather, it is a way in. Mary Dietz (1992) writes:

> [I]t is best to say that this is a vision fixed not on an end but rather inspired by a *principle*—freedom—and by a political *activity*—positive liberty. That activity is a demanding process that never ends, for it means engaging in public debate and sharing responsibility for self-government. (p. 77, emphasis added)

The principle and the activity together cut the democratic path, defining it in a most rudimentary way. Individual freedoms (rights; "negative liberties" or freedoms *from*) are guaranteed, citizens are held to written law, they agree to regard one another as essentially equal and in possession of the full measure of human dignity, and they require of each other a measure of prudent restraint so that change can be accomplished without leaving the path altogether. The path requires that citizens pay some attention to what each other are doing. This is, perhaps, the most difficult path requirement for the many contemporary democratic citizens who wish mainly to be left alone, to be unencumbered by neighbors or priests or parents or, God forbid, the government. Pericles of Athens minced no words: "We do not say that a man who takes no interest in politics is a man who minds his own business; we say that he has no business here at all" (quoted in Thucydides, 1972, p. 147). Jane Jacobs (1961), writing in *The Death and Life of Great American Cities*, lets no community member wriggle free from the shared path, which she invokes as the city sidewalk:

> In real life, only from the ordinary adults of the city sidewalks do children learn—if they learn it at all—the first fundamental of successful city life: People must take a modicum of public responsibility for each other even if they have no ties to each other. This is a lesson nobody learns by being told. It is learned from the experience of having *other people without ties of kinship or close friendship or formal responsibility* take a modicum of public responsibility for you. (p. 82, emphasis in original)

Jacobs speaks in the same anti-idiotic register as those we met in Chapter 1.

This path, this shared path, relies on personal qualities of the sort Plato asked about over 2,000 years ago when the idea of the city was taking shape: "Are there not some qualities of which all the citizens must be partakers if there is to be a city at all?" Minimally, these qualities are:

- A sense of the "inescapable network of mutuality" and "inter-being"
- Practical judgment (everyday, situated intelligence)
- A shared fund of civic knowledge (e.g., knowing the conditions that have undermined democracies in the past)
- A shared fund of civic know-how (e.g., deliberation skills and the disposition to use them)
- A thirst for justice for others and for oneself

Beyond the minimum, King and Thich Naht Hanh bravely and outrageously urged love. Even in his relatively brief 1963 March on Washington address, King added: "There is something I must say to my people who stand on the warm threshold which leads into the palace of justice: In the process of gaining our rightful place, we must not be guilty of wrongful deeds. Let us not seek to satisfy our thirst for freedom by drinking from the cup of bitterness and hatred. . . . We must not allow our creative protest to degenerate into physical violence. Again and again, we must rise to the majestic heights of meeting physical force with soul force" (Gandhi's *satyagraha*) (1963b, p. 1).

These qualities may occur naturally in humans. I do not know. The historical record—with its countless subjugations of one group by another, its ethnic cleansings on every continent—surely indicates otherwise. I am sympathetic, therefore, with Dewey, who argued that these qualities must be "created," and this can be done "only by education" (1916/1985a, p. 93). On the other hand, if these qualities are natural in humans—a birthright—which is the Buddhist point of view (e.g., Hanh, 1988; Trungpa,

1991), then they need not be created but, because they are deeply buried, uncovered. Either way, the qualities must be nurtured. While they can be nurtured in families they cannot be fully developed in them, for there is too little diversity within a family and too narrow a perspective. Here is the mandate for civic education in schools, on city sidewalks, and other public spaces where children from different families, faiths, races, cultures, and language traditions find themselves on common ground.

Pluralism/Assimilation

I have sketched two "advanced" ideas so far. The first, participatory citizenship, tries to take popular sovereignty seriously. It emphasizes forms of public agency beyond voting and requires, in turn, a kind of democratic education that would form, or at least inform, such activity. The second concentrates on democracy as an ongoing way of shared living rather than an achievement that needs only protection and celebration. According to this view, it is the path itself—the tradition of "increasing liberty and rising hope" (Rorty, 1999, p. 121)—that needs protection and deserves celebration. The third idea, to which I now turn, concentrates on the critical juncture of democracy and diversity.

My colleague James A. Banks, the eminent African American scholar of multicultural education and social studies education, often tells the story of his own schooling in Arkansas during the 1940s and 1950s in a society marked by racial segregation that was supported by law, custom, and police power:

> We learned about liberty and justice in school, and said—repeating the Pledge of Allegiance in our segregated school each morning—that our nation had "liberty and justice for all. . . ." My African American teachers and my parents, who were practicing democrats within a racially segregated society, taught me that I was somebody, that I must believe in myself, and that if I worked hard, kept the faith, and kept my eyes on the prize I could become anything I wanted to be. . . . The faith that my parents and teachers had in democratic ideals and in the possibilities of a democratic society—and the ideals of freedom that were promoted by the Civil Rights movement as I was coming of age—were decisive factors that enabled me to live in an apartheid society and yet believe in the possibilities of a democracy. (1996, p. xii)

This stark juxtaposition of apartheid and democratic ideals, of reciting the Pledge of Allegiance while standing in a racially segregated school, underscores why the first two ideas—participation and path—are insufficient. They leave key questions unanswered. Who is and who is not participating, and on whose terms? And, how wide is the path?

Contemporary democratic theorizing is rejecting the longstanding assumption that traditional democratic institutions have solved the "problem of diversity." Drawing on postmodern literatures, contemporary work sponsors a more serious treatment of diversity than was allowed under the toleration model. The newer work, if one can speak generally of it, acknowledges willingly, rather than reluctantly, the plain fact of pluralism. It seeks release from the brethren's assimilationist habit and, more generally, the timeless, illiberal, monistic attempt to melt away differences, contradictions, and conflict. The newer work is relevant to rethinking citizenship and citizenship education because it articulates conceptions of difference and commonality that are not grounded in the fear of dissolution.[4]

Here, then, is the third idea. Liberal democracy's basic tenets of human dignity—individual liberty, equality, and popular sovereignty—need to be preserved but extended and deepened within a new sense of citizenship that is not subtly or overtly hostile to pluralism. This is a citizenship that embraces individual differences, multiple group identities, and a unifying political community all at once. The task ahead is to recognize individual and group differences *and* to unite them horizontally in democratic moral discourse. This discourse is more than "rights talk"—insistence on "my" or "our" rights. Rights talk is included, for rights are a defining attribute of the democratic path; but the needed discourse includes as well sentences geared to the common life that secures the uncommon life, "the whole which alone can bring self-sufficiency," as Aristotle (1958, p. 6) wrote. This is a discourse not only of authenticity but of responsibility, deliberation, and duty. Here is Dewey's (1927) vision of a "larger public" that embraces the "little publics." Let us be clear that the larger public is not a broad-based *cultural* comradeship. In modern, culturally diverse societies, this is both unrealistic and undesirable. When pursued by dominant groups, the wish for cultural homogeneity becomes assimilationist or, pulling all stops, a repressive, totalitarian, murderous campaign. (There are ample examples in the historical record.) "The problem that lies at the heart of totalizing theories," writes Ruthann Kurth-Schai (1992), "is the attempt to address difference by subsuming it within a greater whole . . . (and) the acceptance of diversity as a state to be transcended" (p. 155). Stalin's and Mao's purges, the Holocaust, the atrocities by the Khmer Rouge, Serbs, and Taliban all are monstrous examples of attempts to "transcend" diversity and create a utopia of sameness—"a society with a single, blocklike structure, solid and eternal" (Berman, 2001, p. 19). Following the terrorist attack of September 11, 2001, the Rev. Jerry Falwell blamed it on diversity, on "the pagans, and the abortionists, and the feminists, and the gays and the lesbians who are trying to make that an alternative lifestyle . . . all of them who have tried to secularize America, I point the finger in their face and say, 'You helped this happen'" (Goodstein, 2001, p. 1–2).

Dewey (1927) understood that the larger public is, in effect, a moral grid that binds citizens together in a broad political (again, not cultural) comradeship. The larger public not only tolerates the little publics *but actively fosters them as a democratic necessity.* Little publics are the voluntary associations based on religion, ethnicity, gender, language, race, sexual orientation, hobbies, labor—interests of all sorts, some of which are incompatible from one group to another. The state is the larger public, and it is formally distinct from the little publics. "For support and comfort and a sense of belonging, men and women look to their groups" (Walzer, 1992b, p. 67). This is as it should be. But for their rights, mobilities, and freedom to change their associations, they look to the state. This, too, is as it should be. The democratic journey in a pluralist society, then, requires of citizens the disposition to create "a unity of individuals alongside the diversity of groups" (p. 68).

In order to attain some measure of success, this project needs to include a critique of those forms of liberalism that make genuine pluralism impossible. (It must also examine those forms of pluralism that make political community impossible.[5]) Two forms of liberalism that unnecessarily impede pluralism require immediate attention. First, there is liberalism's old garrison mentality when faced with diversity and, second, its neutrality premise. Liberal democracy holds *pluribus* as a central tenet while at the same time denying, punishing or, at best, tolerating diversity. According to the principles of liberal democracy, unity arises from diversity. Yet in actually existing democracies, numerous groups live on the outskirts of the political community and are not by any stretch of the imagination included in the *unum.* Liberal democracy celebrates pluralism as a present, ongoing, and necessary feature of a democratic state while persistently "short-changing" women (American Association of University Women, 1992), people of color, the poor, gays, and lesbians. Unity is celebrated at the same time that, as Banks's Pledge of Allegiance narrative clearly shows, inclusion is denied or frustrated. By any measure, this is a stunning contradiction. Yet it is the logical conclusion of the forces discussed earlier: fear of dissolution combined with an accomplishment view of democracy. *E pluribus unum,* recall, is held to be an accomplishment; any serious attention to diversity today, therefore, is unnecessary and will result, in this view, in what Arthur Schlesinger (1992) called "the disuniting of America."

Second, there is liberal democracy's neutrality premise. Accordingly, in one's role as citizen, one is an abstraction—an *it*; a *cipher* (Gray, 1992)— of indifferent sex, race, social class, religion, national origin and, in some polities, sexual orientation; the state, meanwhile, is color-blind, gender-blind, and so on. This official blindness is an enormously good invention, to be sure, and perhaps the finest of the Enlightenment. The countless numbers of people over the millennia who have perished in state-sponsored religious warfare, the women who have been burned at the stake, the heathen who have been converted at gunpoint, all the subjects who have been tortured at the king's and pope's pleasure—all these bear silent witness to the wisdom of state neutrality. Neutrality is the state's way of embracing—being bigger than and outside of, though caring for—all the little publics, rather than being nothing more than one of them that has gained power over the others and now insists on assimilation to its ways.

Yet, while the neutrality premise helps protect individual liberty from state and majority tyranny, it impedes the full flowering of pluralism. In societies where group identities are politicized and matter greatly in the conduct of public affairs, which is the case everywhere, state indifference serves especially the interests of whichever groups presently enjoy positions of power—often the majority culture. Official state neutrality disguises actually existing power imbalances and often shifts attention to the supposed deficits of the excluded groups. In this way, political formulations that pretend neutrality tend to reproduce the status quo.

As for the converse—forms of pluralism that impede political community—two are paramount. First is the refusal to walk the path with other groups, conjoining in order to create the larger public, a democratic political framework; second is the reification of group identity. As for the first, the identity politics that inevitably come with pluralism sometimes replace liberalism's excessive self-interest with a new politics of group interest. This can be an advantage, as for example when African Americans and Latinos take a defensive and vigilant stand against continued oppression and demand inclusion in the larger, overarching public. But it can be a disadvantage, too, as when individuals are forced to comply with a currently enforced group identity (e.g., "Act like a lady!" "Be a man!") or when groups try to secure their own betterment without regard for the common good. In the latter case, we have group idiocy and its suicidal inattention to the commonwealth.

As for the second, pluralism must always beware the essentializing tendency in both progressive and traditional theorizing that would make group identity into something natural and biological, as if etched in a DNA string. Not only are ethnic identities not inborn; they are circumstantial and, to an extent, voluntary. This point has always been rather easily grasped where social class identity is concerned, as Anne Phillips (1993) notes. Modern people don't generally believe that one's class is fixed or eternal. This is why people can at least imagine class mobility. Ethnicity, religion, and gender, however, are not so flexibly defined, and the tendency has been to reify them. To do so solidifies what are actually fluid and dynamic cultural identities. The more naturalized the group identity, the more likely are its members—*especially if the group is in a position of dominance in the social hierarchy*—to mistake their particularity for a universal norm, and the less apt they may be to negotiate or modify some of their customs for the sake of the larger public. Ethnocentrism is the historical norm, is it not? Conversely, ethnic pride movements by people of color and other historically oppressed groups most often have as their aim inclusion in that larger public, not separation (Asante, 1998; Banks, 1997; Okihiro, 1994; Sizemore, 1972; Takaki, 1993). Reification of group difference can impede the creation and maintenance of the larger public, then, particularly when it is done by members of the privileged, dominant group—the White middle class in the case of the United States—for members of this group are in a position to use the social, economic, and political power they enjoy to exclude other groups.

Even if pluralism is a democratic necessity, still it is not the whole of life. In democracies, people must also be citizens—stewards of the body politic. Otherwise, there can be no pluralism, no liberty; only isolation, domination, and subjugation.

In an interesting way—some find it paradoxical—liberty and democracy rely on diversity; they *need* it. James Madison saw this in the plainest way: a multiplicity of minority factions keeps any one from tyrannizing the whole of society. Minority factions, therefore, are not a problem in a democracy; rather, the majority is the problem. That is the challenge to which he applied himself. Only when diversity is mediated politically through the commonwealth of shared citizenship are all manner of mutually acceptable differences—liberty—assured. It is an old argument, dating in modern times at least to Machiavelli (Berlin, 1998), and it is central to the liberalism of John Locke through Martin Luther King Jr. I will take this up in more detail in Chapter 5, where I will try to show that diversity is a necessary asset in democratic group discussions.

CONCLUSION

E pluribus unum—alongside the many, the one—is continually a timely idea. It could serve well as the centerpiece of a reconceptualized citizenship education curriculum. In this chapter, I have focused on this idea centrally, as well as on several others on which this main idea depends—namely, participation, path, and diversity. I have not tried exactly to pin down definitions, for these are essentially contested ideas, and anyway, I want to contribute to discussions, not dictionaries. The discussions I have in mind involve teachers, principals, curriculum coordinators, and parents who are wondering whether it would be worthwhile, and what it might mean, to educate students for democratic citizenship. The little publics take care of the education of their own members to the norms and values of their groups; the larger public—where citizenship occurs—must do likewise.

If I have succeeded in sketching the contours of a deepened and expanded conception of democratic citizenship, then the following summary should make sense. The citizenship education literature rests on a conventional conception of democratic citizenship and of the unity/difference (oneness/manyness) tension in particular. That conception is limited in two ways. First, there is its liberal-Federalist emphasis on containing political difference in such a way that the political world of the brethren—those already inside the *unum*—is sheltered and stable; second, there is its tendency to minimize social and cultural diversity, as though these were different matters entirely. This is a nominal and exclusive notion of democracy, one driven by fear of difference and dissolution. It has adverse consequences, and it is these consequences, exemplified in the three opening scenes of this chapter, that call out for something better or, using the term of the young Tiananmen Square protester, for something "advanced."

Among these adverse consequences are three that should be of keen interest to educators: first, a tenacious bias for assimilation, which is a bias against *pluribus*, against identity formation outside the brethren's ken; second, an impoverished notion of citizenship that involves little more than civic voyeurism—watching other people (elected representatives) act like citizens; and third, the evaporation simultaneously of strong cultural pluralism and the sort of vigorous political framework necessary to secure it.

It is possible to rework the nominal and exclusive conception of democracy using three ideas in particular. They are building blocks for a more wholesome conception that brings both difference and democracy into a single frame as parallel phenomena (Figure 2.1). One of these building blocks concerns the kind of participation for which citizens need to be educated. Here is the tension between direct involvement in public life and spectatorship. Contested is the meaning of popular sovereignty. The advanced idea retains representatives but asks citizens to do more than merely elect them and then, as Tocqueville observed, lapse into dependency for another 4 years. It opens up a new civic space for direct and cooperative involvement in public life—for participatory democracy. A related building block concerns the citizen's outlook on (or stance toward) democracy. Here is the tension between viewing democracy as an attainment needing only protection and a way of life that a people are trying to achieve together. Contested here is the meaning of public life and the selves that compose it. The advanced idea is that citizens emerge from idiocy to puberty, thereby regarding themselves as having a public

Figure 2.1. Tensions in a Pluralist Conception of Democratic Citizenship

direct / spectatorship

Participation

path / accomplishment

Outlook

pluralism / assimilation

Difference

---

life in which they are challenged to manifest as democrats. This requires them to reflect on public life and to form it anew, again and again, in community service, social action, and deliberation. The third building block is the tension between pluralism and assimilation. Contested here is whether the "little publics" are a threat or an aid to the "big public" and, hence, the desirability of fostering them rather than only, at best, tolerating them. Contested, in brief, is the meaning of *e pluribus unum*. The advanced idea is that this motto means something other than shying away from difference in the name of a defensive unity. It means the political one alongside the cultural many. With this meaning, difference ceases to be a threat to community.

The implications of a deepened and expanded conception of democratic citizenship for educators can only be imagined, for that is its own democratic path. The program suggested here has a straightforward theme: it would educate children for political oneness and cultural diversity, with the understanding that these exist parallel to and in support of one another. Attempts to transcend this relationship would be dropped, for reasons that by now should be clear.

The citizenship curriculum in the schools, to the little extent one has been deliberated, developed, or implemented, typically covers the documents and procedures of republican government. Assimilation, accomplishment, and spectatorship appear generally to undergird the treatment. Avoided are sustained curriculum and instruction on the central principles and histories of democracy, the problems to which it was put forward as a solution, the conditions that support and undermine this path, the deliberative arts of hammering out law and public policy together, the cultural diversity within societies, and the consequent tensions between oneness and manyness. In a reconceptualized democratic citizenship education curriculum, this largely avoided realm would be explored alongside the history, promise, and perils of republican government. Fortunately, educators need not start from scratch. Helpful curriculum work of various stripes—all of it necessary, none of it sufficient—has been done. The subsequent chapters in this book detail the core of that work, and an historical sample is collected in *Educating the Democratic Mind* (Parker, 1996c). Still, it is the *conceptual* discussion that is needed most critically, I believe—the rationale-building and clarification of meanings that are at the heart of curriculum deliberation.

In the next chapter, I will further specify the non-idiotic life—the citizen's life—as *enlightened political engagement* and explore different ways of achieving that goal, both in school and out.

Toward Enlightened
Political Engagement

"In '56 and '57, night after night I sat down and wrote out a citizenship
education program which would help illiterates learn to read and
write, so they could register to vote."
—Septima Clark (1984, p. 152)

I want to articulate in this book a concept that is, I believe, central to teachers' work as the primary educators of "we the people." So far, I have suggested this concept by discussing its opposite, idiocy, and then contrasting
this with the non-idiotic life, the citizen's life—for example, the work of
Martin Luther King Jr., Mohandas Gandhi, Jane Addams, Thich Naht Hanh,
or the citizenship educator whose quotation opens this chapter, Septima
Clark, who developed education programs in the early years of the Civil
Rights movement. In Chapter 2, I detailed three "advanced" ideas that help
to sustain the non-idiotic life: *path* (democracy is more a project than an
accomplishment), *participation* (popular sovereignty is not a spectator sport
or something one contemplates but doesn't actually do), and *pluralism* (diversity both supports liberty and is itself a kind of liberty, and it nurtures
the democracy we are trying to create).

In this chapter, I want to further specify the non-idiotic life, the citizen's
life, as *enlightened political engagement*. I do this to further specify the curriculum goal of democratic education, and also to explore different ways
of achieving that goal. My plan is to step beyond the territory most familiar to multicultural/democratic citizenship educators long enough to set
alongside it additional and complementary ways of achieving that goal;
then I will turn back to the more familiar territory and try to organize it in
a way that emphasizes four intersecting priorities: knowledge, engagement,
caring, and justice. First, I define enlightened political engagement. Second, I look beyond schooling altogether to other powerfully educative sites:
social class and the voluntary community associations that young people
join or find themselves in—basketball teams, churches and temples, 4-H
clubs, neighborhood associations, and so on. Third, I consider schooling

in two parts: one focuses simply on years of school attendance without looking at what goes on inside schools or at the differences between schools; the other takes us inside schools to curriculum, climate, social relations, and all the formal and informal activity that comes to mind with the term "school." Pulling together non-school associations, school attendance, and inside-school variables under one roof should help explain how the citizen identity and enlightened political engagement are cobbled together across various means. We could also imagine a set of educational policy recommendations drawn from across the array; this I venture at the conclusion.

ENLIGHTENED POLITICAL ENGAGEMENT

Before looking at these multiple approaches, let us look more closely at the goal for which they are a means. My general concern in this book is to use education to combat idiocy, which is self- and familial-indulgence at the expense of the common good. Put differently, idiocy is paying no attention to public affairs—more broadly, to the social and natural environment—even when this inattention undermines one's own liberty. Put positively, our goal is educating people for the role of democratic citizen—for walking the democratic path in a diverse society. These are citizens who have met the challenge of "puberty," as we saw in Chapter 1, and are capable therefore of responding creatively, willingly, and genuinely to the central citizenship question of our time, which was introduced in Chapter 2: *How can we live together justly, in ways that are mutually satisfying, and which leave our differences, both individual and group, intact and our multiple identities recognized?*

A principal attribute of the non-idiotic life, the life of the citizen, might be called *enlightened political engagement*.[1] The concept has two dimensions—democratic enlightenment and political engagement—and together they suggest something like wise participation in public affairs or "reflective civic participation" (Newmann, 1989). Enlightened political engagement is not easily won and it is never won for all time; one works at it continually (path), through one's actions with others (participation), and purposefully with others who are of different ideology, perspective, or culture (pluralism).

Both dimensions matter. *Political engagement* refers to the action or participatory domain of citizenship. Included are political behaviors from voting or contacting public officials to deliberating public problems, campaigning, and engaging in civil disobedience, boycotts, strikes, rebellions, and other forms of direct action. *Democratic enlightenment*, by contrast, refers to the moral-cognitive knowledge, norms, values, and principles that shape this engagement. Included are literacy, knowledge of the ideals of democratic living, knowing which government officials to contact about different issues, the commitment to freedom and justice, the disposition to be tolerant of religious and other cultural differences, and so forth. Without democratic enlightenment, political engagement can move in dangerous directions (Ku Klux Klan members were and are, unfortunately, engaged). Knowledge, values, and attitudes—together, character or virtue—are the ballast that a democratic citizen brings to the action that he or she undertakes. Enlightened action is enlightened because it is aimed at the realization of democratic ideals. Unenlightened action undermines them.

Of course, the faculty called *judgment* or principled reasoning is required to distinguish between enlightened and unenlightened political engagement (Beiner, 1984). Judgment is required because drawing that distinction is not a matter of applying rules or recipes. Accordingly, reasonable people of good judgment may disagree vehemently about which course of action is best in a given circumstance. Should the majority be permitted to do whatever it wishes? Of course not. This would surely undermine democratic ideals, as political theorists from Aristotle to Madison and King have argued so well. But should corporate power be restrained? Should wealth be further redistributed? Should groups have rights or are rights only for individuals? Should women have reproductive freedom? Should voting be required? Should ex-felons be disenfranchised? These are highly contested issues *among* democratic citizens.

With this rough goal statement in hand, we are ready to look at two realms of democratic citizenship education: non-school initiatives and school initiatives. As we do so, the goal will be further elaborated.

SOCIETY AND ENLIGHTENED POLITICAL ENGAGEMENT

With or without schooling, societies socialize their young. They enculturate them; they initiate them into the elders' conventions of knowing, valuing, believing, and behaving. These are the familiar terms deployed in the social sciences to explain social reproduction. The hothouses of this activity are the socializing forces and agencies in society—the immediate and extended family, churches and temples, workplaces, clubs, schools, television, movies, social class, the ubiquitous marketplace, and advertising. The people who set the conditions and ends of this socializing activity, to the extent it can be controlled, are parents, clergy, older siblings, bosses, appointed and elected officials, corporate moguls, publishers, television producers, teachers, and so forth. In a complex, industrialized society, the array of socializing agents is broad and tangled, and citizenship education is spread across that array. Let me zero in on two key non-school citizenship-education sites: social class and voluntary associations. The latter is embedded in the former.

Social Class

"Poverty," as Joel Spring put it so simply, "is a major barrier to free access to ideas and education" (1989, p. xi). Social class membership locates one in a web of circumstances, relations, biases, and achievement expectations that are closely linked with citizenship knowledge, behaviors, and attitudes. The most disadvantaged citizens socially and economically (in the United States, women, African Americans, and the poor) are also "the least informed, and thus least equipped to use the political system to redress their grievances" (Delli Carpini & Keeter, 1996, p. 18). Affluent citizens, by contrast, are much more likely to know officials and the rules of the game, and they use both to their advantage, sometimes skewing the whole political community in their favor.

In both cases, people's ability to learn about and influence their community is shaped by their location in the economy. Whether children go to school, where they go, what they are taught there, by whom, how, and with whom—all these fundamental points of educational opportunity are predicted substantially by a non-school variable: social class membership. One of the surest ways to improve inner-city citizenship education is not by tinkering with curriculum and instruction but by ending inner-city poverty (cf., Anyon, 1997).

Voluntary Associations

I was born in a non-profit Seventh Day Adventist hospital in Denver, Colorado, and raised in a working-class United Methodist family in a suburb south of Denver. I joined bands and orchestras at school, belonged to the Cub Scouts and then the Boy Scouts, went to a summer camp run by a nearby Baptist church and another run by the United Methodists, raised money for the Salvation Army every Christmas, volunteered for the political party in which my parents were active, and listened to my parents talk about *their* organizations, from political parties to the League of Women Voters and the local parks-and-recreation board—all this by the time I left junior high school. I didn't appreciate then and have only begun to appreciate now (thanks to a burgeoning literature on it) that this joining activity, and all the groups available to me for joining, was an important aspect of the civic culture that democracies require. (The democratic path is not built on thin air.) French sociologist Alexis de Tocqueville (1848/1969) visited the United States in the middle of the 19th century and was bowled over by all the joining:

> Americans of all ages, all stations in life, and all types of disposition are forever forming associations. There are not only commercial and industrial associations in which all take part, but others of a thousand different types—religious, moral, serious, futile, very general and very limited, immensely large and very minute. Americans combine to give fetes, found seminaries, build churches, distribute books, and send missionaries to the antipodes. Hospitals, prisons, and schools take shape in that way. Finally, if they want to proclaim a truth or propagate some feeling by the encouragement of a great example, they form an association. In every case, at the head of any new undertaking, where in France you would find the government or in England some territorial magnate, in the United States you are sure to find an association. (1848/ 1969, p. 513)

Americans not only join groups to do things, they even join them to abstain from doing things they think they shouldn't be doing. One might imagine that they would simply not do it, whatever it is; but they join with others to not do it—to not do it *together*. This baffled Tocqueville:

> The first time that I heard in America that one hundred thousand men had publicly promised never to drink alcoholic liquor, I thought it more of a joke than a serious matter and for the moment did not see why these very abstemious citizens could not content themselves with drinking water by their own firesides. In the end I came to understand that these hundred thousand Americans, frightened by the progress of drunkenness around them, wanted to support sobriety by their patronage. . . . One may fancy that if they had lived in France each of these hundred thousand would have made individual representations to the government asking it to supervise all the public houses throughout the realm. (p. 516)

The point is that we not only live our daily lives embedded in the grip of class membership; we live them also in small groups of all sorts. Warmer than the sociologically correct term "groups" connotes, they are *communities*. They exist in the intermediate realm between the overarching political community, on the one hand, and the individual and family, on the other. They are civic spaces, and "civil society" is the term now used to describe the combined mass of these organizations—the vast, deeply layered network of them.

A vibrant civil society—the existence of a vast array of voluntary associations—is one of the keys to making a democracy work. Why? These informal, voluntary associations compose a social infrastructure where social life proceeds "on its own" in a sweep of different directions. In them, non-governmental yet civil relationships are made and nurtured. The people in "we the people" are constituted, and relationships that extend beyond the family are created and maintained (contrast this with the *amoral familism* idiocy introduced in Chapter 1).

Just as important, safety and a sense of self-worth can be found in such groups. For many poor inner-city youth especially (but not exclusively), these safe spaces provide ground in a world without ground, stable relationships in a world where there may be few. According to Heath and McLaughlin (1993), arts and athletics are often the favorite activities in non-school youth associations, for these provide

> planning, preparing, practicing, and performing—with final judgment coming from outsiders (audiences, other teams in the league, and the public media). A sense of worth came from being a member of a group or team noted for accomplishment; a sense of belonging came from being needed within the organization—to teach younger members, to help take care of the facility, plan and govern activities, and promote the group to outsiders. (p. 24)

Furthermore, criticism of mainstream norms and practices can flourish in these groups. They have been called "free spaces" (Evans & Boyte, 1992) because of their potential for unrepressed, candid talk. Totalitarian rulers of the kind seen in 20th-century Germany, China, the Soviet Union, Cambodia, Afghanistan, and so forth had to destroy such groups as the first order of business. Freedom of speech and press was denied, as was freedom of assembly. The civic spaces between government, on the one hand, and individuals and families, on the other, were razed. Government power was thus unbridled, and virtually no organizations remained that could check or balance it. Criticism of public officials and protest activities of any sort were, of course, criminalized. Those who dared to organize or speak out were imprisoned in jails or mental institutions or murdered.

Voluntary organizations, then, are civic spaces, safe spaces, and free spaces. Together they compose the infrastructure or seedbed of democracy. Without them democracy cannot take root, for they provide the fertile medium for the root to grow.

There are two object lessons on this point. The first, briefly, is found in the totalitarian-turned-democratic states of eastern and central Europe. Here, the democratic infrastructure was devastated by the former tyrannies, the fertile medium destroyed. Churches and temples were closed along with other venues of association. With the fall of the Berlin Wall in 1989, the overarching political trajectory of those states was changed to a democratic mode and freedom of assembly was guaranteed in constitutions. *Yet, they flounder because civil society is still weak.* The totalitarian systems were grand exercises in wiping effective social organizations off the map. This is a lesson not only about the importance of civil society to creating and maintaining a democracy but about the difficulty of growing back a civil society once it has been killed off.

The second object lesson is more hopeful, and it reveals the agency and efficacy of voluntary associations—their ability to affect the larger society. Perhaps the most vivid object lesson in U.S. history is the generative role of African American churches in the Civil Rights movement. The Black church served as a *movement center.* According to Aldon Morris (1984), this is "a social organization within the community of a subordinated group, which mobilizes, organizes, and coordinates collective action aimed at attaining the common ends of that subordinated group" (p. 40). Any social movement has one or more movement centers. The Black church was not the only movement center within the Civil Rights movement; Black colleges played a significant role, too, as David Halberstam (1998) illustrates.

While the variety of churches in the African American community is staggering, mirroring the social, political, and economic diversity of that community, still the churches had numerous institutional commonalities. "For one thing," Morris writes, "they all had the responsibility of spiritually and emotionally soothing an oppressed group" (1984, p. 11). These were African American churches, after all, and regardless of their differences their members were and are the most oppressed of all subordinated groups in North American save, perhaps, Native peoples. This commonality modifies any claim of variety among Black churches. Indeed, E. Franklin Frazier (1963) referred to the Black church as a nation within a nation and, therefore, a political force to be reckoned with:

> As a result of the elimination of Negroes from the political life of the American community, the Negro Church became the arena of their political activities. . . . The church was the arena in which the struggle for power and the thirst for power could be satisfied. (p. 43)

The rest is history, as the saying goes. From the church network and its political arm, the Southern Christian Leadership Conference, along with Black college campuses, sprang the movement. Just this one scene from Halberstam's (1998) history of youth involvement in the Civil Rights movement conveys the point in all its subtlety. Picture a desegregation sit-in at a Nashville, Tennessee, lunch counter:

> To the students themselves, the experience was nothing less than exhilarating. John Lewis had been scared before the first sit-in. There were two things

which helped him get through. The first was his absolute certainty that what they were doing was right. The second was that he was not alone. He was with his friends, the closest friends he had ever had in his life. *He had sat there in the first Baptist Church right before the sit-in began* and had looked around, and he could tell how nervous all his colleagues in the core group were. . . . The reality of what they were about to do had finally set in. They were about to go up against the full power of the city of Nashville. (pp. 105–106, emphasis added)

Postcommunist eastern Europe drives home the lesson that a broad and deep network of social relations is necessary if democracy is to take root and if democratic practices are to be workable and sustainable. The role of the Black church and Black college in the movement drives home the lesson that voluntary associations are not static but generative. They can and often do push the status quo to grow toward the fuller realization of its own ideals. They can pressure democracies to make good on their promissory notes, as we saw in Chapter 2. As Gary Okihiro (1994) wrote, these groups have been anything but static. To the contrary, they have helped produce and clarify the core values and ideals of the nation: "The core values and ideals of the nation emanate not from the mainstream but from the margins—from among Asian and African Americans, Latinos, and American Indians, women, and gays and lesbians" (p. ix). In other words, voluntary associations are not only civic or public, as well as relatively safe places for their members; they are relatively free spaces of unrepressed and candid criticism of mainstream society. The democratic potential of voluntary associations exerting themselves on mainstream norms and values cannot be underestimated. Historically, subordinated groups have been "key staging grounds for interventionist politics—from the small group meetings of the early women's movement to the 'free pulpits' of Black churches in the Deep South during the civil rights era, to the 'liberated zones' of independence movements in the third world" (Trend, 1995, p. 10).

One learns in voluntary associations three important things that bear directly on the developing citizen's identity. First, one associates with others who are more diverse than one's family members. One is exposed to a wider and more complex social arena in which one's own perspective becomes one of many. The idiosyncrasy of one's family life can be seen in the reflective mirror of a broadened social horizon, and *pluralism* becomes—to some degree—a fact in one's own life. Second, one engages problems that stretch beyond one's own and one's family's. One becomes involved in the public realm, what Dewey called the public and its problems (1927). The public's problems are wider than the family's—police protection, food and water supply, sanitation, libraries, schools, hospitals, and so on. Even

in a choir, the members must deliberate with one another the practice sched-
ules, artistic differences, and goals and strategies that may never surface
at home. In 4-H clubs young people are planning fair entries, electing club
presidents, working with adult leaders, and so forth—associating for purposes that go well beyond familial relations. Likewise, in the youth associations studies by Heath and McLaughlin (1993), young people are taking
care of the facility and planning activities. Third, in voluntary associations
one learns norms of deliberating across differences, norms that allow conflict without threatening the group's existence. That is, one learns civility
or mannerly conduct. Such conduct differs dramatically from group to
group and setting to setting, of course: the manners of a bowling league
will differ from those of a Quaker meeting. Swearing and teasing may be
rewarded in one but forbidden in another, for example. Still, socially sanctioned conduct proceeds at full steam, decisions get made, and the group's
future is not put at risk.

Voluntary organizations can be bad for democracy as well as good.
The object lesson in the United States is provided by the Ku Klux Klan.
In Germany, Nazi organizations overtook what was a democratic society—the Weimar Republic. What is learned in voluntary associations,
then, can undermine liberal-democratic ideals. The larger political community may emphasize liberal values such as toleration, for example, and
a local church group may support this by taking young people on respectful visits to other churches and temples. Another church group at the same
time might preach that members of other faith communities are sinners
bound for hell. The larger political community may value gender equality while a patriarchic men's club teaches that "the home is a man's castle."
Nancy Rosenblum (1994) writes,

> Liberal government does not require the internal life of every association
> to conform to public norms and practices by prohibiting discrimination, en-
> forcing due process, encouraging liberal private life (outlawing polygamous
> marriage as "patriarchal"), favoring democratic authority (congregational
> churches over hierarchic ones or worker control over other forms of man-
> agement). Liberalism does not command strict congruence "all the way
> down." (p. 540)

To summarize, the young learn much about citizenship, for better or
worse, outside school. Location in the socioeconomic class hierarchy compels children to learn and not learn particular things; it places them in a
particular social niche that allocates both a school building and, inside it, a
school experience. Meanwhile, membership in multiple voluntary groups
potentially deepens one's understanding of pluralism, placing one in overarching moral grids that extend well beyond the family.

SCHOOLS AND ENLIGHTENED POLITICAL ENGAGEMENT

Schools are potentially rich sites for citizenship education. They present both a formal curriculum—a planned scope and sequence of teaching and learning that can be aimed directly at the development of enlightened political engagement—along with daily situations of living together "in public" outside the family. Schools, then, are both curricular and civic spaces, and both can be marshaled toward the education of democratic citizens. But before peering inside schools, let us look at something that educators interested in curriculum and school climate typically overlook: the effect of simple school attendance on the development of enlightened political engagement.

School Attendance

By simple school attendance I mean nothing more than *years* of school attendance, ignoring what goes inside schools and all the attendant variability. (I acknowledge that school attendance is no simple matter for students or their parents, particularly disabled or challenged students and students in poor city schools. I use the term "simple" only to distinguish going to school from the more complex matters of what goes on inside schools and the variability between schools.) Political scientists who are interested in citizen development call this variable "educational attainment" or "level of schooling." Using mainly survey research, they find again and again that years of schooling is the chief predictive variable of citizenship knowledge, attitudes, and behavior—in other words, enlightened political engagement. In fact, there is probably no single variable in the survey research literature that generates as substantial correlations in such a variety of directions in political understanding and behavior as years of schooling. It is *"everywhere the universal solvent,"* political scientist Philip Converse writes, *"and the relationship is always in the same direction"* (1972, p. 324, emphasis in original; see also Lazarsfeld, Berlson, & Gaudet, 1944; Nie, Junn, & Stehlik-Barry, 1996; Verba & Nie, 1972). As for the indicators used in this body of work, there are a total of seven, five of which are associated with political engagement and five of which are associated with democratic enlightenment (there is some overlap, as shown in Table 3.1).

The first set, indicators of political engagement, is concerned with citizens' ability to participate in popular sovereignty—to engage in politics and to influence public policy. These five are knowledge of current political leaders, knowledge of current political facts, political attentiveness, participation in difficult political activities, and frequency of voting. The citizen who pays attention to public issues and knows the names and addresses

**Table 3.1. Correlations between Citizenship Outcomes and Years of Formal
Education Completed**

Citizenship outcome	Correlation	Dimension
Knowledge of principles of democracy	.38	Democratic enlightenment
Knowledge of current political leaders	.29	Political engagement
Knowledge of other current political facts	.37	both
Political attentiveness	.39	both
Participation in difficult political activities	.29	Political engagement
Frequency of voting	.25	both
Tolerance	.35	Democratic enlightenment

Source: Nie, Junn, and Stehlik-Barry, 1996

of her current elected and appointed officials and contacts them now and
then is better positioned to influence public policy than the citizen whose
engagement begins and ends with watching political spectacles on television and/or voting. The second set, indicators of democratic enlightenment,
is concerned with citizens' understanding of and support for the norms and
ideals of democratic political community. These five are knowledge of
principles of democracy, knowledge of current political facts, political attentiveness, frequency of voting, and tolerance. The citizen who knows that
tolerance of diversity is crucial to making a democracy work possesses
knowledge that is directly consequential for living together cooperatively
in a pluralist society. This knowledge should, for example, restrain her from
advocating a state religion or the incarceration of political dissidents—both
standard practices in authoritarian states. It should help her to argue not only
for her own rights but for the rights of others, especially those with whom
she disagrees or whose cultural life she finds repugnant. What could otherwise be a kind of political engagement dedicated to self-aggrandizement
at the expense of the common good (idiocy) is moderated by a grasp of
democratic principles and one's obligations to the political community.

Table 3.1 displays correlations between years of schooling and these
two sets of citizenship outcomes based on data from the 1990 Citizen Par-

ticipation Study (Nie, Junn, & Stehlik-Barry, 1996). They reveal a positive and consistent relationship between school attendance and the seven citizen outcomes. This is survey research, recall, so let me give examples of the questions used. The first indicator, "knowledge of principles of democracy," was measured by three questions: One asked respondents to identify a constitutional guarantee dealing with the Fifth Amendment; another asked them to distinguish between democracy and dictatorship, and the third to give the meaning of "civil liberties." The seventh indicator, political tolerance, was defined as "a willingness to permit the expression of ideas or interests one opposes." There were four questions: Respondents were asked if they would allow someone to make a speech in their community who called for letting the military rule the country or who was against all churches and religions, and they were asked whether books should be removed from the library when they advocate homosexuality or argue that Blacks are genetically inferior to Whites.

To be sure, these seven characteristics of enlightened political engagement do not capture the full range of desired citizenship outcomes. Deliberative competence, such as the ability to make policy decisions with citizens who are culturally different from oneself, which is the subject of Chapters 5, 6, and 7, is not addressed. Nor is the commitment beyond "tolerance" to fight for inclusion of groups historically marginalized. Still, they are headed in the right direction, and I suspect that none would be excluded from a more complete list.

But *why* does simple school attendance predict enlightened political engagement? Norman Nie and his colleagues (1996) conducted a path analysis to develop an explanatory model. They reached the following conclusions: First, school attendance influences political engagement by allocating access to political resources. Citizens with more schooling get more access than do citizens with less schooling. This is because schooling positions a citizen in the sociopolitical network. This network is like a giant stadium with a stage at the front. Those persons with more schooling generally are placed closer to the stage where it is easier to hear and be heard and become a player oneself.

What about the democratic enlightenment a citizen will or won't bring to his or her place in the stadium? (Recall, participation alone is not necessarily pro-democratic.) A high school or college graduate may have won a seat close to the civic stage but lacks the liberal understanding of democratic community needed to use that position for the common good rather than as a power base from which to launch his or her private agenda. As with the engagement dimension, enlightenment is also correlated positively with school attendance, but the path now, according to Nie and his colleagues, is cognitive rather than positional. Knowledge of principles of democracy and the disposition to tolerate dissent are explained by formal schooling's positive impact on political knowledge and attitude. (When kids are taught these things, they stand a better chance of learning them.) There are two explanatory paths, then, in this attempt to reason why educational attainment has its well-established positive ties to citizenship outcomes: social network positionality and intellectual attainment. On this analysis, schooling is important for democracy because it gives one relatively more power *and* ideas about how to use it.

Educators who labor to shape school curricula and climate toward critical and democratic ends may find this school attendance data annoying. Perhaps they presume school attendance, for that battle seems largely to have been won thanks to the struggles first to create public schools and then to desegregate them. Accordingly, educators concentrate on practices internal to school buildings, on inequalities between affluent and impoverished schools (and between high and low tracks in the same school), on the effects of teaching quality, building leadership, materials availability, funding, the local policy context, and on the battle against racist and sexist practices embedded within the culture of the school. However, were educators to take a broader view of democratic citizenship education, they would not dismiss the role of school attendance in positioning citizens to exercise power and to shape how that power is exercised. They would take seriously two social reform movements that have been eclipsed in recent decades: increasing the school-retention (high-school graduation) rate and making higher education available to all, either free of charge or on a sliding scale.

Inside Schools

Asked why they ignore the phenomena to which teachers and students devote their days and educational researchers devote their careers—namely what goes on *inside* schools—political scientists could respond, "We don't need to look inside schools; attending them is what matters, and we have the data to support this claim." But there exists also a conceptual habit that might help to explain how they manage not to peer inside at curriculum, instruction, and the quality of school life. These researchers operate within a discipline that subsumes education within the concept *political socialization*, and political socialization studies generally are concerned with *unconscious* social reproduction. They are guided by a descriptive-explanatory aim, whereas the aim of educators is conscious social reproduction and transformation. The currency of educators is not description so much as prescription—reform, renewal, transformation. Educators are concerned to intervene in history and intentionally shape society's future—increasing the literacy rate, strengthening citizens' ability to analyze social issues, deepening their grasp of constitutional principles, exposing racism, creating equal access where there has been only limited access, and so forth. When citizenship education is assimilated into political socialization, it is easy, as Amy Gutmann (1999) observes, "to lose sight of the distinctive virtue of a democratic society, that it authorizes citizens to influence *how* their society reproduces itself" (p. 15).

Democratic citizenship educators of all stripes act on this virtue and prescribe an array of interventions toward increasing some aspect or other of enlightened political engagement. There are a good number of empirical studies among this work,[2] but the bulk of it is theoretical and philosophical. Underlying debates (e.g., which should be emphasized: enlightenment or engagement?) fuel ever more literature on what *ought* to be done to educate democrats, and it is this amelioration-oriented literature that I want to explore in this section.

It is a sprawling literature. Two prominent attempts to organize it are by Barr, Barth, and Shermis (1977) and Cherryholmes (1980). Barr, Barth, and Shermis described three traditions of citizenship education inside schools: citizenship transmission, social science, and reflective inquiry. The first affirms existing political institutions and ideals (e.g., the rule of law, civil liberties, critical thinking, tolerance) and seeks to deploy education in their service, intentionally passing them to succeeding generations. The second and third are reform initiatives that endeavor to replace the transmission model. The social science tradition aims to help young people acquire the knowledge and methods of inquiry esteemed by the social science disciplines. The desired citizen can form and test hypotheses about social and political life; she can evaluate data, reason historically, and has mastered some of the central concepts of each discipline. This model is exemplified by Edwin Fenton's (1967) work and others in the New Social Studies movement. The third tradition seeks reform in a more activist direction: to develop citizens capable of rational decision making in public policy contexts. It is exemplified by Shirley Engle's famous article, "Decision Making: The Heart of Social Studies Instruction" (1960) and Hunt and Metcalf's (1955) curriculum that focused on those social problems that have been closed off from open and critical discussion (society's "closed areas").

Cleo Cherryholmes (1980) reviewed largely the same literature but from a different epistemological standpoint. He argued that *each* tradition described by Barr and colleagues was epistemologically naïve—the third (reflective inquiry) as much as the first (citizenship transmission); and the second (social sciences) more so than the other two. All three assume positivism; all three ignore the relationship of knowledge to power—to social position, interests, and ideology. Reflective inquiry gets the bulk of Cherryholmes's criticism, for while it admirably educates students to grapple with society's problems, it fails to work out a methodological stance that would allow citizens "to gain a critical perspective on solutions for which they and others strive" (p. 136). In other words, it engages students in social problem solving without enabling them to think about which problems are worth solving, according to whom, to what ends, and in whose favor. Cherryholmes thus delineates two basic approaches to citizenship education inside schools: critical and non-critical.

These two analyses of inside-school citizenship education are helpful as far as they go, but I want to supplement them by highlighting a set of tensions that speak more directly to the content of educators' current debates—feminist critiques of traditional citizenship education, for example, and the tension between teaching about democracy and teaching democratically. My organization of this literature can be summarized as follows: Inside schools, there are both curricular and extracurricular approaches, and within each is a central tension. This makes four basic clusters of approaches to democratic citizenship education within the schools (see Figure 3.1).

Curricular Approaches

Let us begin with two curricular approaches, looking at both their common characteristic and the central opposition that divides them, then move to the two extracurricular approaches, again looking at the common characteristic and the central opposition. Curricular approaches to citizenship education focus on intentional (conscious) curriculum and instruction in schools—on what educators have planned for students to learn in school and how students are to be helped (instructed, coached) to achieve those objectives. These include the three traditions described by Barr, Barth, & Shermis (1977) and they cut across the critical/non-critical distinction described by Cherryholmes. There can be both critical and non-critical treatments of a reflective inquiry curriculum, for example. One need only compare Engle's (noncritical, 1960) to Apple's (critical, 1975) work.

The central opposition within the curricular cluster today is *participation* versus *transmission*. Participation approaches seek to engage students in the actual activity of democratic politics rather than, as is the case with transmission approaches, preparing them for it. Participation advocates ask incredulously: How can young people possibly learn to be democratic citizens in non-democratic schools? On the participation end of the curricular dimension is involvement *in* democracy; on the transmission side is learning *about* democracy. The work of Shirley Engle (1960), Fred Newmann (1975), and Richard Pratte (1988), among others, suggest the participation approach; the work of Paul Gagnon (1996) and the committee that produced

Figure 3.1. Curricular and Extracurricular Approaches

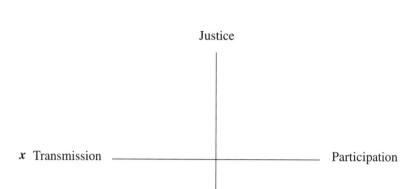

x = curricular dimension

y = extracurricular dimension

the *National Standards for Civics and Government* (Center for Civic Education, 1994), among others, suggest the latter.

Gagnon's main concern is that children should know the past because
"historical knowledge is the precondition for political intelligence" (1996,
p. 243). He urges teachers to "leap at (Thomas) Jefferson's argument" that
the general education of citizens should be chiefly historical. Quoting Jefferson,

> History, by apprising them of the past, will enable them to judge the future; it
> will avail them of the experience of other times and other nations; it will qualify
> them as judges . . . and enable them to know ambition under every disguise it
> may assume; and knowing it, to defeat its views. (quoted in Gagnon, 1996,
> p. 242)

Transmission advocates are not found only among conservative educators. Transmission is alive and well among critical educators who focus

on multicultural and pro-labor curricula. For example, the problem with an Anglocentric curriculum is that one perspective is uncritically transmitted rather than multiple perspectives being transmitted critically. The problem with a curriculum that celebrates generals and entrepreneurs but says nothing about labor, antiracist struggles, or economic democracy is not that a set of information is being transmitted but that it is the wrong set or that it privileges a single perspective (one that uncritically advantages the status quo) rather than multiple, competing perspectives that open up the inquiry to other possibilities (see Stanley, 1992). In this vein, the prominent Canadian socialist educator, Ken Osborne (1995), wrote a damning review of a new book on democratic education. He observed that many authors in the collection held forth on "democracy" and "democratic education" without defining it substantively, instead viewing it as a set of activities. One contributor to the book, Osborne tells us, wrote that "democracy is best taught as a process and best learned through active participation in decision-making. . . ." Osborne responds:

> There is, of course, a certain truth to this notion of democracy as process, but it takes us only so far. It is obviously true that a richer and more powerful democratic life will depend on a higher level of civic engagement than now exists. However, it is equally true that democracy involves more than simply "empowerment" and "participation," for fascists, racists, and assorted other anti-democrats can, and often do, feel highly empowered and participative, and also feel highly committed to a certain sense of community. The fundamental question must be this: once students are empowered and are ready to participate, what will they use their skills and powers to do? What will ensure that they will use them in the interests of democracy? (p. 122)

It should be noted that there is considerable overlap between the transmission and participation camps. Participation advocates typically want the Socratic tradition of critical thinking to be transmitted somehow from one generation to the next along with liberal values (e.g., liberty, tolerance, equality, justice) and institutions (e.g., rule of law, separation of church and state). Yet, inside the school, they don't want this transmission to eat up so much instructional time that none is left for deliberation, service learning, and direct political action (three kinds of participation) on real social problems both inside and outside the schoolhouse. Conversely, transmission advocates typically want students to participate in political activity, but they worry that without in-depth understandings of democratic principles this activity will be impulsive and unwise. Using the terms established earlier, we could say that at one pole of this curricular tension is political engagement, and at the opposite pole is democratic enlightenment.

Extracurricular Approaches

Extracurricular approaches involve the implicit or informal curriculum of the school. They focus not on what students should be learning directly from classroom instruction but on what they should be learning indirectly from the governance and climate of the classroom and the school. The common characteristic of extracurricular approaches is a concentration on the norms by which adults and young people in the school relate to one another and by which decisions on school and classroom policies are made. Toward the goal of cultivating democratic citizens, egalitarian and caring relations are prescribed over authoritarian and formalistic relations; cultural pluralism over assimilation; classroom and school climates that are open to the free expression of opinions and controversy over climates that encourage conformity and agreement; and student engagement in school and classroom governance over exclusion from such decision making. The rallying cry here, similar to the participation end of the curriculum dimension, is that it is absurd to teach about democracy without practicing it.

What would divide this apparently cozy group into opposing camps? Plenty. The central opposition among the extracurricular approaches today is between two social goods: caring and justice. The work of Nel Noddings (1992) and Donna Kerr (1997) suggests the former; the work of Lawrence Kohlberg (Power, Higgins, & Kohlberg, 1989) and Myra and David Sadker (1994) suggests the latter. Kohlberg delineated a conception of morality as just (fair; principled) reasoning, which he specified as the ability to imagine oneself in another's shoes—to take the perspective of others with empathic understanding. Students can develop in their ability to reason justly, Kohlberg found, given the right kinds of classroom and school support. This support is exemplified in the pedagogic setting he created and studied in his later work, following his sociological turn, called the "just community" (this will be discussed in the next chapter).

For Noddings and Kerr, a keen sense of fairness is not the central moral requirement of democratic citizens; there is more importantly a realm of care, which is relational, responsive, and concrete versus intellectual, imaginative, and abstract. Kerr (1997) writes,

> [T]he democratic psyche, formed in human relationships, is both receptive of the other and self-expressive. Genuine hope for democracy is grounded in this circuit of recognition. To jump over this reality in favor of talk of civil society and the requirements of political life is to fail to acknowledge the psychic and social realities in which democratic relations take root, when they do. . . . If democracy is to have substance [rather than being superimposed

upon human relationships], it can come only through the development of relations of mutual recognition and regard. (pp. 81–82)

This opposition among the extracurricular approaches is not a simple feminist/non-feminist one. Feminists are found on both sides of the justice/caring debate. For example, the Noddings/Kerr strand of feminist analysis is "maternalist"—grounded in the virtues of mothering—according to feminist political theorists like Mary Dietz (1992), Nancy Fraser (1995), and Anne Phillips (1991). By contrast, the latter articulate a strand of feminism that does not shy from reason, argument, and politics. "There are crucial distinctions between being a citizen and being a nice caring person," Phillips writes (p. 160). An ethic of care can lead (and historically *has* led) caregivers to neglect their own welfare.

The main tension on the extracurricular dimension, then, is between a worry on the one hand that the moral and political struggle for social justice and inclusion has edged out an ethic of care, and on the other, a worry that social justice will not be won, nor institutionalized repression dismantled, by caring people.[3]

To summarize, four sets of inside-school approaches are formed by intersecting two dimensions of inside-school democratic citizenship education: curricular and extracurricular activity. The resulting four quadrants should be helpful for making sense of several contemporary debates within the educator community about how best to nurture democrats. While I am aware that I have not exemplified the four quadrants fully, I want to stop here so that I can take up another related issue. If I may make just one more point first, however, about where this effort to conceptualize the inside-school approaches could go next, it would be to add a *third* dimension to the matrix: the critical/non-critical dimension that was mentioned earlier (e.g., Cherryholmes, 1980). Imagine Figure 3.1 now becoming a three-dimensional representation of the four quadrants. Doing so would create a near and a far version of each of the four quadrants for a total of eight (see Figure 3.2). We would then have a critical and a non-critical variation of each of the four quadrants. For example: In the *non-critical* variant of the upper right quadrant, we might place Shirley Engle's (1960) seminal work on decision making; in the *critical* variant of the same quadrant, we could place Michael Apple's (1975) also-seminal work on conflict.[4] In the *non-critical* variant of the lower right quadrant, we might place community service programs that help children perform good deeds, such as canned food drives for the hungry; in the *critical* variant of the same quadrant would go projects with social justice goals and a commitment to reclaiming lost personal histories (Giroux, 1993; Wade, 2000). Related to this, on

**Figure 3.2. Curricular, Extracurricular, and Critical/Non-critical
          Dimensions**

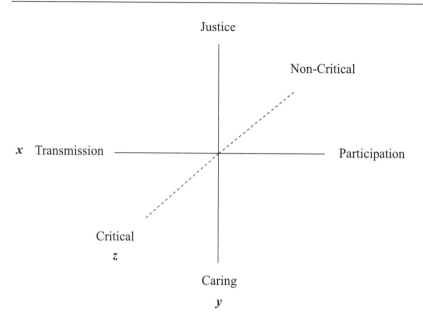

x = *curricular dimension*
y = *extracurricular dimension*
z = *near-far dimension*

the *critical* side of the upper-left quadrant, we would hope to see serious study of the kind of economic system that makes food drives necessary generation after generation.

When compared to the citizenship effects of simply attending school, we see in the inside-school quadrants a multifaceted array of *intentional* educational activity—conscious social reproduction—the combined effect of which ought to supplement school attendance effects, maybe even over-take them. This is not only a conceptual but also an empirical matter, of course, and the necessary research question would go something like this: Can a multifaceted democratic citizenship education program inside schools add something more to the development of enlightened political engagement than what already is contributed by school attendance alone?

CONCLUSION

History gives democracy no advantages. All democracies are weak and short-lived, and no actually existing democracy is an ideal democracy. Most are minimalist democracies: most adults are allowed to vote in elections that are more or less fair, by which representatives, most of them rich, win their seats in visual media performances. Attempting in the face of this to educate for principled democratic activism—for enlightened political engagement—is ambitious, yet a moral necessity.

How to do it? Not every strategy has been considered, but three of powerful consequence in the battle against idiocy were explored: involvement in voluntary associations can provide youth with safe yet public spaces; by staying in school, young people position themselves closer to the political stage; and within schools, both curricular and extracurricular activity can democratically enlighten and engage them.

The three approaches—group membership, school attendance, and inside-school activity—present an apples and oranges problem, which makes awkward my effort to place them within the same analytic framework. The third is consciously intentional and prescriptive, while the first two are descriptive and explanatory. These first two are not really "approaches" to the extent this term implies goal-oriented (intentional and strategic) action. Still, I treat them as approaches for the reason that the variables and dimensions they identify are consequential; they contribute to the development of particular citizenship knowledge, skills, and attitudes, whether they intend to or not.

Let us see, finally, if policy directions might be culled from the three approaches taken together. This strikes me as a worthwhile effort because it incites our imagination toward the big picture rather than only a piece of it, and it does so in a way that is responsive to the practical question, What can we do? On my attempt to do this, eight policy recommendations emerge. The first two derive from the first approach, society. The third and fourth represent the second approach, school attendance. The final four represent the third approach, inside schools, with one prescription each for the four clusters within it. Were we to add the third dimension, critical/non-critical, we should be able to derive 16 recommendations.

Arena A: Society

1. Tackle inner-city miseducation by tackling inner-city poverty.
2. Involve young people in a rich array of associations, and involve them in governance (planning, deciding, implementing, evaluating) therein.

Arena B: School Attendance

3. Increase the high school graduation rate.
4. Make higher education available to all.

Arena C: Inside Schools

Curricular

5. Require high-quality civics/government courses and hold students accountable for learning this subject matter.
6. Infuse the curriculum with decision-making opportunities.

Extracurricular

7. Afford students opportunities to deliberate actual classroom and school problems.
8. Create a caring social environment at school.

Across the array of efforts to cultivate enlightened political engagement, where should educators focus their attention? What are the priorities? "All of the above" seems to me the best response: Fight poverty and fund education, involve youth in civil society, fight for equal access to schools and strive to keep youth in school through high school and college, and provide multidimensional citizenship education inside schools. To this list, we should add that rather than shying from diversity in communities, schools, and curricula, we should support it vigorously, and foster it as a democratic force and a necessary condition for freedom.

These recommendations are meant only to suggest what might be done on multiple fronts, simultaneously, to educate democratic citizens. The point here is to bring young people into and through "puberty"—that is, to introduce them to public life and to cultivate public citizens, not idiots. Because democracy is tenuous and unsure, because most democracies are short-lived, because tyrannies and ethnic strife are not uncommon—for these reasons, the cultivation of democrats is not to be wished away as a natural by-product of attending to other things, such as raising scores in reading and math. Real attention needs to be paid, and in several directions at once.

Promoting Justice: Two Views

"How can you advocate breaking some laws and obeying others?" The answer lies in the fact that there are two types of laws: just and unjust.
—Martin Luther King Jr. (1963a, p. 82)

What if we seriously were to commit ourselves to educating children and youth to become enlightened and engaged democratic citizens? With all the social and psychological forces compelling them (and us) toward a life of comfortable idiocy, this would be an extraordinary aim. Were we to be successful, it would be an extraordinary achievement. What would that work entail? How would it look and feel? These questions guide the remaining chapters of this book. The present chapter delves into one aspect of that project: the task of educating just citizens. These are citizens who are principled and compassionate, who refrain from harming or exploiting others, and who believe it is their duty both to protect just institutions and to prevent injustice. "To sit passively by while injustices are committed, or democratic institutions collapse, in the hope that others will step in, is to be a free rider," writes Will Kymlicka (1999, p. 14). The idiocy of free ridership becomes clear even to free riders when they realize that having not looked out for their neighbors, there comes a day when there are no neighbors left to look after them. This is the point made so compellingly by the Protestant pastor Martin Niemoller when asked how the Nazis accomplished what they did: first taking over a state (Germany), then wreaking havoc on other states and engineering the Holocaust. Niemoller said it happened this way:

> First they came for the Communists, but I was not a Communist so I did not speak out. Then they came for the Socialists and the Trade Unionists, but I was neither, so I did not speak out. Then they came for the Jews, but I was not a Jew so I did not speak out. And when they came for me, there was no one left to speak out for me.[1]

There are a number of promising ways of educating for justice. One basic way of organizing them, as we saw in the last chapter, is to sort them into two groups: those oriented to engagement itself and those oriented to enlightenment. One aims to help students form particular understandings of justice (e.g., that "injustice anywhere is a threat to justice everywhere" [King, 1963a, p. 77]). The other aims to engage students in decision making and action on shared problems. An instructional approach drawn from the first group is the Socratic Seminar, which is a method of shared inquiry into the ideas, issues, and values expressed in powerful works of art, literature, and music.[2] For example, high school students might read and discuss King's "Letter from Birmingham Jail" (1963a) and attempt, by exploring one another's interpretations, to understand how King distinguishes between just and unjust laws. They could turn next to another famous jail scene, the dialogue about Socrates' final days as depicted by his student, Plato (1992b), in *Crito*.[3] Socrates' friend, Crito, visits him in his cell shortly before he is to be executed by drinking poison. "I can get you out of here; I've bribed the guard," offers Crito. Socrates replies that he'll accept the offer of escape only if he and Crito can, after thinking it through together in dialogue, agree that this would be the right thing to do, the just thing to do. Both King and Socrates display the highest imaginable respect for, and understanding of, the law. Both are in jail because of it. The behavior of each rides on his sense of justice. One was assassinated, the other executed. Each holds up a mirror in which students, if they are inquisitive and imaginative and have good discussion partners and a capable seminar leader, might clarify their own conceptions of justice.

An approach drawn from the second group is the Just Community. Here, students become involved in school and classroom governance, deciding with one another how they will treat one another, what norms and values will govern their behavior together. There are examples of this approach from across the school grades. They center on encouraging students, whether kindergartners or 12th graders, to deliberate with one another the norms and values of group life that will govern their conduct with one another. This requires a basic shift in the school climate and decision-making apparatus, to be sure. Students come to *experience* popular sovereignty firsthand and on their own terms.

I admire both approaches. I attempt to apply them in my own teaching, and will highlight several examples in subsequent chapters. But we should not overlook the fact that deploying either one of them presupposes that we have grappled with the meaning of *justice*, that we ourselves have attempted to think it through, that we have searched for a personal understanding of what it means to do the right thing. Whether teachers choose to steep their students in the ideals and strategies set forth in accounts of inspiring individuals who under the most difficult circumstances struggled to advance justice, or to engage students in decision making in which they must work out just solutions to the problems of living together—whichever way teachers go, even if they go both ways, they cannot go far or well without an understanding of what they are attempting, without a working theory of justice.

This chapter is devoted to that, to helping readers draw out and reflect upon their preconception of justice and, perhaps, to clarify and rebuild it somewhat by considering diverse points of view on the subject. Toward that end, I provide two reasonable yet contrasting viewpoints: One is mainly a psychological conception of justice, the other mainly sociological. The first centers on individual psyches, the second on social structures. The first is concerned with the cognitive-moral development of individuals, in which moral development is viewed as part and parcel to intellectual development; the second is concerned with the moral condition of whole societies, in which the moral development of individuals is viewed as an appendage to the way society is organized. The first worries about how just individuals such as King and Socrates got that way (and Jane Addams, Gandhi, Thich Nhat Hanh, and so on), concentrating on their psychological development. The second worries about how different social systems are organized to privilege certain groups—the ruling class or culture of power—while subordinating others. The first offers a theory of just individuals, the other a theory of just societies. The first will be more palatable to most readers, perhaps, because individualism is the dominant ideology of contemporary American life. It existed before our births; we were born into it and grew up and formed our ideas and values within it. Few of us can escape that fundamental bias in our thinking. Even if we were protected from it in families and faith communities (and even that is highly unlikely), still these institutions couldn't keep out television, pop radio, and the market economy. The social historian Richard Sennett (1974) writes, "Few people today would claim that their psychic life arises by spontaneous generation, independent of social conditions and environmental influences. Nevertheless, the psyche is treated as though it has an inner life of its own" (p. 4).

There is a fundamental tension here. Each view, in the eyes of the other, has a blind spot: "Individualists" emphasize the sovereignty and autonomy of persons, but they do so *as if* individuals were not actually the products of different ways of organizing society over which individuals have little control. Meanwhile, "socialists" emphasize the underlying social situations that determine how and to what ends individuation takes place, but they do so *as if* these situations themselves were not interpreted and dealt with differently by different individuals and transformed continually by the theories and actions of these individuals. Each in its own way ignores the other. In *The Ethics of Ambiguity* (1948), French existentialist Simone de Beauvoir tries to capture the way we might feel this tension in real life—in the conditions of our daily living: "It is in knowledge of the genuine conditions of our life," she reminds us, "that we must draw our strength to live and our reason for acting" (p. 9). These conditions are the basic material we work with, the daily delights and burdens of existing with one another. But at the heart of these conditions, she finds a tragic ambiguity: We experience ourselves as sovereign subjects, agents taking action within and against the social structures that surround and engulf us—from the family to the schoolhouse; the workplace, legal, and economic systems—yet also as objects crushed by these forces, "crushed by the dark weight of things" (p. 7). We understand ourselves as unique, choosing persons, yet we know we are positioned as a cultural, socioeconomic, and racial "type," formed in and by a particular social milieu riddled with unequal power relations. We feel that our actions make a difference, yet we know that the circumstances of our activity are not of our choosing. We assert ourselves and effect change, yet we are also helpless.

To make the distinction between the two frames more vivid, I will provide a striking case of each. From the psychology corner, I feature moral-justice developmental theory as it was worked out by the developmental psychologist Lawrence Kohlberg and his colleagues. From the sociology corner, I feature historical-materialist theory as it was developed by the sociologist Karl Marx and his colleagues. Each is controversial, and each has much to say about justice, one through the individualist lens and the other through the socialist lens. Each has been contested by legions of critics (and upheld by legions of advocates).[4] I am not concerned here to summarize these criticisms or to offer an additional criticism of my own. Rather, by setting them beside one another, because each is provocative and coherent in its unique style, we might perceive the criticism of one by the other and thereby clarify what we mean by justice and what we intend to do when teaching for it.

JUST INDIVIDUALS

Following the assassination of Martin Luther King Jr., a group of children ranging in age from 8 to 16 years was asked, "When the killer is found, how do you think he should be treated?" The older children thought the killer should receive a "fair trial" and be punished "according to the law." Younger children thought the killer should receive specific, usually extralegal punishment (Siegel, 1977). For example, the killer should be "turned over to the Negroes and let them take care of him. " And, "Let Mrs. King kill him," and "Dr. King was killed by him so the same thing should happen to him." In response to the questions, "Why do you think Dr. King was shot? What made the person do it?", the older children more often gave answers indicating abstract political thinking (e.g., "He was killed because he tried to do something for the Negroes"), while the younger, less abstract, more concrete thinkers typically personalized the shooting (e.g., "He hated King" and "Because a riot might have went on in his neighborhood and wrecked his home, and he thought Dr. King started it"). Specific punishments and personal motives are concrete representations of the event whereas the ideal of justice mediated through a fair trial and the rule of law is, to say the least, abstract.

This study illustrates one of the truisms of developmental psychology: As children mature, their reasoning evolves from preconcrete to concrete and from concrete to abstract, and this movement incorporates both the physical and social worlds—that is, their reasoning about which of two glasses contains more soda pop as well as their reasoning about what should happen to someone who accidentally spills one of them. From about age 2 until about age 6, most children "follow" rules; that is, they obey them through imitation, not understanding. By ages 7 to 10, most children are understanding in a rudimentary way that rules are important regulatory mechanisms in social life. On the playground, for example, changing the rules after a game has begun can be just cause for a fight. The accusation "That's not fair!" is wielded confidently by many children of this age. By adulthood, some people (around half) develop into fully abstract thinkers capable of reasoning in complex terms about a fair trial, due process, equal opportunity under the law, and the like. In *The Moral Judgement of the Child* (1965), Jean Piaget writes: "All morality consists in a system of rules, and the essence of all morality is to be sought for in the respect which the individual acquires for these rules" (p. 13). How does this concrete-to-abstract journey progress? Why do some people travel the full course while others do not?

Several philosophies tell us that justice is latent in the soul—the seed for justice is already planted in human nature. Buddhism is based on this view, as is Western philosophy in the lineage of Socrates. It follows pedagogically that what is already there can be *drawn out* in good teaching-learning settings but not imposed. Piaget and Lawrence Kohlberg extended and qualified that tradition within the discourse of cognitive developmental psychology, both providing evidence (Kohlberg's data were both cross-cultural and longitudinal) for the view that individuals become more just as they proceed through stages of development. But what is the underlying idea of justice that accompanies this concrete-to-abstract evolution in our thinking as we grow and develop? We will understand it first implicitly by examining Kohlberg's theory of cognitive moral development; that is, we will derive it from Kohlberg's stage-wise description of the natural evolution of a sense of justice. Then we will understand it explicitly by examining the decision-making method employed at the highest level of development in Kohlberg's scheme.

First, we should understand that cognitive developmentalism is one of several psychological theories about how humans know and learn. Other theories, to name only two, are behaviorism and biological maturationist theory. Kohlberg argued that cognitive developmentalism overcomes a dichotomy between these two by asserting a dialectical, or interactive, model of human development (Kohlberg & Mayer, 1972). This model considers human knowing to be a function of increased *capacity* to know that results from the interaction of an always changing individual and an always changing environment.

Second, we should understand that Kohlberg was a Piagetian. Piaget's well-known theory holds that one's way of learning and knowing develops naturally and hierarchically through an invariant sequence of stages. No one skips a stage, but development can be arrested at any stage. Each stage is a qualitatively distinct, integrated thought system, and each is more complex, inclusive, and thus more powerful than preceding stage. Upward stage movement occurs as one constructs a satisfactory response to the experience of disequilibrium—confusion or being stuck on a problem or dilemma one is facing. There are plenty of problems, naturally, because the friction of person and environment interacting engenders all manner of conflict as the person struggles to understand what is happening and to respond. According to Piaget, the only satisfying escape from confusion is further cognitive development: The way out of the present disequilibrium is the construction of a new way of knowing within which the conflict dissolves and equilibrium is restored. Each predicament becomes, thereby, fertile ground for the next resolution, and one's way of making sense of the world is thus "drawn out." Both the knower and the known develop in such a way that objects (whether toys, glasses of soda pop, parents, friends, or games) are known anew by a new knower—what Kegan (1982) calls *the evolving self*. Eventually, this evolving self

> can construe the world propositionally, hypothetically, inferentially, abstractly. It can spin an "overall plan" of which any given concrete event is but an instance of "what might be." This rebalancing, often the hallmark of adolescence, unhinges a concrete world. Where before the "actual" was everything, it falls away like the flats of a theater set, and a whole new world, a world the person never knew existed, is revealed. The actual becomes but one instance (and often a not very interesting instance) of the possible. (p. 38)

Imagining Alternatives

The implications of the evolving self for enlightened political engagement—that is, social criticism and action—is my chief concern here. To repeat, "any given concrete event is but an instance of 'what might be.'" The present situation, the status quo, "becomes but one instance . . . of the possible." The evolved self is not likely to take the given social situation as anything other than one setup among an array of possibilities. Perceiving a perniciously racist and segregated society, the freedom marchers of the Civil Rights movement imagined an alternative. Perceiving a rapidly globalizing marketplace in which corporate heads were making the new game rules, protestors of the World Trade Organization (WTO) imagined an alternative. Perceiving the fantastic rich-poor gap in the United States today, pockets of opposition across the country are imagining alternatives.

Kohlberg's theory of moral imagination and moral reasoning, as we have seen, is an extension and qualification of Piaget's dialectical, stage-wise conception of intellectual development. As an individual's reasoning about the physical world evolves, Kohlberg argues, so does his or her capacity for reasoning about the world of people and relationships and, in particular, justice (Kohlberg, Levine, & Hewer, 1984a, 1984b). Before we can regularly consider others' perspectives in our reasoning about issues of fairness, our mode of perception and judgment must have been developed beyond egocentricity, beyond idiocy. We must be capable intellectually of accommodating the other as another subject: another thinking, feeling agent. In Piaget's terms, the transcendence of the infant's unabashed egocentrism requires the set of abilities called *concrete operational thought*, central to which is *reciprocity* or the ability to see two dimensions of a problem simultaneously. So, the concrete stage makes possible an advance from justice-as-obedience to justice-as-equal exchange. Further cognitive development, from concrete to abstract reasoning, permits yet another qualitative advance in our sense of justice from *concrete reciprocity* to *ideal reciprocity* (Kohlberg, 1971). This entails imagining yourself in another's role and considering what you would want from that perspective. This is represented in the colloquialisms "putting yourself in the other person's shoes" and understanding where someone is "coming from." As the evolving self develops the intellectual capacity for ideal reciprocity, the Golden Rule is for the first time comprehendible not as an admonition to treat others as they treat you (concrete reciprocity) but to treat them as you would want to be treated if you were they. Now we can take the perspective of others with less egocentric and ethnocentric distortion. Now, too, principled reasoning such as that expressed in the U.S. Constitution or the Seneca Falls declaration of the rights of women or King's "Letter" can at last be comprehended.

Perspective taking is an act of moral imagination: One cannot actually walk a mile in another's shoes, but one can try to imagine his or her life conditions. It is in this light that King (1963a) wrote in the "Letter": "Injustice anywhere is a threat to justice everywhere. . . . Whatever affects one directly, affects all indirectly" (p. 77). And, it is in this light that Thich Nhat

Hanh (1988) said, "You cannot just *be* by yourself alone. You have to inter-be with every other thing" (p. 4). Imagining oneself in another's place is the moral opposite of egocentricity and ethnocentricity. It is the key to moving from idiocy to puberty.

From Idiocy to Puberty

Kohlberg's research (Kohlberg, Levine, & Hewer, 1984a & 1984b) in-dicates that at each cognitive stage individuals have a distinct conception of right and wrong embedded in a distinct capacity for role-taking, or tak-ing the perspective of others. At stage one, an individual is behaving rightly if she is obedient and escaping punishment. At stage two, she can take the perspective of another person, but only in the limited sense of fair exchange. Here, two wrongs can indeed make a right, and "What's in it for me?" is compelling logic. "You scratch my back and I'll scratch yours" and "an eye for an eye" are slogans of fairness according to a stage two reasoner. Com-mon among children in middle school (and not that rare in adults), stage two morality compels us to do what is necessary to please *ourselves*. Write Mosher, Kenny, and Garrod (1994), "The fundamental goal at stage 2 is to maximize personal gain and to minimize losses in any interaction with oth-ers. Greed, self-protectiveness, and opportunism are part of this way of thinking" (p. 43).

At stage three, our morality becomes conventional. We become social beings. Our view of right and wrong shift from the instrumental hedonism and concrete reciprocity of stage two to a view that is bound up with "what others think"—peers and family members, the neighbors, the people at church or temple, youth group members, and adult mentors. This is an important advance, as any parent knows, yet it is its own cause for con-cern. A different sort of problem emerges, often with the force of a loco-motive. Now, peer pressure and the drive to conform govern one's view of right and wrong. Right action is that which pleases others and is ap-proved by them. Kohlberg calls this "good boy/good girl morality" because it heralds the shift to thinking about right and wrong in terms of group norms and approval.

Conventional morality continues at stage four, but the reference point can shift from the concrete peer group to abstract, imagined groups such as "my country" or "humanity." Now individuals are concerned about how various groups in society define right and wrong and how the laws and moral grid of the overarching political community—the larger public—hold soci-ety together into a moral commonwealth that, paradoxically, protects diver-sity. This is an enormous advance over the prior stage of development. Pluralism and tolerance make sense for the first time, and the rule of law is revered as the glue that makes diversity and liberty, *pluribus* with *unum*, possible. Fixated at this stage of development, however, is the adult who believes that the law is necessarily right. Not until an individual's reasoning has developed to the postconventional fifth stage is she freed from reading the status quo—for example, the law—as if it were a moral commandment. At the fifth stage she is capable of principled reasoning and, therefore, the ability to evaluate a law or any other social situation in its light.

Individuals who are locked into stage four reasoning will not likely conceive two types of law as did King in the "Letter": just and unjust. Instead, they might espouse a law-and-order idea of justice: *Rather than deriving their conception of law from justice, they will derive their conception of justice from the law—extant law.* They will assume that the law mirrors justice. On this view, moral people obey the law; immoral people do not. Individuals operating at the stage four conception of justice will be entangled, therefore, in the status quo, be it just or not. Consequently, an interest in moving the law forward toward justice (i.e., a commitment to envisioning different ways of organizing society that might advance the common good while leaving our differences intact) is not likely to arise because these individuals are confined to maintaining conventions without the additional, transcendent capacity to interrogate their assumptions and contrast them with alternatives that may be more just. By contrast, individuals who have moved to postconventional reasoning have moved from law-obeying (right or wrong) to law-making or principled reasoning.

Both national and cross-national data (Kohlberg, Levine, & Hewer, 1984a; 1984b) show that preconventional reasoners (stages one and two) are oriented rigidly to obedience and punishment avoidance. They have virtually no concern for group welfare or the common good—not because they are mean people but because their moral reasoning has not developed sufficiently. Most, but not all, of these reasoners are children. Conventional reasoners (stages three and four) are also oriented rigidly, but now to systems of law that are considered fundamental to group welfare and social order, both the immediate group (stage three) and the abstraction called "society" (stage four). These reasoners have advanced beyond morality as law obeying and punishment avoidance to morality as law maintenance. Relatively few people are cognitively and morally capable of anything beyond this conventional rationality—capable, that is, of understanding King's a forementioned response when he was asked, "How can you advocate breaking some laws and obeying others?" Postconventional reasoners can, in other words, figure out two things: (1) which laws need to be maintained and which need to be changed because they are unjust, and (2) what is the right thing to do when there are no laws. Tapp and Kohlberg (1971) found that postconventional reasoners

viewed rules and laws as norms mutually agreed on by individuals for maxi-
mizing personal and social welfare. They judged laws should be obeyed either because of rational considerations or because they are coincident with
universal principles of justice. The perspective offered a coherent, responsible guide to social change and the creation of new norms: Those that
served no purpose or were unjust should be changed; those that violated
fundamental individual rights and universal moral principles could be le-
gitimately broken. (p. 85)

This language, "preconventional *reasoners*" and "conventional *reasoners*," is for convenience only. Actually, a stage of development is not
fixed. Individuals move in and out of stage behavior as social contexts
change.[5]

What Educators Can Do

Moving from this explanatory theory of cognitive-moral growth to an
education theory, Kohlberg and his colleagues (Power, Higgins, & Kohlberg, 1989) reasoned that not all social environments are equal—that they
act differently on the evolving knower, some encouraging more development than others. Which social conditions best support growth toward
postconventional principled reasoning? Kohlberg concluded, and this is
the essence of his education program, that frequent and extended involvement in discussions of genuine value conflicts would promote development. But some elaboration is needed. First, whereas Kohlberg's earlier
work (e.g., Blatt & Kohlberg, 1975) emphasized the use of hypothetical
value conflicts or dilemmas, his later work ("The Just Community": Power,
Higgins, & Kohlberg, 1989) argued for authentic value conflicts derived
from the activities of the group. Second, the discussion group needs to be
heterogeneous in its members' stages of development so that all discussants may have exposure to reasoning and social perspectives different
from their own, thereby increasing the likelihood of genuine exchange and,
therefore, intellectual conflict and disequilibrium. Third, a discussion
leader is needed who can comprehend and present reasoning at various
levels. In school settings, this is typically the teacher. Along with diversity in the student group, the leader can increase the likelihood that each
student encounters reasoning that effectively probes and challenges his
or her own. Fourth, the discussion group needs to be free of coercion, because perspective taking requires the social conditions of genuine dialogue.
(Domination-free discussion cannot simply be assumed. Doing so perpetu-
ates inequities by denying them.[6]) Finally, because justice is "drawn out"
rather than "driven in," these discussions need to be dialogic. That is, discussants need to be engaged in conversation and debate about one

another's reasoning rather than ignoring others' reasoning while reiterating their own arguments—a phenomenon Berkowitz (1981) called *alternating monologues*.

To summarize, the evolving self is an increasingly imaginative and empathic self who—thanks to social and intellectual attainments that are the product of particular kinds of mind/society interactions—is successively better able to take into consideration others' perspectives in determining what is fair and what is not. Such evolution can be encouraged. The key seems to be a combination of problems and conflicts (never in short supply!) and competent deliberation on them with the persons with whom we are experiencing these problems and conflicts. Kohlberg's work has contributed greatly to our understanding of these matters (and for this reason I am featuring it here), but the complementary work of many others could be considered as well.[7] Let us look briefly at just one of these now: the theorizing on justice by John Rawls (1971). His work targets specifically the problem of social equity in fair deliberation.

Reversibility

The notion of justice-as-perspective-taking, coupled with the five conditions described just now, make rather clear what this conception of justice entails both as an idea and a set of pedagogical practices. To teach for justice on this view a teacher could have students grapple with the advanced moral reasoning of the likes of Socrates, Gandhi, Hanh, Addams, and King (e.g., in Socratic seminars, dramatizations, book clubs, etc.), *and* expose students to one another's reasoning, right there in the classroom in discussions of classroom rules and problems (e.g., the Just Community approach). But let us try to clarify further the conception of justice that undergirds both sets of practices.

In *A Theory of Justice* (1971), John Rawls lays out an account of social justice based on a novel approach to social contract theory. Social contract theories typically posit, as a thought experiment, an imagined "initial choice situation" (a "state of nature") as a means by which social justice, given human nature, might be imagined. Two of the most famous of these thought experiments were composed by the Enlightenment philosophers John Locke and Jean-Jacques Rousseau. Rawls criticized both of them for imagining flawed initial choice situations that would not engender fairness in the arrangements agreed to therein. Rawls then advanced his own initial choice situation that maximizes the likelihood of fair agreements. In his original position, people make decisions about social problems (e.g., who gets what; how should law breakers be sanctioned) behind a veil of ignorance. This veil prevents participants from knowing the roles they occupy, including their social positions and accompanying advantages and disadvantages, once the veil is lifted. The veil thereby erases inequity and forces impartiality into the discussion since the discussants do not know whether, after the veil is lifted, they will be strong or weak, rich or poor, man or woman, Black or White, immigrant or native, captain or corporal, able or disabled, Gentile or Jew, European or Asian, ex-convict or senator, and so forth. A decision made under such circumstances is more likely to be fair because participants choose in such a manner that they can live with the choice after the veil is lifted and they find themselves in a particular situation.

Kohlberg (1979), citing Rawls, calls this justice as reversibility or ideal reciprocity. Reversibility means "changing places with." It is the criterion of justice implied by the Golden Rule: You cannot figure out what is the right thing to do until you consider being on the receiving end of your actions; that is, "it's right if it's still right when you put yourself in the other's place" (Kohlberg, 1979, p. 258). Reversibility requires both dialogue and impartiality as conditions for working out social justice. Kohlberg spells out Rawls's meaning as *ideal* perspective-taking or "moral musical chairs." This means "going around the circle of perspectives involved in a moral dilemma (a value conflict) to test one's claims of right or duty until only the equilibrated or reversible claims survive" (p. 262). Claims that are not reversible, that are not fair from all perspectives, are dropped from further consideration.

Rawls uses the example of cutting cake to illustrate reversibility at work. The just citizen who is put in the role of cake cutter would cut it knowing that he or she would ask another person to distribute the pieces, thus placing himself or herself on the receiving end of any indiscretions in the cutting. Knowing that the distribution of pieces of cake would be blind, it makes no sense to be anything but scrupulously fair in the cutting.

As the capacity for taking the perspective of others with less egocentric distortion develops in a stage-wise fashion, our ability to know others as they are and to imagine their suffering increases. We "develop" our way out of the idiocy that makes other people nothing but projections of our own mind or objects to be used to make us happy, safe, or rich.

JUST SOCIETIES

King (1963a) writes in the "Letter": "I am sure that none of you would want to rest content with the superficial kind of social analysis that deals merely with effects and does not grapple with underlying causes" (p. 78). This statement propels us from considering how principled postconventional reasoners got that way—how they *develop*—to a consideration of "underlying causes" set not in the variables of psychological growth but in the material conditions of life, the way social systems are organized.

It is important, then, to counter the psychological approach to justice with a socioeconomic approach. The former is convincing in its conception of justice as perspective taking (imaginative reversibility; the Golden Rule; what Buddhists call compassion or exchanging oneself for others [e.g., Khyentse, 1993]) and its explanation of why only a few of us develop to the postconventional moral level of a King or a Socrates. However, it lacks a critical sociological treatment of morality, which is to say an analysis of the interaction of values, knowledge, history, and the social positions and situations in which people actually live, such as race, ethnicity, gender, and social class. The last of these today gets less sociological attention even than race and gender. bell hooks bluntly states: "Nowadays it is fashionable to talk about race or gender; the uncool subject is class" (2000b, p. vii). Let us turn, then, to approaches that talk directly about that. An exemplar is the socioeconomic approach of Karl Marx (1867/1990), called "historical materialism."

Marx's scholarship seems to be imbued with an abiding concern for justice. Its central concern is domination of the poor by the rich and exploitation of workers by owners. This is not a morally neutral stance! And it seems clear that Marxism's prognosis of a socialist transformation of society was not merely put forward as objectively inevitable, but as desirable. Stuart Hampshire (1977) captured this moral concern:

> For me socialism is not so much a theory as a set of moral injunctions, which seem to me clearly right and rationally justifiable; first, that the elimination of poverty ought to be the first priority of government after defense; secondly, that as great inequalities in wealth between different social groups lead to inequalities in power and in freedom of action, they are generally unjust and need to be redressed by governmental action; thirdly, that democratically elected governments ought to ensure that primary and basic human needs are given priority within the economic system, even if this involves some loss in the aggregate of goods and services which would otherwise be available. (p. 359)

Accordingly, a Marxist critique of the Piagetian/Kohlbergian scheme of moral development and its postconventional conception of justice as principled reasoning based on skillful and compassionate perspective taking would not, it would seem, oppose moral theorizing *per se* since moral theorizing lies at the heart of Marx's work as well. But, according to many in the school we might call "classical" or "scientific" Marxism, such is not the case.

A materialist science of society holds that objective material conditions—social arrangements or structures—account for social and psychological life. In *Capital* (1867/1990), Marx is explicit:

> Here individuals are dealt with only in so far as they are personifications of economic categories, the bearers of particular class-relations and class-interests. My standpoint ... can less than any other make the individual responsible for relations whose creature he remains, socially speaking, however much he may subjectively raise himself above them. (p. 92)

This is no denigration of the value of individuals, but only a description of how they come to be. Marx asserted matter-of-factly that individuals' minds are organized and furnished by the objective class conditions of their lives, and that to know those conditions—the underlying social structures—is to know the people who live within them and are their embodiments. Subjectivity, then, can be inferred from material conditions. Know my material conditions, and you will know my state of mind. Individuals, in this view, are *epiphenomena*—the tip of the iceberg, skin-deep expressions of underlying socioeconomic causes. Studying epiphenomena as though they were the source, while ignoring the source (material structures) is the very sort of illusory activity of which materialist critics, including but not limited to Marx, charge modern social scientists (see also Freire, 1970; Habermas, 1971; and Jacoby, 1975).

Here is the point. Moralities—codes of right and wrong conduct, conceptions of justice—are in this view epiphenomenal. Conceptions of justice and the whole of moral theorizing are aspects of subjectivity, and subjectivity is an effect of underlying socioeconomic causes. We think otherwise, that morality is fundamental to personal and social transformation, only because *ideology* (the false beliefs that legitimize current inequalities as sensible and good [Cormack, 1992]) requires that we think otherwise. That is, the preservation and legitimacy of the way society is organized now—the status quo—requires people to believe that individual moral judgment matters. This is the base/superstructure model at the heart of the Marxist critique of the status quo. The socioeconomic system is the base, and everything else—the superstructure of education, the political and legal system, people's beliefs, norms, and values—is built atop this foundation.

Marx has been widely accused in the West as having spoken against the individual and against morality when we could say instead that he wrote as a social scientist endeavoring to describe and explain the causes and conditions for both. In his view, impoverished human relations, including today's prejudices against women, homosexuals, and people of color, and the huge imbalance between haves and have nots—all of these exist as logical extensions of a socioeconomic structure and are not, then, moral problems to be overcome through individual moral development. Similarly, in Plato's (1992a) famous cave allegory, the way out of the cave is not to be found in scrutinizing ever more closely and cleverly, let alone striving to change, the shadows on the cave wall. What is needed instead is close analysis of the way ideology functions to make the shadows appear real and reasonable, lodging them in common sense where they are taken for granted. Marx accused fellow social scientists of being preoccupied with justice and, in particular, with the just distribution of resources when they ought instead to have been concerned with the causes of these effects in underlying conditions of production. This materialist science, then, is amoral. It needs no moral theory since its purpose is to reveal and explain social structures and their effects, one of which is moral theorizing.

Let me take this one step further. If the first scientific-socialist criticism of moral theorizing is that it is epiphenomenal, the second is that it is dangerous. Why? Moral hierarchies carry with them the potential for the repression of those who fall short of the hierarchy's moral ideal. Stalinism is a case in point, argues Andrew Collier (1981). Stalin was morally indignant at social conditions that impeded the rise of a just society. The carnage justified on behalf of that moral righteousness is well known. Other examples can be cited, from the Crusades to Mao's Cultural Revolution, the Terror of the French Revolution, the Holocaust, and the contemporary campaigns of the Christian Right and the Islamic Right against pluralism. Pol Pot's Khmer Rouge in Cambodia exterminated countless numbers of so-called corrupt individuals who failed to exemplify in one way or another the moral ideals of that revolution. Even the Klan in America justified its virulent racism, its lynchings and church bombings, on *moral* grounds.

Scientific socialism, then, takes morality to task not only for being epiphenomenal but for opening the door to red terror, then reactionary terror, to terrorists of the left and right, to fascists and communists, to the Khmer Rouge and the Klan, to religious fanatics, and to impassioned zealots around the world who justify killing children on behalf of some "great mission" to "purify the world."

Further developing this basic amoral position, others have argued that while it is true that Marx roundly condemned capitalist structures for being inherently exploitive of labor, he did not condemn them on moral ground (Tucker, 1969; Wood, 1972–1973). Marx never called them unjust or unfair and never criticized them for abrogating workers' rights. This apparent paradox can be understood by seeing that Marx did have a theory of justice, but one that was radically historical. That is, justice is always to be understood as an appendage of a particular historical era and accompanying social arrangements and, more specifically, relations of production. Justice under feudalism is feudalist justice, justice under capitalism is capitalist justice, justice under socialism is socialist justice, and so on. Marx thought slavery was unjust in capitalist societies since it violated capitalism's own standards, but that the exploitation of labor was not unjust, since that is the essence of capitalism. Using one social arrangement's moral principles to judge another's is a mistake, for doing so fails to grasp the materialist underpinning of justice.

What we have here is a cogent line of critique that would reject the moral theorizing of Kohlberg and Rawls not by contesting its particular conception of justice, as some have done (e.g., Gibbs, 1979, Gilligan, 1982), but by drawing a line around the whole concern and calling it false consciousness: much ado that serves mainly to mystify everyone into thinking that individuals make a difference when, in fact, individualism is a shadow on the wall. The activity of civic virtue, of knowing and doing the common good, is fine as far as it goes, but it doesn't go very far because it is actually an effect of something much more powerful. As a cause, it is impotent. To summarize, justice is at best a trivial concern and at worst dangerous ideology that obscures rather than discloses real injustice. It fails to inform us that the market economy has stolen the common good and, with it, our minds and, therefore, the sense of vision and capacity for critical thinking needed to reinvent society.

CUTTING THROUGH CONVENTIONAL WISDOM

Considering cognitive-moral developmentalism and historical materialism together, bringing them both to the table, ought to help us enlarge and rethink our understanding of what it means to be "teaching for justice." That is my hope. The ideal of civic virtue, defined as knowing and doing the common good, and with it justice, defined as fairness, requires that we distinguish the common good from the common bad, that we distinguish fair from unfair laws, that we tell right from wrong, that we not only refrain from acting unjustly ourselves but take action against injustice wherever we find it. None of this is easy. But is it mainly a matter of cognitive-moral growth? Is it mainly a matter of developing the capacity for principled reasoning, including reversibility—the ability to imaginatively take the perspective of others? On this view, "puberty" marks the evolution from "me-centered" to "we-centered" consciousness. At last, one can be a law-abiding citizen. And what follows that, if development is not arrested, is postconventional or principled reasoning when, at last, one can make and change laws as justice requires. King (1958) supports this developmental view, at least in part, when he tells the story of his own "intellectual pilgrimage to nonviolence."

> I had grown up abhorring not only segregation but also the oppressive and barbarous acts that grew out of it. I had passed spots where Negroes had been

savagely lynched, and had watched the Ku Klux Klan on its rides at night. I had seen police brutality with my own eyes, and watched Negroes receive the most tragic injustice in the courts. All of these things had done something to my growing personality. I had grown perilously close to resenting all white people. (p. 90)

Yet, he supports the material view as well, at least in part. "I had also learned that the inseparable twin of racial injustice was economic injustice," he wrote in the very next sentence (1958). He tells us that he worked for two summers in a factory that hired both Blacks and Whites. His father was against it ("he never wanted my brother and me to work around white people because of the oppressive conditions"), but doing it allowed King Jr. to see firsthand that economic injustice cast a wide net: "I . . . realized that the poor white was exploited just as much as the Negro" (p. 90). He appreciated Marxism's "protest against the hardships of the underprivileged" and its "concern for social justice" (p. 93). But he rejected Marxism's secular materialism, which "has no place for God. This I could never accept. . . . History is ultimately guided by spirit, not matter" (p. 92). He also rejected its deprecation of individual freedom: "I am convinced now, as I was then, that man is an end (not a means) because he is a child of God. Man is not made for the state: the state is made for man. To deprive man of freedom is to relegate him to the status of a thing" (p. 93).

Still, King (1958) credited Marx with making him "ever more conscious of the gulf between superfluous wealth and abject poverty" and ever more committed to "a better distribution of wealth" (p. 94). Ultimately, he expressed profound disappointment with *both* capitalism and communism, mainly because of the unacceptable societies and states of mind both produce:

> Capitalism is always in danger of inspiring men to be more concerned about making a living than making a life. We are prone to judge success by the index of our salaries or the size of our automobiles, rather than by the quality of our service and relationship to humanity—thus capitalism can lead to a practical materialism that is as pernicious as the materialism taught by communism. (pp. 94–95)

King's commitment to a fairer distribution of wealth made him many enemies, both Black and White. It was one thing to struggle against racism, quite another to struggle against capitalism. But he found both unjust. Racial segregation was bad enough; class segregation went hand in hand with it and supported it all the way. His were postconventional, principled judgments, of course. This was moral reasoning, not racial reasoning (West, 1993b). Meanwhile, conventional wisdom—the common sense of the day—supported *both* segregation and capitalism.

Scientific Marxists will claim that King's judgments were superficial aspects of a capitalist ideology the purpose of which was to safeguard the capitalist status quo. This claim makes little sense, however, when we consider that postconventional wisdom, as King displayed so clearly, has the ability (by definition) to cut through conventional thinking, to see the situation differently, to disrupt and challenge it. Individuals are not only predetermined personifications of the economic base; they are also agents who think, who reflect on their situations, and who act. Of course, thought and action are in some measure determined by social circumstances, and people's choices are confined in some measure to predetermined options; but they do think, they do choose, they do act. Indeed, *only* subjects can do these things. Maxine Greene (1995) writes, "Only a *subject*, after all, can choose—can decide to break from anchorage and insert himself or herself into the world with a particular kind of identity and responsibility, a particular mode of valuing what lies around and straining toward what ought to be" (pp. 70–71). To fail to see this is to misconstrue causes as effects. In fact, we are cause *and* effect, both subjects *and* objects. This was Beauvoir's (1948) point, the "tragic ambiguity."

The truth of the matter of individuation, development, and choice, on the one hand, and socioeconomic conditions on the other, appears to me to lie somewhere in combination of the two. By "in combination" I mean to intersect the two (subjectivity/socioeconomic structure; individual/environment; psychology/sociology) in such a way that their interdependence becomes clear.

Iris Marion Young (1997) captures this combination. She invokes the work of the French existentialist, and Beauvoir's friend, Jean-Paul Sartre (e.g., 1948). Interpreting Sartre, Young writes that "agents are always free insofar as they choose to make of themselves what they are, but they always must do so within an unchosen historical and social situation" (p. 405). "Thrownness" is a term often used in existential writing for the unchosenness of the situation into which one is born or in which one finds oneself. Young writes, "We find ourselves positioned, thrown, into the structured field of class, gender, race, nationality, religion, and so on, and in our daily lives we have no choice but to deal with this situation" (p. 391). We are positioned. We find ourselves at the intersection of a number of social conditions (White, male, middle class, college professor, husband, brother, Buddhist, Democrat, urban dweller— these would be some of my own social positions); and this positioning conditions who we are. Yet this positioning does not *determine* or *define* subjectivity—one's identity—as the scientific Marxists insist. Young writes:

> Individuals are agents: we constitute our own identities, and each person's identity is unique. We do not choose the conditions under which we form

our identities, and we have no choice but to become ourselves under the conditions that position us in determinate relation to others. We act in situation, in relation to the structural conditions and their interaction into which we are thrown. Individuals can and do respond to and take up their positioning in many possible ways, however, and these *actions-in-situation* constitute individual identity. (1997, p. 392, emphasis added)

Even Louis Althusser (1984), one of the most trenchant historical materialists, suggested that "actions-in-situation" are not only possible but frequent. He argued that the superstructure has a "relative autonomy" (p. 67), meaning that what sits atop the basic economic system of production and distribution has some amount of independence. This allows elements of the superstructure actually to challenge and cause changes in the base rather than always doing its bidding. Accordingly, economic structures and human agency "should be seen as intertwined frameworks of social action. Changes in one result in changes in the other. Economic change results in ideological change, but this latter change can itself lead to further economic change" (Cormack, 1992, p. 14). Together, they form a complex social totality—a whole that is incomplete when one is missing the other.

In sum, individuals can and do act on history. But to do so in ways that advance justice they must not only understand the present situation but be able to evaluate it in such a way that they can choose whether and how to act for transformation. Here is the combination of facing up to the generative power of social conditions *and* a well-developed sense of justice with which one might be capable of judging them.

An analogy may help to convey this interdependence. The analogy concerns setting a clock to display the correct time. The fact that you have learned to tell time and have determined what the correct time is, obviously, will help you know where to set the hands on the clock. So say the individualists. The same knowledge and ability is not pertinent, however, if the clock is broken. So say the socialists. You could set the clock, but it wouldn't do any good; first, you should fix it. Still, "you can't know if you have fixed the clock if you don't know the correct time" (Reiman, 1981, p. 310). This is the point the scientific Marxists seem to have missed. Neither Stalin, Hitler, the Klan, nor the Khmer Rouge knew the correct time.

CONCLUSION

The task of educating just citizens—citizens who are principled and compassionate and who can, therefore, tell the difference between just and unjust laws and, more broadly, between decent and cruel ways of treating one another and who are, therefore, capable of enlightened political engagement—requires a conception of justice that is capable of discerning injustice not merely at the surface of social life but in the underlying modes of relating. In short, a conception of justice must be thoroughgoing and critical. This requires that it see through the spells cast by ideology so that injustices that are legitimized by it might be revealed. Otherwise, tragically, individuals develop out of preconventional hedonism into conventional puberty, developing further, perhaps, the ability to see around and through common sense, only then to limit the power and reach of that achievement to trivial concerns and issues floating on the surface of social life. A developed sense of justice should not be wasted on choosing between tweedledum and tweedledee; rather, returning to Beauvoir (1948), it ought to promote efforts to "surpass the given towards an open future" (p. 91). Justice so conceived is necessary to the broader quest for the virtuous citizen and the good society. Its particular contribution to this quest is its capacity for recognizing patterns of domination and unfairness that may be lodged comfortably in everyday life and for working toward alternative ways of living together.

In my judgment, the developmental model of a sense of justice that matures, given the proper social interaction, from the concrete, egotistic, preconventional level to the abstract, compassionate, postconventional level, makes good sense. Here we have a compelling explanation of the role of intelligence in moral reasoning, and it is supported by an empirical base of considerable depth and breadth. Further, the conception of justice as reversibility describes a democratic, equitable form of discussion—*deliberation*, the central concept of the next chapter—that not only helps resolve interpersonal dilemmas fairly but also can contribute to the larger task of cutting through conventional wisdom and interrogating the fairness of present and proposed social policies.

Aside from making good sense as a theory about how just individuals evolve, it has desirable consequences in educational settings: Educators are more likely to orchestrate classroom and school environments in ways that bring diverse students into meaningful dialogue about the real problems of schooling/living together. These ways, to review, are:

- Students are engaged in discussions of genuine value conflicts that arise in the course of relating to one another at school.
- Discussion groups are heterogeneous so that each student has the benefit of exposure to reasoning and social perspectives different from his or her own.
- The discussion leader is skilled at comprehending and presenting reasons and perspectives that are missing—countering preconventional ideas with conventional ideas, conventional with postcon-

ventional, and advocating (some) positions that are being drummed
out of consideration.
- The discussion group is free of domination, gross and subtle, because
  perspective taking requires the social conditions of genuine exchange.
- Because justice is "drawn out" rather than "driven in," discussions
  are dialogic. Discussants are engaged in conversation about their
  reasoning, not alternating monologues.

What the materialist analysis makes quite clear, however, is that both
the theory of development and its conception of justice, along with its pedagogical applications, are hollow when history and the crushing weight of
social conditions are ignored and when a developed sense of justice is not
applied to a critique of the status quo. Without these connections, even a
developed sense of justice is destined, under the weight of present conditions, to be reserved for the relatively trivial dilemmas of our private lives
while the public sphere, in which those lives are nested and upon which
they depend, continues its demise.

Our challenge is to comprehend individuation in its social context. On
the one hand, there is individual cognition, which appears to evolve toward the more complex operations needed for principled thinking and the
capacity for taking others' perspectives in dialogues about mutual problems. On the other hand are social institutions—the structures of relating
within which individuals become individuals and of which subjectivity is
a distillation. This subjectivity/structure tension cannot be eased without
peril. The classical Marxist argument considers subjectivity—the psyche
and, with it, one's sense of justice—epiphenomenal. While not entirely
untrue, the argument is partial and reductionistic. It denies the subjectiv-
ity/structure tension and, consequently, contributes little to an understanding of how humans might judge one social formation against another. It
fails to account for the variation in individuals' responses to the circumstances into which they are thrown and their varying ability, returning to
the broken clock analogy, to tell the correct time. The subjectivist position,
also not untrue, is also partial. Today it enjoys free reign in a sweeping
societal craze Russell Jacoby calls a "cult of subjectivity" (1975, p. 119): a
world of choices, will, luck, and merit, or their lack; a world that believes
all you need to do to get ahead is work hard or get lucky; a world that is
fixated on money and how to get it; a world that tolerates and condones
greed and a wealth gap of unspeakable proportions.

Rather than easing the tension between the two, the prudent course
seems to me to be one that synthesizes them into one whole. The list of
ills that we face, from the hedonism of consumerism to terrorism and

myriad dominations of class, gender, race, religion, sexual orientation, language, and ethnicity, cannot be understood exclusively as a crisis in individual moral development or an expression of a flawed social order. The either/or approach can do little more than advocate one side of the tension as an antidote for the other. To reject this approach is to reject the passivity of classifying for the activity of critical thinking, which can hold the subject/structure tension dialectically. To seek virtue and social justice is to understand that the individual and the community must be known simultaneously. While not an easy task, and steeped in ambiguity, it seems the only reasonable alternative to the blind spots of either pole.

Months before his assassination, Dr. King gave his own account of this synthesis in a speech delivered in Atlanta on August 16, 1967, *Where Do We Go from Here?*

> We must honestly face the fact that the movement must address itself to the question of restructuring the whole of American society. (Yes) There are forty million poor people here, and one day we must ask the question, "Why are there forty million poor people in America?" And when you begin to ask that question, you are raising a question about the economic system, about a broader distribution of wealth. When you ask that question, you begin to question the capitalistic economy. (*Yes*) And I'm simply saying that more and more, we've got to begin to ask questions about the whole society. We are called upon to help the discouraged beggars in life's marketplace. (*Yes*) But one day we must come to see that an edifice which produces beggars needs restructuring. (*All right*) It means that questions must be raised. And you see, my friends, when you deal with this you begin to ask the question, "Who owns the oil?" (*Yes*) You begin to ask the question, "Who owns the iron ore?" (*Yes*) Now, don't think you have me in a bind today. I'm not talking about communism. What I'm talking about is far beyond communism. . . . (*Yeah*) What I'm saying to you this morning is communism forgets that life is individual. (*Yes*) Capitalism forgets that life is social. (*Yes, go ahead*) And the kingdom of brotherhood is found neither in the thesis of communism nor the antithesis of capitalism, but in a higher synthesis. (*Speak*) [*applause*] It is found in a higher synthesis (*Come on*) that combines the truths of both. (*Yes*) (1967b, pp. 8–9)

Can We Talk?

The importance of a genuine dialogue is that it permits a more
accurate diagnosis of the problems at hand.
                                         —Azizah Y. Al-Hibri (1999, p. 42)

A public space is created when people come together in speech
and action and try to bring into existence an "in-between" among
themselves.
                                         —Maxine Greene (1996, p. 28)

Harry, a sophomore in an experimental Just Community school, reflected
on his decision to get involved in school governance:

> I really like the diversity in the school. There are so many different groups,
> different cultures. But . . . there are certain places where you feel intimidated
> when you walk by. We need to do something about those. We can't just abol-
> ish the turf areas, but we can encourage more and more people to walk by
> them and use the stairs. . . . We can have discussions so that people can talk
> about their fears. (Mosher, Kenny, & Garrod, 1994, p. 140)

Admirably, Harry considers fear. As emotions go, fear goes far and deep.
It is an intelligent emotion, of course, warning us of danger. But it is crip-
pling, too, and one of the primary causes of prejudice. It "leads members of
groups to avoid interacting with outgroup members and causes them dis-
comfort when they do" (Banks et al., 2001, p. 10). Racism, anti-Semitism,
sexism, and homophobia each, in its own way, is rooted in fear; and fear,
not surprisingly, fuels catastrophic outbursts of social hysteria.[1] When a
population fears crime, for example, or a food or water shortage, a plague
or an attack by hostile forces—when basic fear of this sort strikes, norms can
dissolve and tolerance can give way to rounding up "the usual suspects"
and persecuting scapegoats. The rise of Hitler in Germany during a time of
economic crisis and resentment following World War I is an object lesson in
European history. The surge of White lynchings of Black males in the southern United States during the final decade of the 19th century, when cotton

prices were collapsing and White masculinity was threatened; and, 50 years later, the imprisonment of Japanese Americans during the Second World War—these are object lessons in U.S. history. Regrettably, there are more, from Salem to Senator McCarthy to attacks on Muslim Americans following the terrorist attacks of September 2001 on New York and Washington, DC. No society has managed to escape fear's grip. No society can hold itself above fear, the causes of fear, or the consequences of fear.

For our purposes here, what Harry makes clear is that a school is not a private place, like our homes. The "places" he refers to are public places. Former kindergarten teacher and moral philosopher Vivian Paley (1992) writes, "The children I teach are just emerging from life's deep wells of private perspective: babyhood and family. Then, along comes school. It is the first real exposure to the public arena" (p. 21).

Schools are places where diverse children are gathered. Their diversity runs the gamut from language and religion to ability and intelligence, race and social class, gender and sexual orientation, and disability. Catholics, Protestants, Muslims, Baptists, Buddhists, Hindus, Jews, animists, agnostics, and atheists are there, as are the various schools of thought *within* each of these groups, alongside students who haven't the slightest concern for religion. Chinese, Vietnamese, Arab, Mexican, Anglo, and African American students are there, and more. Affluent and working class, rich and poor, gifted and challenged—all may be there. Some students were thrown into socially privileged groups, others not. Some have never been on the outside of mainstream society, others have never been on the inside. Some are hard at work on a second or third language; others might possibly get by on one, especially if it is English and they are White. This diversity at school is increasing steadily. In 1982, Whites composed 73% of the student population. Ten years later their proportion was down 10% to 63% (Pratt, 2000). Looking ahead, estimates vary: Pallas, Natriello, and McDill (1989) predict that by 2020 the proportion of White students will be 56%. Garcia and Gonzalez (1995) estimate that by 2026, the proportion of students of color in U.S. schools will reach 70%, roughly the inverse of the proportion today.

This buzzing variety does not exist, as Paley notes, in "a private place, like our homes" (1992, p. 21). It exists in places where diverse people congregate, places where people who come from numerous private worlds and social positions are brought together on common ground. These are places where multiple perspectives and personal values are brought into face-to-face contact around matters that "are relevant to the problems of living together," as Dewey put it (1985a, p. 200). These are mutual, collective concerns, not mine or yours but ours. These arise in public places— places such as schools. This is why public schools can, like no other place in society, nurture *puberty.*

Compared to home life, schools are like village squares, cities, cross-roads, meeting places, community centers, marketplaces. When aimed at democratic ends and supported by the proper democratic conditions, this interaction in schools can help children develop the habits of thinking and caring necessary for public life—the courtesies, tolerance, respect, the sense of justice and knack for forging public policy with others *whether one likes them or not*. If students are fortunate—if the right conditions, both social and psychological, are present and appropriated—they may even give birth to critical, postconventional consciousness. Without the formation of these habits, anything approaching a vigorous and flourishing democratic civic life is put desperately at risk. *Civic, civilization, civility, citizenship*—all derive from the Roman word for *city*.

This, then, is the great democratic potential of the public places called schools. As Dewey (1916/1985a) observed, "The notion that the 'essentials' of elementary education are the three R's mechanically treated, is based upon ignorance of the essentials needed for realization of democratic ideals" (p. 200). Used well, schools can nurture these "essentials"—the qualities needed for the hard work of living together freely but cooperatively and with justice, equality, and dignity. Schools can do this *because* of the collective problems and the diversity contained within them. Problems and differences are *the* essential assets for cultivating democrats.

But how actually to accomplish this? Looking back through the historical record and across the cultural landscape, three actions seem to be key: First, increase the variety and frequency of interaction among students who are different from one another. Classrooms often do this naturally, but these and other opportunities can be deepened and expanded and their quality improved. Second, orchestrate these contacts so that competent public talk—*deliberation* about common problems—is fostered. This is talk about two kinds of problems: those that arise inevitably from the friction of interaction itself (Dewey's "problems of living together") and those grounded in the academic controversies at the core of each subject area in the school curriculum. Third, clarify the distinction between deliberation and blather and between open (inclusive) and closed (exclusionary) deliberation. In other words, expect, teach, and model competent, inclusive deliberation. Concentrate not only on the open expression of honest viewpoints but on the receptive practice of listening. I will conclude the chapter with an explanation of why diversity is a social good and, specifically, an asset to any deliberation.

INCREASING INTERACTION

First, the congregation must be created. This mixing can be staged in two public arenas within the school: the classroom and the common areas of the school at large. In both, students should be mixed in various kinds of groups. These groups should be temporary and task oriented.[2] Fixed groups, in which students are separated *permanently* for whatever reason (ability, prior knowledge, behavior) should be avoided. Why? Because separating students permanently for whatever reason does not build a civic culture. The isolated group lacks the plural reference points, the larger common interests, and the multiple levels of reasoning—the buzzing variety—of public life.

Here are a few examples of interaction in both arenas. Within classrooms: (1) primary children are all brought to the rug and gathered around the teacher to share their work with one another; (2) students in a science class, who have been taught cooperative skills, work in teacher-assigned cooperative learning groups to compose biographies of Galileo; (3) middle-school children work in teacher-assigned pairs to practice a skill, recite a poem, or interpret a chart or essay; and (4) high school students gather for band and choir classes.

Schoolwide interaction: (1) Middle and high school students gather in after-school clubs and teams, in assemblies, on the playground and in the lunchroom, and at school events and presentations, such as dances, plays, pageants, athletic games, band and choir concerts. (2) Elementary school students are assigned to cross-grade teams to care for and clean an area of the school. A team might have five children, one each from grades 1–5, with the fifth grader as leader. (This is a time-honored school activity in Japan, where it is considered part of the "moral education" program.) (3) Middle school students make signs saying "Please Vote, We Can't Yet" and take them to the street corner to encourage passing motorists to vote in an upcoming election. (4) A diverse committee of 9- and 10-year-olds is organized to greet new students on their first day, showing them the lunchroom, lockers, gym, and so forth.

But interaction alone—mere contact—is not a sufficient condition for nurturing the wherewithal to walk the democratic path together in a diverse society. This has been made abundantly clear in studies involving racial contact, where contact alone has been shown just as often to *increase* racial antagonism and stereotyping.

FOSTERING DELIBERATION

Gordon Allport's (1954) highly influential study of prejudice produced a theory of *effective* contact (as opposed to mere contact) that influenced a generation of cooperative learning researchers (e.g., Aronson et al., 1978; Cohen, 1994; Johnson & Johnson, 1985; Slavin, 1995). Allport concluded that prejudice is reduced when contact situations have three characteristics (summarized in Banks, 2002):

- They are cooperative rather than competitive.
- The individuals experience equal status.
- The contact is sanctioned by authorities such as parents, principals, and teachers.

Accordingly, it is one thing to attend a Friday night dance with a diverse group of classmates, but quite another to plan the dance together—to choose the music, set the atmosphere, coordinate the setup and breakdown, and make all the other decisions that planning action always entails. Here is the second key: Beyond gathering students into numerous temporary, task-oriented groups, there needs to be ample opportunity for them to *deliberate* together. The word "deliberation" derives from the Latin word *libra*, for scale. It means "to weigh," as when weighing alternative courses of action and trying to decide which policy would be best for all concerned. Deliberation ends, therefore, not in action itself but in a decision to take a particular course of action. Forging that decision together, reasoning together, generating and considering alternatives together: this is deliberation. It is, practically speaking, discussion with an eye toward decision making.

Before deliberation begins, the parties to it have experienced a problematic situation together, and this is what motivates the deliberation in the first place. And in addition to the problems themselves, what brings participants together is dialogue. Nicholas Burbules (1993) writes:

> Dialogue is not a matter of two isolated persons who simply decide to start talking with one another. . . . Once constituted as a relation, the dialogical encounter engages the participants in a process at once symbiotic and synergistic; beyond a particular point, no one may be consciously guiding or directing it, and the order and flow of the communicative exchange itself take over. The participants are *caught up*; they are *absorbed*. (p. 21)

A deliberation is creative. It is an occasion—an experience—that happens between persons.[3] It is not defined solely by its substantive aim, which is to choose wisely and fairly a course of action, nor solely by the deliberative methods employed, but also by the way it constitutes a relationship—a purposeful relationship that requires some measure of getting to know one another, presenting ourselves to one another, expressing opinions and reasons for them, and listening, whether we are particularly fond of one another or not. Consequently, deliberation is not only a means to an end (reaching a decision), but an end in itself, for it creates a particular kind of democratic public culture among the deliberators. When a diverse group of people deliberate together, they create a new "we" in which differences are regarded as an asset, listening as well as expressing occurs, stories and opinions are exchanged, and a decision is forged together. In this way, deliberation is a *public-building activity*. "Publics" are groups that come together to decide what to do about common problems.[4] As Maxine Greene (1996) wrote, "a public space . . . is *created* when people come together in speech and action and try to bring into existence an 'in-between' among themselves" (p. 28, emphasis added). This captures the generative role of deliberation. It is not merely a technical procedure for deciding policy on classroom and school problems, but a way of taking advantage of the fact that students are congregated in schools so as to cultivate democracy. Schools are public places, but without decision making on shared problems an actual public consciousness is not born; there is interaction and congregation, perhaps, but not deliberation and the creation of genuine in-betweens.

To further clarify what deliberation is and is not, we should distinguish it from its cousins. Deliberation is not the only way for publics to decide the question, "What should we do?" *Voting* is another way. In a plurality, the alternative that receives the most votes wins; in a majority system, a decision is not reached until one of the options wins at least 51% of the votes. Either way, the give-and-take of discussion is not required. In the electronic at-home voting systems being considered in numerous nations, the decision could be made by individuals having utterly no interaction with one another, let alone deliberation with one another. *Debate* is another way for groups to make decisions without the benefit of discussion. The proposals being debated were not forged by the group that is debating them, but by subsets (e.g., debate "teams") of the group. And, these alternative proposals were formed before the debate got underway. *Negotiation* is a third way. Here discussion is involved, certainly, but the group is assuming competing interests and the discussion is guided by calculating constantly the gains and losses of each interest group. As in debate, there is not actually one group, but at least two groups present in the same forum engaged in an adversarial contest. Deliberation, by contrast, involves everyone in the group forging together the alternatives and making a decision. It should not be confused with situations in which people who have already formed their opinions gather to advocate and defend them, nor with alternating monologues (whether autobiographical or expository) where there is sequential talking but no listening, let alone perspective taking and empathy.[5]

Deliberation, in sum, creates an in-between space—potentially a solidarity across differences; a "we"—among people who are not necessarily friends or relations but who need to accomplish a goal that requires joining together. Elementary and middle school students are in an ideal setting to deliberate classroom and school policies together. High school students should be doing this as well, but they should also be deliberating pressing domestic and foreign policy questions, from environmental issues to questions of "free trade," haves and have-nots, and war and peace.

Here are a few examples. I begin with classroom examples, featuring the work of Vivian Paley, then move to schoolwide examples, featuring the work of JoAnn Shaheen. Because both Paley and Shaheen provide examples drawn from elementary schools, I will in the next chapter focus on deliberative education in secondary schools.

Classroom Deliberation

First, consider the similarities across the following examples: (1) Primary children are brought to the rug and grouped around the teacher to consider a classroom rule that the teacher or another student has proposed. (2) High school students study and deliberate ethical controversies in U.S. history, such as the causes of the Salem witchcraft hysteria or Supreme Court cases concerning civil rights. (3) Students in teacher-assigned cooperative learning groups gather information on an assigned topic after deciding the fairest and most effective division of labor. (4) Students hold weekly homeroom meetings (they rotate the role of discussion moderator) to weigh classroom and school policies regarding cheating, stealing, violence, and vandalism. (5) High school seniors take a rigorous course called "Senior Problems," in which they deliberate pressing domestic and international policy questions. In each case, interaction—mixing—is combined with the mainspring of public building: deciding how to act.

The first example, from Vivian Paley's work in primary classrooms, deserves a closer look at this point because it (1) clarifies the look and feel of actual classroom-based deliberation while (2) revealing how entirely possible it is to do such work in everyday classroom settings, even with the youngest children. Paley, who is now retired, was a kindergarten teacher in Chicago for many years. Readers are probably aware of her keen descriptions of children's thinking and moral reasoning from her many popular books. Her approach to public life—to the creation of the in-between—is to focus on the lived problems that her children experience in the classroom and on the playground. In *You Can't Say You Can't Play* (1992), Paley facilitates an ongoing deliberation about whether to have a particular classroom rule. She tells the kindergartners of a rule she is considering, not one she has decreed, and engages them in an ongoing inquiry about the rule, lasting for months. The inquiry focuses on two questions: Will the rule work? Is it fair? These questions are compelling, moral questions for the children. They have memories and opinions immediately. She brings the children to the circle often to deliberate whether the rule should be adopted, and she interviews older children to ascertain their views, and then brings these views back to her kindergartners who, of course, are terribly impressed that *their* issues are of such interest to the older children.

One day, Paley (1992) informed her class that she was considering a new classroom rule, which she had written on a poster that read, YOU CAN'T SAY "YOU CAN'T PLAY." She said, "I just can't get the question out of my mind. Is it fair for children *in school* to keep another child out of play? After all, this classroom belongs to all of us. It is not a private place, like our homes" (p. 16). The children greeted the proposed rule with disbelief. "Only four out of twenty-five in my kindergarten class find the idea appealing, *and they are the children most often rejected.* The loudest in opposition are those who do the most rejecting. But everyone looks doubtful . . . " (p. 4).

Notice here that Paley communicates to children that the classroom is a public place and that how we conduct ourselves in such a place is somehow unique. In public places, we have to be concerned with the common good, not just private interests and personal preferences. We are obliged to act with civility and to engage one another with care for the in-between. To repeat: "The children I teach are just emerging from life's deep wells of private perspective: babyhood and family," she says. Selfishness and jealousy are natural to both conditions. "Then, along comes school. It is the first real exposure to the public arena." (p. 21)

> *Mrs. Paley:* Should one child be allowed to keep another child from joining a group? A good rule might be: "You can't say you can't play."
>
> *Ben:* If you cry people should let you in.
>
> *Mrs. Paley:* What if someone is not crying but feels sad? Should the teacher force children to say yes?
>
> *Many voices:* No, no.
>
> *Sheila:* If they don't want you to play they should just go their own way and you should say, "Clara, let's find someone who likes you better."
>
> *Angelo:* Lisa and her should let Clara in. . . .
>
> *Lisa:* But then what's the whole point of playing? (pp. 18–19)

Soon, Mrs. Paley traded classes with a second-grade teacher for a little while. She asks those children's opinions about her class's plan. "I've come to ask your opinions about a new rule we're considering in the kindergarten. . . . We call it, 'You can't say you can't play.'" These older children know full well the issue she is talking about. Examples and some vivid accounts of rejection spill forth. They are fully engaged in the discussion because it is a problem that they both recognize and feel. Many children believe it *is* a fair rule, but that it just will not work: "It would be impossible to have any fun," offers one boy.

Later, she goes to a fourth-grade class for their advice. These students conclude that it is "too late" in their lives to give them such a rule. "If you want a rule like that to work, start at a very early age," declares one fourth grader. "Yeah, start it in kindergarten," someone says. "Because they'll believe *you* that it's a *rule*. You know, a law" (p. 63).

Paley takes these views back to the discussion circle in her own classroom. Her children listen, enthralled, to her retelling of the older children's views. In the Socratic spirit, gently, she encourages them to support their views with reasons, and to listen carefully to and respond to the reasoning of other children, both classmates and older children. In this way, she orchestrates the birth of an in-between.

Schoolwide Deliberation

Let's leave the classroom environment and consider the broader social environment of the whole school, with its inner and outer spaces, its hallways and playgrounds, cafeterias and stairwells, classrooms and library, main office, gymnasium, and so forth. Consider the similarities across the following examples: (1) student councils, with multiple rotating delegates from homerooms, meet regularly in the school library to identify problems, decide policies, and plan activities; (2) cross-grade teams meet weekly to decide on, plan, do, and reflect on a community-service project; (3) classrooms in each wing of the school congregate as "houses" within the larger school, planning joint projects, setting policy, and solving common problems. In each case, as in the classroom examples, interaction is combined with the mainspring of public-building: deciding how to act.

The first example above, involving student advisory councils (SAC), is from Cottage Lane Elementary School in New York, where school and school district educators created a council system that turns these too-often mechanical, staid bodies into something approaching vigorous deliberative publics. JoAnn Shaheen (1989), a school district administrator involved at Cottage Lane, describes one of the meetings. "Are you delegates or representatives?" she asks the gathered SAC members. She knows from years of experience that it is a tough question, and an important one to the success of the deliberation at the council meeting and at the homeroom meetings from which the delegates are sent to council meetings and to which they return with results of the discussions. Douglas, a fifth-grade boy who has been involved in the councils for several years, responds to her question. "We are delegates. We can't just say what we want to tell only about our own problems. We must talk about the class's problems" (Shaheen,

1989, p. 361). Shaheen agrees. When the group of delegates from each classroom walks in the door to a council meeting, "it is as if all their classmates and teacher walked in with them." This is because in classroom meetings the children have already raised and deliberated the issues that the delegates now bring to the council meeting. Here she describes a meeting of the fifth-grade student advisory council ("Big SAC"):

> It is an important day. . . . The first meeting of the school year of Big SAC 5 is about to begin. Three delegates and one visitor from each of the seven 5th grade classrooms enter the dining hall. They sit down at a table on which a placard has been placed with the name of their home-base teacher. Each group of four has notes (from their classroom meetings). One or two delegations carry notes on oversized chart paper. Some delegations have notes scribbled on notebook paper. . . .
>
> The principal of the school and I open the meeting. Roll is called. It is quickly ascertained that there are three delegates and one visitor present from each classroom. Another delegate has been selected jointly by the principal, the teacher of the gifted/talented, the home-base teacher, and me to assure that all kinds of children, who might not otherwise have been elected but whose profile is important to the problem-solving purpose of the Student Advisory Council [SAC], are included from each classroom. . . . It is understood that, during the school year, each child in the classroom will have attended at least one SAC meeting. (1989, p. 361)

Shaheen then explains to the group that "we need to take a few minutes to inform everyone present about our purpose and function—who we are and what we are to do." She asks, "Are you delegates or representatives?" "What does advisory mean?" "Why are we doing this?" She clarifies the purpose: to identify problems and try to solve them. "I remind delegates and visitors that SAC will not plan parties, special field days, school fairs, contests, community outreach projects, money-making projects. We will do nothing in SAC that might distract us from our one purpose—to identify problems and try to solve them" (p. 361).

Shaheen and the principal call for reports from each classroom. Earlier, in preparation for today's meeting, each class was asked to spend time at its class meeting listing "the ten best things about Cottage Lane" and "the ten things most in need of improvement." It becomes clear that there are recurring problems. "Just as the delegates predicted, the principal and I hear things that we did not know and that surprise us," Shaheen said. This same meeting was repeated in the fourth grade SAC. Soon after, a meeting was held between central office administrators and small delegation of SACs 4 and 5. The director of facilities listened to children explain bathroom-related problems, an assistant superintendent listened to problems in food service. In this school district, every elementary school has an SAC system. First ("Little SAC 1") through fifth graders are involved in SACs, with each grade level having its own "so that children may take ownership of their school and be empowered and feel empowered to take responsibility" (p. 362).

Another council structure that contributes to this same goal is the Due Process Board. Whereas the SACs help children identify, frame, and try to solve problems that arise in the course of interaction at school, the due process boards involve students in deliberating problems related to justice. "If children believe they have been treated unjustly, they can request a meeting of one of the due process boards." Typically, the boards deal with interpersonal conflicts—taking property, playground mishaps, and racist comments. There are boards at the third, fourth, and fifth grades. They meet during lunch, and meetings last no longer than 15 minutes. A child whose actions are in question is encouraged to bring a friend who may be either a child or an adult.

I intend these examples—Paley's classroom meetings; Cottage Lane's schoolwide councils—only to outline the general features of actually existing deliberations in classroom and school settings from the vantage point of the educators who facilitate them day in and day out. Let me turn now to the third key in the project to realize the democratic potential of the public spaces called schools: deliberative competence.

STRIVING FOR INCLUSION AND GENUINE EXCHANGE

Deliberation with diverse others hopes to bring into existence a wise decision to act, certainly wiser than what results when people do not think together about the problems they face. This is its point. A "we" is deciding an issue, and each member will be bound by it. Whether the issue arose on the school playground or in the classroom, the student advisory council, or communities outside the school, right action is the goal. This is *praxis*. As Aristotle (1985) put forward, *praxis* is action, but not just any action. It is morally committed action. Some end product is being brought into existence by this action, but the end product is not a thing (a loaf of bread; a hubcap). When that sort of thing is brought into existence, the action is *poiesis* (instrumental action; making something). With *praxis*, the desired end is right action, such as a decision about what a "we" should *do* in a particular set of circumstances.

A central idea of deliberative democracy is reversibility, introduced in Chapter 4. Reversibility is an ideal form of reciprocity and means changing places with—perspective-taking, genuine exchange. It requires inclusion, dialogue, and imagination. Without inclusion, there can be neither dialogue nor reversibility. People with diverse perspectives, opinions, and life experiences must actually be at the table and, once there, equal to one another and engaged in communication. As Habermas (1990) has said, "nothing better prevents others from perspectivally distorting one's own interests than actual participation" (p. 67).

In the previous chapter, five conditions of good deliberation were identified. These emerged from Just Community projects, in which democratic governance became a way of life in actually existing high school settings (Power, Higgins, & Kohlberg, 1989). Not aiming only for individual moral development, these projects aimed to change the school culture—its hidden curriculum (Jackson, 1968)—and, in this way, to change both the group and the individual. "For even if the values of justice were discussed in classes (this itself would be a significant advance), if the students perceive that getting along in school runs by a quite different set of norms, they will tend to perceive the latter as the real rules of the game and the former as nice talk one engages in with teachers" (Power et al., 1989, p. 21). To review, the conditions are:

- Students are engaged in decision-making discussions involving genuine value conflicts that arise in the course of relating to one another at school. (For example, the children in Mrs. Paley's care, when deliberating the rule she proposed to them, faced the conflict between the obligations of care and fair play, on the one hand, and the freedom inherent in playtime, on the other.)
- The discussion group is diverse such that each student has the benefit of exposure to reasoning and social perspectives different from his or her own.
- The discussion group is free of domination, gross and subtle, by participants who were thrown into privileged social positions, because perspective taking requires the condition of genuine exchange.
- The discussion leader is skilled at comprehending and presenting reasons and perspectives that are missing—countering preconventional ideas with conventional ideas, conventional with postconventional, and advocating positions and perspectives that are absent, inarticulate, or being drummed out of consideration.
- Because justice is "drawn out" rather than "driven in," discussions are dialogic—discussants are engaged in conversation about their viewpoints, claims, and arguments, not in alternating monologues.

Each of these is a tall order, and a host of competencies—knowledge, skills, and dispositions—are involved: listening as well as talking, striving to understand points of view different from one's own, challenging ideas

and proposals rather than persons, admitting ignorance, slowing the rush
to decision so as to clarify or reframe the problem or gather more information, courageously asserting unpopular views, supporting claims with reasoning, drawing analogies, encouraging others to participate, noticing and
seeking missing perspectives and arguments, even appreciating the principle attributed to Voltaire: "I disapprove of what you say, but I will defend
to the death your right to say it." Rather than addressing each condition
and the many competencies involved, I will explore in some depth the last
condition—discussions are dialogic—as it implicates all the others and
presents a number of special difficulties. I will narrow my focus to the receptive dialogic competence of *listening across difference*.

When I use this phrase I am picturing many situations: the included
and excluded students in Paley's kindergarten classroom; Catholic and
Protestant high school students in Belfast brought together by members of
a reconciliation project; Chinese immigrant students and fourth- and fifth-
generation WASP students in a suburban Vancouver middle-school student council meeting; Black and White students having a "conversation
about race" in a 12th-grade government course in Seattle. In a shorthand
way, we might think of listening across difference as a skill, but I hope to
make clear the knowledge and dispositions involved as well. Three concepts will be central in what follows: *epistemic privilege*, *social perspective*,
and *diversity as a deliberative asset*. My goal is to underscore the real difficulties of dialogue across difference while affirming the possibility, the
necessity, and the hope for success.

Listening across Difference

Each individual in deliberation needs to listen. The greatest difficulty
here often arises for discussants who, relative to other discussants, were
thrown into privileged social positions (i.e., individuals who enjoy relatively more social status, often without awareness that they do). Consider
this testimony, for example, by an African American teacher:

> When you're talking to white people they still want it to be their way. You
> can try to talk to them and give them examples, but they're so headstrong,
> they think they know what's best for *everybody*, for *everybody's* children. . . .
> It's really hard. They just don't listen well. (quoted in Delpit, 1995, p. 21)

Every effort must be made to educate all students to listen across difference, of course. But because privileged persons possess the fruits of privilege—political, cultural, and economic power—and can, therefore, do the
most harm, they especially need to learn to listen. They are uniquely obliged
to listen without egocentric or ethnocentric distortion.

Uma Narayan (1988) writes, "Given the way difference works, it is hardly surprising that insiders and outsiders may often have very different understandings of what is involved in a situation or issue" (p. 41). By "insiders" Narayan refers to members of historically oppressed groups (e.g., the poor, gays and lesbians, women, people of color); "outsiders" are non-members. Non-members do not share in the oppression. People are insiders or outsiders in relation to specific forms of oppression—racism, sexism, compulsory heterosexuality, and so on. When the children are deliberating Mrs. Paley's proposal that a child shouldn't be permitted to say "You can't say you can't play" (1992), there are both insiders and outsiders in the deliberation. Children typically excluded from play (e.g., Clara) are the insiders, and those typically doing the excluding (e.g., Lisa) are the outsiders—as far as this issue is concerned. When discussing sexual harassment in school or at the workplace, girls and women are usually the insiders, boys and men the outsiders. Using the terms "insider" and "outsider" has the distinct advantage of turning upside down the conventional usage by according dialogic privilege to the oppressed—what Narayan calls *epistemic privilege*: Members (insiders) have an unparalleled vantage point from which to understand and articulate the experience of oppression. They have a more immediate knowledge of their oppression, to be sure, than non-members. It is "right there" for them; it is not an act of imagination but observation, memory, and feeling. This knowledge is, therefore, more subtle, nuanced, and (regrettably) precise than even the highly empathic knowledge of an outsider, even one who is listening carefully and is capable of reversibility. The insider carries a burden, obviously, but less obviously a *complex* burden. He or she "pays a heavy social and psychological price that no outsider pays" (Narayan, p. 40); consequently, dialogue among outsiders and insiders can be loaded with difficulty. The two groups do not share power equally and are not, therefore, equally vulnerable. Consider deliberations on sexual harassment:

> When, for instance, men totally blame women for the sexual harassment and sexual terrorism from which they suffer, they wholly deny the validity of the insiders' understanding of such harassment as something inflicted on them. The insider will most often respond emotionally to such attempts to negate her understanding—with anger, tears, etc. The issue, to the insiders, is not a purely theoretical one, and their anger and pain at what they have to endure become exacerbated by the seeming inability of even well-intentioned outsiders to see their point of view. (Narayan, p. 41)

Emotions and intentions both are involved in dialogue across difference, and listening cannot avoid either of these and still be called listening. Taking emotions seriously has long been a feminist commitment in politics and education. Applying that commitment to deliberation has the advantage not only of helping participants hear and respect one another's emotions in deliberation—fear, grief, hurt, vulnerability, violation—but also signaling outsiders that some caution is needed to avoid causing or dismissing emotional turmoil among insiders. Narayan (1988) details some ways that outsiders unintentionally do this, chief among which is by (unintentionally) denying the validity of the insider's understandings of and responses to a situation.

Consider the sexual harassment case again. Heterosexual men sometimes reason that women are responsible for harassment by men because they look attractive—the way they dress, their makeup and physique, hairstyle, and so forth. These men may not perceive a woman's understanding of harassment as something originating from men, from the harasser, and inflicted upon women. In response to this denial, the insider understandably has an emotional response: hurt, frustration, exasperation, anger— each compounding the violation. The validity of this response also might be denied by the outsider. First was the denial of the insider's view of the situation; now, adding insult to injury, is denial of the feelings that arise in response to that denial. This second volley of denial can take several forms, Narayan suggests. One is dismissal of the emotion as irrelevant or irrational. Another is to accuse the insider of trying to manipulate the situation with emotion (e.g., crying to win sympathy). A third is to accuse the insider of "paranoia"—of imagining oppression when none exists, or exaggerating what little may exist rather than ignoring it and getting on with life.

Or consider the following passage from King's (1963a) "Letter from Birmingham Jail." The letter was written, now using Narayan's meaning of the term, to "outsiders"—to White clerics who wanted King to leave Birmingham; in order to negotiate rather than engage in direct action, and to "wait." To these sympathetic, well-intentioned outsiders, King wrote: "Perhaps it is easy for those who have never felt the stinging darts of segregation to say, 'Wait'" (p. 81). Having not been on the receiving end of oppression, they can say things that those who are regularly on the receiving end would never say. That sentence is followed immediately by the longest sentence in the "Letter," in which King tries to give the insider's view through a series of brutal social facts:

> But when you have seen vicious mobs lynch your mothers and fathers at will and drown your sisters and brothers at whim; when you have seen hate-filled policemen curse, kick and even kill your black brothers and sisters; when you see the vast majority of your twenty million Negro brothers smothering in an airtight cage of poverty in the midst of an affluent society; when you

suddenly find your tongue twisted and your speech stammering as you seek
to explain to your six-year-old daughter why she can't go to the public amuse-
ment park that has just been advertised on television, and see tears welling
up in her eyes when she is told that Funtown is closed to colored children,
and see ominous clouds of inferiority beginning to form in her little mental
sky, and see her beginning to distort her personality by developing an unconscious bitterness toward white people; when you have to concoct an
answer for a five-year-old son who is asking: 'Daddy, why do white people
treat colored people so mean?'; when you take a cross-country drive and find
it necessary to sleep night after night in the uncomfortable corners of your
automobile because no motel will accept you; when you are humiliated day
in and day out by nagging signs reading 'white' and 'colored'; when your
first name becomes 'nigger,' your middle name becomes 'boy' (however old
you are) and your last name becomes 'John,' and your wife and mother are
never given the respected title 'Mrs'; when you are harried by day and
haunted by night by the fact that you are a Negro, living constantly at tiptoe
stance, never quite knowing what to expect next, and are plagued with
inner fears and outer resentments; when you are forever fighting a degenerat-
ing sense of 'nobodiness'—then you will understand why we find it difficult
to wait. (1963a, pp. 81–82).

King concludes with an insider-to-outsider plea: "I hope, sirs, you can
understand our legitimate and unavoidable impatience."

But can the White clerics understand? Can *I* understand? Can my good
will, my good intentions, see me across the bridge between my privileged
social position—White, middle-class, male—to King's, and help me understand? Can an in-between be created across the gulf that separates outsider
and insider, privileged and oppressed? This is no easy matter, to be sure,[6]
especially for outsiders for whom the insider is often what Azizah Y.
Al-Hibri (1999) calls an *inessential Other*:

> So inessential is this Other that, even when included in the discussion, it is
> rendered remarkably indistinguishable and voiceless. It is allowed into the
> discussion only through the voice and perceptions of the dominant 'I' (the
> outsider). Given these ground rules, it is hard to have a serious discussion
> or reach a democratic resolution of existing conflicts. (p. 42)

Narayan (1988) argues that "good will is not enough" (p. 34). When
individuals or groups resolve sincerely to understand the experience of
persons whose oppression they do not share, this is of course a useful
and wholesome intention. It indicates both knowledge of the reality of
the oppression and some sort of willingness to put effort into listening.
This resolve may lay an important foundation on which trust may eventually develop. It will not, however, "solve or resolve the thousands of

problems that are going to crop up in discussion and communication. . . .
The advantaged would be wrong to expect this to be sufficient to cause
strong, historically constituted networks of distrust to simply evaporate
into thin air" (p. 34). All of the very reasonable grounds for mistrust on
the part of insiders, reinforced through decades of "good intentions" by
(some) outsiders—intentions that are nonetheless wedded to intransigent
structures of power and privilege—will not dissolve thanks to an outsider's sincere attempt to listen anew.

Are there strategies that might consciously be enacted to take us—any
one of us, but outsiders especially—farther than "good will" can take us
and, therefore, make genuine deliberation, complete with contention and
disagreement, more achievable? Might norms be implemented by which
outsiders can hear and challenge insiders' understandings and responses
without denying their validity and authenticity? If not, then dialogue de-
volves to alternating monologues: insiders and outsiders telling stories to
which one another listen politely. This is far from deliberation because the
group is not thinking together about how to frame and solve a problem.

There are several such strategies. Narayan (1988) suggests epistemic
privilege, as well as "methodological humility" and "methodological caution." Each strategy aims for honest and open deliberation across difference.
Each aims to surpass denial, invalidation, and alternating monologues.
Epistemic privilege, as we have seen, means that insiders have better knowledge about the nature of their oppression than outsiders. To grant epistemic
privilege in a discussion is an act of human-hearted generosity that assumes
this is the case. This does not mean that insiders' knowledge is beyond question—beyond dialogue—as that would suggest that insiders' claims cannot
be mistaken or need clarification, which is nonsense. Narayan explains:
"Members of an oppressed group, like human subjects in general, can always be mistaken about the nature of their experience. Other members of
the very same group may differ in the way they perceive or interpret certain
incidents. . . . [N]ot all of them can be right, and at times, it may even be that
all of them are wrong" (p. 37). To grant epistemic privilege, then, does not
absolve an outsider from critical listening and responding nor, conversely,
infantilizing the insider by removing his or her statements from criticism and
challenge, reducing him or her to a storyteller. Rather, it calls on the outsider
to exert effort to absorb the details of the insider's understanding of and
response to an event—to come seriously to grips with the litany of "whens"
in King's statement, for example, and the sense of attack in a woman's experience of sexual harassment.

> Having members of the oppressed group as friends, sharing in aspects of their
> lifestyle, fighting alongside them on issues that concern them, sustaining a

continuous dialogue with them, etc. can all help non-members develop a more sophisticated understanding of what a form of oppression involves. But "outsiders" who do none of the above, who simply have an abstract sort of goodwill towards members of the oppressed group, are unlikely to have much of a clear or detailed awareness of the forms in which that oppression is experienced. (Narayan, p. 37)

"Methodological humility" and "methodological caution" are additional strategies that can be intentionally implemented by an outsider when listening to an insider share an understanding of a situation or propose a solution. If I am *humble* while listening and responding, I realize that I am very likely missing something—that my understanding is probably incomplete. I remind myself that there is more I must learn, and that I am probably, albeit unintentionally, distorting what I am hearing. What appears to me to be a mistake on the part of the insider, or "paranoia," would probably make more sense to me if I had a better grasp of the details and the situation. Similarly, if I am *cautious* when listening and responding, I will engage carefully so that I am not denying or dismissing the validity of the insider's point of view, nor even appearing to do so; that is, I am careful not to violate the premise of epistemic integrity.

In *Is Multiculturalism Bad for Women?*, Susan Moller Okin (1999) reviews the feminist case against the great monotheisms—Judaism, Christianity, and Islam—for their "attempts to justify the control and subordination of women" and their "characterizations of women as overly emotional, untrustworthy, evil, or sexually dangerous" (p. 13). As evidence, Okin cites two stories: the creation of Eve from Adam and the fall of Adam. In a response to Okin, Al-Hibri (1999), the founder of Muslim Women Lawyers for Human Rights, chides Okin for lacking both humility and caution and, consequently, producing a distorted "Orientalist reductionist approach to Islam" (p. 42). Okin sees Islam not on its own terms, says Al-Hibri, but as projected through biblical eyes:

> The Qur'an nowhere says that Eve was created out of part of Adam. In fact, the Qur'an clearly states that males and females were created by God from the same *naf* (soul or spirit). . . . The story of the fall of Adam is also different in the Qur'an. *Both* Adam and Eve were tempted by Satan, and both succumbed. The story is thus about the human condition. It is not about gender. By missing these important differences, Okin attributes to Islam a position based on biblical analysis. (p. 42)

My emphasis here on the receptive act of listening should not imply an absence of talking—of asserting opinions and expressing reasons, advancing arguments, telling stories, and challenging or clarifying the claims and arguments that others are making. To the contrary, making proposals and evaluating those already on the table are central activities of deliberation without which there would be little to listen to or exchange. However, in deliberation no one is relieved of the obligation to listen, neither insider nor outsider, and the difficulty of listening across difference escapes no one, for no one lacks a social perspective—a cultural and intellectual "home base" from which he or she thinks and feels and observes the problem at hand.

Even Thich Nhat Hanh approaches listening with humility and caution. I say "even" Thich Nhat Hanh because his decades of mindfulness-awareness practice (meditation) have cultivated his listening ability in a most direct and precise way. Still, when he was asked shortly after the September 2001 attacks on the World Trade Center and the Pentagon what he would say if he had a chance to "speak to Osama bin Laden," he responded:

> If I were given the opportunity . . . the first thing I would do is listen. I would try to understand why he had acted in that cruel way. I would try to understand all of the suffering that had led him to violence. It might not be easy to listen in that way, so I would have to remain calm and lucid. I would need several friends with me, who are strong in the practice of deep listening, listening without reacting, without judging and blaming. In this way, an atmosphere of support would be created for this person and those connected so that they could share completely and trust that they are really being heard. After listening for some time, we might need to take a break to allow what has been said to enter into our consciousness. Only when we felt calm and lucid would we respond. (2001, p. 1)

The first thing Thich Nhat Hanh would do was listen, not talk. Even then it would be difficult to listen well, so he consciously implements strategies that should help.

The Deliberative Advantages of Diversity

To educate children and youth in the deliberative arts is to educate them in the anti-idiotic obligation to pay attention to shared problems and to listen, respect, and work skillfully with the plurality of perspectives that are present in any public space. This applies as much to Vivian Paley's kindergarten classroom as to an after-school community center, a church choir practice, 4-H Club, or legislative body such as the city council.

Now that we have looked at strategies for competent (fair, skillful, attentive) public decision making across difference—actual strategies that can be practiced and evaluated and deepened—let us turn, finally, to a claim that undergirds this push toward competence: *A plurality of social perspectives is a social good and a deliberative asset, not a problem to be overcome.* Let us consider two questions. First, what is a social perspective? Second, why is a plurality of social perspectives a social good and a deliberative asset? Neither of these are impractical or "merely theoretical" questions by any stretch of the imagination, for both deal directly with how educators plan and conduct discussions in their various settings: in classrooms (from kindergarten through college), in schools (curriculum committees, student councils, faculty meetings, site council meetings, parent conferences), and in our communities (voluntary organizations, jury duty, neighborhood meetings, and city councils).

Social Perspective

We saw in the previous chapter that individuals are "thrown into" unchosen historical and social situations. We are positioned in already-structured fields of social class, race, gender, nationality, religion, sexual orientation, first and second language, and so forth, and we have really no choice but to deal with the situation in which we find ourselves—in this life, in this moment. As I stated in Chapter 3, I was born of working-class, English-speaking WASP parents in Englewood, Colorado, brought up in the Sunday school classes, summer camps, and youth groups of the Englewood Methodist Church, and schooled in the local neighborhood public schools. I chose none of this. Now, to what extent has this social positioning shaped my identity? I believe it influenced but did not determine my identity. Our social positioning—our "thrownness"—does not *determine* our identities because each of us deals in unique ways with the cards we were dealt, with the circumstances into which we were thrown. Yet our social positioning does matter, of course. It influences, but does not determine, our identities.

Our social position locates us in some social groups but not others, thereby placing us closer to some individuals (e.g., my fellow WASPs in the church youth groups of which I was a member) and, simultaneously, farther from others who are positioned differently (e.g., wealthy WASPs living in other neighborhoods, Jews, Muslims, African Americans, poor Whites, and Hispanics). That is, all of us are positioned closer to persons similarly thrown and farther from persons who were thrown into different situations. This is precisely what constitutes us as members of the same group. Furthermore, the groups into which we are thrown are not equal. They are positioned differently in the socioeconomic hierarchy and the related status hierarchies of race, gender, language, religion, and sexual preference. This inequality of groups matters. It matters because individual

members are differently enabled or constrained in the life possibilities laid
before them; for example, likelihood of admission to college, of sexual
harassment by supervisors, of being stopped by police while driving an
automobile, of being elected to a legislature, of being bullied at school.

Being positioned in one way rather than another, here rather than there,
adds up to a unique social perspective—a unique point of view, a vantage
point, a frame of reference. *Where* one is situated matters in terms of *how*
one sees the world and *what* one attends to in it. Iris Marion Young (1997)
put it this way:

> A social perspective is a certain way of being sensitive to particular aspects of
> social life, meanings, and interactions, and perhaps less sensitive to others. It
> is a form of attentiveness that brings some things into view while possibly
> obscuring others. . . . Perspective is a way of looking at social processes with-
> out determining what one sees. (pp. 394–395; see also Code, 1991; McIntosh,
> 1997)

Two people who are similarly located in society may share a similar perspective, but they probably will experience situations differently and deal
with them and respond to them differently. Position does not determine
identity; still, shared perspective is consequential. While one cannot necessarily infer the content of either of these individuals' opinions simply by
knowing the social groups into which they were thrown, one can rather
safely assume that these two will probably share at least the following: an
understanding of their position in relation to other positions, a point of view
on the history of their group in relation to the broader society, and a posi-
tion-specific view of the way society operates.

A social perspective, then, is a shared way of looking at situations that
is grounded in one's social position(s) without automatically predicting
what one sees. Sharing the same social perspective with others creates a
bond of sorts, an affinity of being similarly positioned, and perhaps due to
similar experiences in that location, a sense of solidarity and sometimes
even agreement on what should be done about particular problems.

Drawing this distinction between perspective (point of view) and identity (subjectivity) is practically useful in attempts to deliberate together the
problems of living together, whether we are participants in such discussions or, as educators and citizens, facilitating them. Why? It acknowledges
the reality and consequences of group membership while arguing against
stereotyping and "the tendency to interpret groups as fixed, closed, and
bounded" (Young, 1997, p. 398). Moreover, it suggests the possibility that
persons who are differently positioned, differently thrown, might nevertheless understand one another and deliberate honestly and equitably to-

gether, though a huge amount of work may be needed. Therein lies the value of strategies such as those recommended by Narayan (1988).

Diversity as a Deliberative Asset

Now the second question: Why is a plurality of social perspectives a social good and a deliberative asset? It may seem strange to ask this question, because in some ways the matter seems to have been settled, especially perhaps with readers of this book. By now, "celebrate differences" has become a popular slogan in American and Canadian education (and elsewhere). But a slogan, while perhaps symbolizing an ideal, is no substitute for understanding or action. Indeed, it is difficult to imagine enlightened political engagement without an understanding of exactly why diversity is necessary to the promise of a vibrant and flourishing democracy. Accordingly, let me try now to unpack the slogan and show why group diversity should not merely be tolerated but *fostered*. Specifically, I show why multiple social perspectives are a necessary resource for deliberation. I offer three reasons: diversity motivates individuals to justify their proposals with appeals to justice, it contributes to social knowledge, and it helps people flower as human beings.

First, diversity motivates individuals and groups, when deliberating public policy, to justify their proposals with appeals to moral principles, especially justice. To understand this claim, we should recall, as we saw in Chapter 2, that diversity protects liberty. Rather than "balkanizing" or "disuniting" us, as assimilationists like to charge, our deep and abiding differences require a political framework that protects these differences and, thereby, encourages them. This is the point of the First Amendment's counter-majoritarian guarantees of speech, religion, press, and assembly. As James Madison (1787/1937) argued in *The Federalist No. 10* at the time of the debate over the ratification of the U. S. Constitution, the plurality of "factions" in society helps prevent tyranny by the majority group. Madison believed that in a large society (in extent of territory and number of citizens) "you take in a greater variety of parties and interests; you make it less probable that a majority of the whole will have a common motive to invade the rights of other citizens; or if such a common motive exists, it will be more difficult for all who feel it to discover their own strength and to act in union with each other" (p. 22). Were it not for diversity, odious monistic groups such as the Christian Right, the Islamic Right, and the Ku Klux Klan could not exist; yet it is the same diversity that prevents these factions from more widely implementing their antidemocratic, antipluralist, theocratic platforms. Liberty and diversity are in this way interdependent.

Accordingly, when collective policies are being deliberated, it is clear that everyone's liberty is at stake, while at the same time there is a common problem to be solved and, therefore, a common interest at stake. For this reason, when we argue for or against proposals in a public forum where a plurality of social perspectives and individual differences are present, we are motivated to appeal to justice. We try to show that our proposals are workable, that they can be implemented effectively, but also we try to show that they are fair to everyone concerned. (Recall Vivian Paley's [1992] two questions to her students when proposing a rule: Will it work? Is it fair?) Others are not likely to accept "I want this" or "this alternative is the best for me" as good reasons for them to accept a proposal. To the contrary, "the need to be accountable to others with different perspectives on collective problems motivates participants in a discussion to frame their proposals in terms of justice" (Young, 1997, p. 403). Whether faculty members are deliberating budget allocations for scarce curriculum resources or children are deciding whether to adopt a classroom rule, "I want this" is at best heard as a preference but rarely accepted as a reason for the group to adopt a policy that will be binding on all. Public reasoning—reasoning in public—thus has its own moral imperatives. Political requests and demands cannot be justified by reference to individual likes and dislikes, provincial values, or religious scripture, and this moral imperative is all the more apparent and necessary when a diverse array of perspectives are present in the deliberation. Melissa Williams (2000) clarifies:

> [D]eliberative democracy aspires to a polity in which public decisions are justifiable to all citizens, and in which all public actors hold themselves accountable to give publicly acceptable reasons in defense of their actions. Although there may be some limitations on the degree to which this aspiration can be met, even in theory, it remains the regulative goal of deliberative democracy. (p. 129)

A second reason why multiple perspectives are a deliberative asset is that they contribute to social knowledge. Group difference increases a diverse society's collective knowledge base and enlightens its public decision making. It does this in at least two ways. One is by enlarging each participant's knowledge of people and perspectives beyond one's own social position and experience. As Williams writes, "pluralism enhances deliberation because it expands the number of alternative understandings of a problem we can entertain in attempting to resolve it" (pp. 131–132). This assumes that participants are listening to one another, of course, and thereby learning—learning how social problems and events look from various perspectives, learning of alternative solutions heretofore unimagined, and learning something about life as it is lived in other social positions. One's horizon is broadened. One's understanding of social life is deepened and widened thanks to a multiplicity of perspectives present in a deliberation, and the problem at hand can be understood in broader terms. As Al-Hibri (1999) puts it in this chapter's opening quotation, "The importance of a genuine dialogue is that it permits a more accurate diagnosis of the problems at hand" (p. 42).

Another way social knowledge is advantaged by group difference is that the presence of multiple perspectives increases the likelihood that dominant norms and beliefs are subjected to observation and critique. It is no coincidence that groups excluded from participation in the larger civic realm have again and again directed the attention of those who are comfortably included to the persistence of injustice and the extent of hypocrisy, and it is they who have demanded that the gaps be closed. The democratic struggle in the United States has relied upon those barred from the *unum* to deepen and extend the democracy that the founders created. As we saw in Chapter 2, it was from the outskirts of the public square, from the "corners of American society," that Martin Luther King Jr. came to Washington, DC in 1963 to say, "We have come to cash this check . . ." (1963b, p. 1). And it was from the Birmingham city jail that he wrote, "We know from painful experience that freedom is never voluntarily given by the oppressor; it must be demanded by the oppressed" (1963a, p. 80). In this sense, the purpose of the Civil Rights movement was not to alter the American dream, nor to revise it, but to fulfill it. The founders may have been the birth parents of democracy American style, but those who were excluded (then and now) became the adoptive, nurturing parents.

When constitutionally protected liberties are vigorously enforced, the primary sources of criticism of established conventions of thought and action are kept alive. To reduce this diversity dangerously removes from public spaces much of the debate, boycotts, and direct action that challenges the status quo. As Carole Gould (1996) put it, to reduce diversity is to undercut "the creativity that issues forth in imaginative critique and rejection of existing agreement and in the generation of new and unexpected frameworks for agreement" (p. 173). This is known especially well, again, by peoples who are excluded from the mainstream culture where the norms of social life are made. These subordinated groups are forced to take advantage of the constitutionally guaranteed freedom of association to do just that—to create "underground" factions where there is the potential for unrepressed, candid discourse. Historically, as we saw in the discussion of voluntary associations in Chapter 3, these have been "key staging grounds for interventionist politics" (Trend, 1995, p. 10). The point here is that without diverse viewpoints there can hardly be constructive or deconstructive criticism of the dominant viewpoint, and without that there can be nothing of the creative problem-solving needed to deal with the actual problems and always-changing circumstances of life.

A third reason why multiple perspectives are a deliberative asset is that they contribute to individual enlightenment. They bring to individual life a sense of the possible. You and I can benefit from the full range of human flowering only if we are fortunate enough to live in close association with others who are different, who embody that range. Otherwise, there is no meaningful choice as to what and who we each will be. As Charles Taylor (1998) writes, "To attempt to impose uniformity is to condemn ourselves to a narrower and poorer life" (p. 153).[7] Moreover, our ability to cut through conventional thinking—to develop morally, to imagine alternatives, and to distinguish just and unjust arrangements—is nurtured through our engagement in deliberations in heterogeneous groups. When Paley's (1992) kindergartners listen to one another in discussion, the diversity of perspectives they encounter stimulates cognitive and moral growth—ideal reversibility. Discussion is more likely to have this effect if each student encounters and listens to reasoning that is somewhat different from his or her own. Therefore—and this will bring us back to classroom practice—teachers should encourage all students to speak during discussions, sharing both opinions and reasons, and help all children listen carefully to what each other are saying. Asking children regularly to paraphrase what others have said is a good way to build the listening habit. "Brandon, what was Neetha saying to the group?" "Jamal, were you listening as Myrna gave her reasons? Please restate them for us." Also, when two children share the same opinion but have different reasons, students should be helped to notice: "You two seem to agree, but for different reasons. Let's try to understand the difference." And, "Who else agrees, but for yet a different reason?"

CONCLUSION

Schools are public places where diversity and common problems come with the territory. In addition, every topic addressed in class is loaded with genuine problems of interpretation and explanation. Teachers and school leaders should exploit this diversity and these problems in order to cultivate the deliberative arts, using the common space to forge positions with others rather than as a platform for asserting and defending positions already formed. This is serious work. The three keys are closely related, one leading to the next on a trajectory of increasing power and depth. Interaction counts for something, to be sure. Better is interaction combined with deliberation on the problems at hand. More powerful still is competent deliberation, especially strategies for genuine inclusion and exchange, without which deliberation has no warrant.

Making Publics, Finding Problems, Imagining Solutions

If you are defending your opinions, you are not serious.
—David Bohm (1996, p. 41)

When people of any age and social perspective "come together in speech and action and try to bring into existence an 'in-between' among themselves" (Greene, 1996, p. 28), we witness the creation of a public space. Idiots shun this activity for any number of reasons—both individualistic and familial.

By definition, an "in-between" is a space that bridges difference; this is what makes it public and dialogic. There is a *path* quality to creating these in-between spaces. Path, as we saw in Chapter 2, implies journey and creativity, work yet to be done, an open future. Listening is key, as we saw in Chapter 5. Listening is one of the least idiotic activities of all: open, receptive, sensitive, leaning forward to hear and see something other than our own clod of assumptions, prejudices, and projections. And difference—pluralism and diversity—is key. "Deliberation matters," writes Anne Phillips (1995, p. 151), "only because there *is* difference; if some freak of history or nature delivered a polity based on unanimous agreement, then politics would be virtually redundant and the decisions would be already made."

This is serious work. If in the middle of it we are busy defending our opinions, we are not serious. David Bohm (1996), quoted at the opening of this chapter, was one of the great physicists of our time and a passionate sage on dialogue. Busily defending one's opinions is at times appropriate, of course, as when engaging "outsiders" (dominant group members) who may practice neither caution nor humility, nor privilege even for a moment an "insider's" experience and perspective. Too often, however, an active defense displaces its complement, receptive listening, and is for that reason "not serious" and not dialogue. Bohm continues:

> If you are trying to avoid something unpleasant inside of yourself, that is also not being serious. . . . There is a story about Freud when he had cancer of the mouth. Somebody came up to him and wanted to ask him about some

point in psychology. The person said, "Perhaps I'd better not talk to you, because you've got this cancer which is very serious. You may not want to talk about this." Freud's answer was, "This cancer may be fatal, but it's not serious." And actually, of course, it was just a lot of cells growing. I think a great deal of what goes on in society could be described that way—that it may well be fatal, but it's not serious. (1996, pp. 41–42)

DELIBERATIVE CURRICULA

If we are to be serious in this work, and practical, then we need courses of study as well as a variety of deliberative forums in which democracy and difference can be experienced directly. In this way, both the transmission and participation dimensions of the democracy curriculum are addressed, as discussed in Chapter 3. Elementary school examples were featured in Chapter 5; here I will concentrate on the upper grades. The suitable courses of study are likely to be inclusive versions of stalwarts such as American history, world history, comparative government, and problems of democracy, along with less common but vitally important and doable courses such as the Civil Rights movement. (The latter was championed by Vincent Harding [1990] as the single most compelling subject matter for developing an understanding of democracy and the rights and responsibilities of democratic citizens.) The deliberative school settings in the high school will differ from Mrs. Paley's gatherings of kindergartners, of course, but their nature will be much the same: students deliberating with diverse peers, in multiple venues, with capable facilitators, on an array of public controversies shared by the students involved.

In this chapter, I will outline a one-semester high school course. Its overall purpose is to teach and learn a generic approach to deliberation that I will call public policy deliberation (PPD). I base it on a particular model of policy deliberation that combines two traditions: the *content selection* approach of the "problems of democracy" and "public issues" traditions in American social studies education, and the *intellectual framework* that is practiced by policy professionals working in public agencies, city halls, and legislatures. The goals of the course are democratic public building and democratic decision making. These two, as we have seen, are interdependent: publics are formed when people come together to solve problems that are held in common. The course has three objectives: (1) to uncover and understand the problems faced by various publics (e.g., classroom and school problems; local, national, and international problems), (2) to imagine, find, develop, and evaluate policy alternatives together, and (3) to choose together a publicly justifiable course of action.

Can It Be Done?

It is not wise to recommend things that cannot be done. That, too, is not being serious. For this reason, before turning to the PPD model we should consider questions that bear directly on the feasibility of implementing it. I will address four: Is deliberation effective? Can teachers teach it? Can students do it? Are there instructional resources?

First, is deliberation effective? The PPD outcomes of concern here, against which effectiveness would be judged, are public building and right action; that is, the empowerment of citizens as agents rather than spectators in policy making—to compose them as a public, not merely a populace—and the enlightenment of citizens so that they might be more likely to choose wise courses of action. While there are longstanding suspicions that "the people" simply cannot rule wisely (see Plato's [1992a] argument in the *Republic*, Madison's [1787/1937] in the *Federalist No. 10*, Schumpeter's [1950] in *Capitalism, Socialism, and Democracy*), there is evidence to the contrary. Recent studies support the ancient Greek belief that public agents come into being through collaborative policy deliberation (Evans & Boyte, 1992; Harwood Group, 1993; Putnam, 1994). Furthermore, researchers find that engagement in this in-between activity changes participants' knowledge and attitudes. Specifically, it changes their perceptions of one another, the problem, and the array of policy alternatives (Doble, 1996; Farkas & Friedman, 1996). These are powerful effects.

Second, can teachers teach PPD? A main finding of instructional research informed by sociocultural theory is that typical performance should not be confused with optimal performance (e.g., Brown, 1996; Wertsch, 1991). Teachers evidently do not typically lead students in the kind of intellectual work PPD involves (Goodlad, 1984; Hahn, 1996; McNeil, 1988; Shaver, Davis, & Helburn, 1979), yet—whether few, some, or most—are capable of doing so. Case studies of exemplary teachers (e.g., Bickmore, 1993; Hess, 2002; Miller & Singleton, 1997; Parker, 2001b; Power, Higgins, & Kohlberg, 1989; Rossi, 1995; Wineburg & Wilson, 1988) show them to be well engaged in several aspects of PPD (e. g., leading discussions of controversial issues; helping students weigh alternatives and adjudicate multiple perspectives; suggesting alternative perspectives, positions, and reasons). Furthermore, research done with the school or department as the unit of analysis (rather than individual teachers) indicates that, despite obstacles, sophisticated teaching and high-quality student achievement does occur (Hill, Pierce, & Guthrie, 1997; Meier, 1995; Newmann & Associates, 1996). These studies in general, and best-practices research in particular, have established "existence proof" for those practices, which in turn helps clarify what is possible given supportive conditions. Still, I am in no position to assure readers that teachers generally possess sufficient understanding of deliberation or pedagogy to teach or lead PPD. Knowledge matters in teaching (Shulman, 1986) and there is every reason to believe that this is true also of teaching deliberation.

Third, can students do it? For students as with teachers, typicality and capability should not be confused. Knowledge of what students are and are not capable of knowing and doing cannot be gleaned from assessments of students at work in task environments where they are neither expected to achieve at high levels of quality nor assisted skillfully in reaching them (Brown, 1996; Wertsch, 1991). Various studies have shown that junior and senior high school students can and do reason well on public issues when given ample support (e.g., Levin, Newmann, & Oliver, 1969; Mosher, Kenny, & Garrod, 1994; Oliver & Shaver, 1974; Parker, McDaniel, & Valencia, 1991; Power, Higgins, & Kohlberg, 1989). When the scaffold (a temporary system of instructional support—assistance—that helps students accomplish more than they otherwise could) is strengthened to include a classroom climate that welcomes dissension and disagreement, students generally respond with more capable consideration of the controversies at hand (Blankenship, 1990; Ehman, 1970; Hahn, 1998; Hahn & Tocci, 1990; Torney-Purta, Lehmann, Oswald, & Schulz, 2001). Whether or not students, in the best of circumstances, can capably deliberate public policy in the fullest sense, working systematically with the aid of a comprehensive analytic model, remains to be seen. The best circumstances do not always obtain, obviously (Kozol, 1992; Onosko, 1991). But there is, again, "existence proof" that favorable circumstances exist for at least some students at some times, and it is on this basis that we may remain hopeful that PPD can be attempted with promising results. Our hope is buoyed as well by the knowledge that Vivian Paley accomplished it routinely with 5-year-olds.

Fourth, are there resources? Among the barriers to creating the sorts of thoughtful high school classrooms PPD requires, three loom large: broad and superficial content coverage, low expectations of students, and lack of teacher planning time (Onosko, 1991). Each of these problem areas, I believe, becomes workable—not solved, but more manageable—with adequate curriculum resources. Thoughtful, policy-relevant resources are needed, especially if public policy deliberation is to rise above "current events" instruction, which often relies on daily newspapers and weekly magazines and too often avoids the problems of race and class as well as a challenging intellectual framework for deliberating them competently.

Fortunately, several resources are readily available that meet both of these criteria. Let me review briefly some of the best of the low-cost resources. I am impressed particularly with the classroom materials published by the *National Issues Forum* (NIF).[1] They have been extensively field-tested with thousands of high school aged youth, both in classrooms and non-school organizations (e.g. rural 4-H clubs). These materials feature authentic public policy controversies and highlight the value conflicts that make them difficult. Each unit in the program centers on an NIF issues booklet familiar to the many adults who participate in NIF "deliberative forums" in libraries, service clubs, and churches and temples. These booklets provide background information on the problem, then present three or four distinct policy alternatives. In this way they draw participants into the deliberative choice-work that is the essence of policy deliberation.

Let's look at one of these booklets. *Remedies for Racial Inequality* (National Issues Forum [NIF], 1990) deals with the persistence of racism and economic disparity. The opening chapter, "Unfinished Business: Racial Justice and Economic Inequality," provides background data, including trends, on racial inequality. One chart, for example, shows that unemployment rates for men, women, and 16–19-year-olds are dramatically racialized. For each of these three groups, African Americans had the highest rate of unemployment (more than twice that for Whites), followed by Hispanics, then Whites. Between 1973 and 1986, it explains, the percentage of African American men employed full time and year-round fell from 44% to 35% and earnings for these men fell by an astonishing 50%. Elsewhere in the opening chapter are survey results that underscore the different social positions and perspectives of African Americans and Whites in the United States. When asked why African Americans have worse jobs, income, and housing than Whites, seven out of ten African Americans—compared to less than half of the Whites surveyed—say the differences are mainly due to discrimination. Following this and other background information, the remaining three chapters lay out alternative courses of action for students' consideration:

- *Choice 1: Civil Rights Strategy: Prohibiting Discrimination, Enforcing the Laws.*
    Our public commitment is to uphold the principle of equality under the law, for people of all races. The government's obligation is to make sure the rules of the game are the same for everyone. But equality of opportunity does not necessarily lead to equal results.
- *Choice 2: Affirmative Action Strategy: Taking Race into Consideration.*
    Equal opportunity is not enough. Government must take measures to ensure equal *results*, even if affirmative action benefits minority groups at the expense of others. Racial equality can be achieved only by allowing preferences for groups that have suffered from discrimination.
- *Choice 3: Ladder Out of Poverty: Helping the Poor, Closing the Racial Gap.*
    Because the obstacles to equality today are chiefly economic,

race-specific remedies are no longer the most promising. Poverty
must be attacked at its roots with aggressive social welfare programs
that help all low income people, even if such programs are costly.
(National Issues Forum, 1990)

I have observed on more than one occasion students in large, racially
and economically integrated urban high schools squirm at the thought of
deliberating with one another the problem of racial inequality *and* stare
blankly at the third of these alternatives. As for discussing racial inequality
with one another, "What is the point?", they seem to ask. I hear White students declare that the whole problem will go away once the current generation of adults dies off. The problem lies with racist grown-ups (in the media,
at home, at friends' homes) and will vanish with them. The magical thinking here rests on the assumption that *they* are racist, not *us*. As for choice
three above, students typically have not made the connection between race
and poverty prior to encountering this section in the booklet. The information on low-income people can be compelling to students of this age, and is
new to many of them. As choice three lays out, even more striking than the
poverty of low-income people is their apartness. This is the central theme in
Michael Harrington's influential book *The Other America* (1963).

NIF materials have been used in one-semester courses devoted entirely
to public policy deliberation.[2] These courses begin with a preparatory unit
introducing students to public controversies—how to define, research, and
discuss them. The class then selects three to five of the available issues booklets (there are more than ten in any year) for in-depth study of about 2 to 3
weeks each. In that period, the class studies the issue and the given policy
options, conducts interviews and other research, and takes relevant field
trips. The culminating activity is one or more deliberative forums at which
class members clarify and argue over the alternatives and try to choose a
course of action. Having been through three or four such policy studies
and forums, students are ready to develop one themselves. They have been
"scaffolded up" to the task. Now students themselves identify and clarify
a problem, assemble background information, search for multiple social
perspectives on the problem, frame three or four divergent policy alternatives, and create a briefing booklet similar to those they have been using.
Finally, they deliberate the issue, deciding on a course of action, or they
trade briefing booklets with another class, studying and deliberating one
another's issues.

Other curriculum materials are helpful in roughly the same way, but
for global rather than national problems. *Choices for the 21st Century*[3] are a
variety of briefing booklets published by the Center for Foreign Policy
Development. Each booklet provides three to four policy alternatives along

with background information. As with NIF materials, the presentation of the issue *through policy alternatives* engages students in the kind of deliberation that has been associated with key outcomes: public building and development of participants' understanding of one another, the array of alternatives, and the problem itself (Doble, 1996; Farkas & Friedman, 1996).

Using NIF or *Choices* materials, teachers can orchestrate student practice on the PPD model, as I will outline in the following section. This strikes me as pedagogically feasible because the task requirements have been simplified. The authors of the materials have developed the policy alternatives; consequently, students are given (and don't themselves have to generate) grist for the analytic mill. They can evaluate the authors' diagnosis of the problem and their representation of stakeholders on the issue, and they can deliberate the options provided. The provision of alternatives by the authors scaffolds the task in a helpful way, modeling for students what an array of alternatives looks like and allowing them to labor at understanding these and at listening to one another. After this, students are ready to have the scaffold removed and to investigate an issue of their own choosing, creating their own briefing booklet.

Exemplary curriculum materials are no panacea, of course. NIF and *Choices* materials are helpful pedagogically in the way they model some of the analytic work for students and handle a good portion of the materials assembly for teachers. Still, teachers' knowledge and beliefs about these materials, the deliberative approach, and democracy in a diverse society all matter tremendously. Teachers need to know, for example, why the materials are designed with an emphasis on policy alternatives and value conflicts, and how to orchestrate students' study and deliberations in both large and small groups. And they need to *believe* in the approach—that both democracy and subject matter understanding are deepened by it, that as we saw earlier, it changes students' perceptions of one another, the problem, and the array of policy alternatives.

A MODEL FOR DELIBERATION IN HIGH SCHOOL

Let me turn to outlining the deliberative model that I propose as the centerpiece of a high school course (or a unit) the purpose of which is that students learn and apply a generic model of public policy deliberation (PPD). The goals here are democratic public building and democratic decision making, and the objectives, again, are to uncover and understand the problems faced by various publics, to develop and evaluate policy alternatives together, and to choose together a course of action. The rationale is that deliberating public problems is the basic activity of creating and sustaining democratic life in a diverse society; that the particular knowledge and habits unique to it should be the possession of citizens from all cultural, linguistic, and racial groups, otherwise access to the democratic path is restricted and the world that *could* have been made is not realized; and that school-based attempts to foster the knowledge, skills, and dispositions of democratic citizenship should be lodged in both the formal and informal curricula of the school.

Content Selection

To the extent that educators can find time and energy to think seriously about curriculum issues, they set about deciding what they want to accomplish and select a sample of content (subject matter) that arguably can help get them there. When planning a course or unit oriented to the deliberation of public policy, advice on content selection is available (e.g., Massialas, 1996; Oliver, 1957). Some of the best came in the first decades of the 20th century when the progressive education movement tried to focus a portion of the school curriculum on the surge of public problems that accompanied industrialization, urbanization, and immigration. The "Problems of Democracy" course was launched in 1916 and became for decades a common 12th-grade course offering in school systems. The 1950s through the early 1970s saw the development of "public issues instruction." Hunt and Metcalf (1955) outlined a curriculum in which students would examine social taboos and other controversial topics. Massialas and Cox (1966) blended inquiry and issues when they invited teachers and students "to participate in the process of inquiry *in order to grow in their predisposition and ability to explore and validate alternatives*" (emphasis added). Oliver and Newmann (1967) introduced teachers and students to the "jurisprudential framework" and distinctions among several kinds of issues that arise in discussions of public problems (definitional, empirical, ethical) and taught them strategies for moving such discussions forward—for example, clarifying an issue, stipulating a definition, and drawing analogies.[4] Newmann (1975) later developed a "citizen action" approach, which taught high school students to exert influence on public affairs.

Recent work has built on this foundation. *Education for Democratic Citizenship* (Engle & Ochoa, 1988), the *Handbook on Teaching Social Issues* (Evans & Saxe, 1996), and *Preparing Citizens* (Miller & Singleton, 1997) are useful resource books for public issues curriculum, instruction, and assessment. The recent *National Standards for Civics and Government* (Center for Civic Education, 1994) expects students to be able to "evaluate, take, and defend positions" on numerous public issues, and in 1998, the National Assessment of Educational Progress began to test students' ability to do just that (National Assessment Governing Board, 1997).

There are two types of content to which more or less equal attention needs to be paid in a PPD curriculum: *topics* and *intellectual frameworks*. In Oliver and Shaver's (1974) terms, content selection "involves two major decisions: What topics will one choose as the basis for selecting specific materials of instruction? What intellectual framework will be used to guide the teacher and, in turn, the student in handling these materials?" (p. 59) Content selection needs to occur deliberately on both fronts; yet daily teaching and learning require an artful synthesis of the two.

Topics

Regarding the first category, the main topical area for PPD is public conflict and related policy controversies. Research methods and findings from the social science disciplines are involved as well, but these are *resources*, not the primary objects of study. Oliver and Shaver's (1974) curriculum, for example, emphasized six areas of public conflict:

- Racial and ethnic conflict
- Religious and ideological conflict
- Security and the individual
- Conflict among economic groups
- Conflict over health, education, and welfare
- National security

Note that each problem area is perennial; each contains potentially many cases across time and space. Careful selection of analogous cases from different historical eras and cultures, but within a single problem area, should help students understand that publics across time and space have had to deal with similar problems.

The second category of content objectives, the intellectual framework, must clarify and structure what is otherwise the black box called "deliberation." Needed is a teachable and learnable conceptual framework in which these problems are to be identified, clarified, and deliberated with an eye toward making or recommending policy decisions. In the next section, I will detail such a framework. But I want to turn first to the content decisions in the venerated and long-lasting "Problems of Democracy" course that was developed in 1916 by the Commission on the Reorganization of Secondary Education of the National Education Association (1916). Like most curriculum programs that have been developed in the United

States, this course did not take seriously the fact of cultural and racial diversity generally or the pervasiveness of prejudice and racism in particular. However, it did treat democracy as a living, participatory endeavor, and it did develop the concept of citizenship education further than it had been before.

Problems of Democracy Course (POD)

A subcommittee assigned to "social studies" worked out a comprehensive curriculum for grades 7 through 12 ending in a "culminating course . . . with the purpose of giving more definite, comprehensive, and deeper knowledge of some of the vital problems of social life, and thus of securing a more intelligent and active citizenship" (Commission on the Reorganization, 1916, p. 52). This became POD. It would rely heavily on what students had learned in a course of study called Community Civics (CC), taken in grades 7 through 9, and in history courses (European and American) taken in grades 7 through 12.

Careful to mollify the several social sciences competing for legitimacy in the secondary school curriculum, the planners decided that POD would not "discard one social science in favor of another, nor attempt to crowd the several social sciences into (POD) in abridged forms." Rather, it would have students "study actual problems, or issues, or conditions, as they occur in life, and in their several aspects, political, economic, and sociological" (Commission on the Reorganization, 1916, p. 53). In this way, students might "acquire the habit of forming social judgments" (practical reasoning), which would necessitate "drafting into service the materials of all the social sciences as occasion demands for a thorough understanding of the situations in question" (p. 56). Here, well-stated, is the concept of the disciplines as curricular resources as distinct from the disciplines as the curriculum.

As for the first content-selection matter, the topics recommended for the POD course were problems, and these problems required for their competent deliberation knowledge formulated by historians and social scientists as well as the students' own critical judgment. Judgment is needed because disciplinary knowledge cannot speak for itself or leap up and apply itself prudently to policy alternatives. Furthermore, problems had to meet the committee's twin criteria for problem selection: immediate interest to the class and vital importance to society. Problems were to have been studied "in some of their aspects and relations" in history and CC courses, but they "may now be considered more comprehensively, more intensively, and more exhaustively" (Commission on the Reorganization, 1916, p. 54).

In particular, they would be studied "from different angles," which were disciplinary vantage points. For example:

1. Economic relations of immigration:
   A. Labor supply and other industrial problems.
   B. Standards of living, not only of the immigrants, but also of native-born Americans who are affected by immigration.
2. Sociological relations of immigration:
   A. Movements and distribution of population; congestion in cities.
   B. Social contributions of immigrants; art, science, ethics.
3. Political and governmental relations of immigration:
   A. Political ideals of immigrants; comparison of their inherited political conceptions with those of the United States.
   B. Naturalization; its methods, abuses. (Commission on the Reorganization, 1916, p. 54)

To its credit, POD exemplifies a way of looking to society's problems for topical curriculum content as opposed to looking at the problems academics are choosing in universities. However, POD planners, for whatever reason—racism, perhaps, or they may have been preoccupied with immigration, the predominant public policy issue of the day—skirted racism itself and the flourishing institutions of Jim Crow in particular. And they did this at a time when lynchings of African American boys and men were at an all-time high. Skirted also was the second category of content selection—the intellectual framework—except to suggest that this is where the academic disciplines become pertinent, each with its particular mode of inquiry. The task of specifying and elaborating an intellectual framework for use in policy deliberation was left to others. The projects in the aforementioned "public issues" era (e.g., Massialas & Cox, 1966; Oliver & Shaver, 1974) took up some of this slack, but an intellectual framework more directly related to public policy deliberation is needed alongside. For that, I suggest an intellectual framework drawn from the field of public policy analysis and tailored to the three objectives of PPD.[5]

Intellectual Framework

Policy analysis is now taught in colleges and universities from the bachelor's to the doctoral level, and in a considerable range of academic units, from political science departments to business and other applied professional schools (e.g., urban planning, public health, education, environmental studies). Entire degree programs in the field of public policy have sprung up over the last 30 years or so, with most of these granting the M.P.P. (Master of Public Policy), or a similar degree. Also, public policy analysis is now often a several course requirement and/or a specialty track within the hundreds of Master of Public Administration (M.P.A.) programs in U.S. colleges and universities.[6]

But a policy analysis model used by professionals working in city halls, legislatures, and county governments may not be appropriate for average citizens like ourselves and our students. We probably need a citizen's model, not an expert's model. Expert models typically assume levels of complexity, competence, and resources that exceed reasonable expectations for lay people. This is true in medicine, law, farming, and school teaching, for example; surely it is also true in public policy. Even with this caveat, the framework used to train professional policy analysts is attractive for its thoroughness, especially the attention it pays to multiple social perspectives.

This framework is best thought of as a mental tool. Students are to learn the tool by applying it several times (as with NIF, three to five times) to public problems that require action. Deciding together *which* action to take is the deliberative goal of the framework; listening to one another to decide what to do about a shared problem is the solidarity-building (public-building) goal.

I have divided the framework into three parts, each part with a number of steps. Each "step" is typically found in the professional's analysis model, and each fleshes out what would otherwise be a simpler three-part model. Each step is best thought of as a window through which students can see particular aspects of a problem and view the problem from different vantage points.

Part I: Identify and explain a public problem
    1. Identify a public problem
    2. Explain the problem
    3. Map stakeholders and their perspectives
Part II: Develop and Analyze Policy Alternatives
    4. Formulate policy goals
    5. Develop policy alternatives
    6. Assess consequences of policy alternatives and evaluate trade-offs
Part III: Deciding What Action to Take
    7. Selection
    8. Political analysis

While the verbal presentation of any procedure is necessarily linear, the procedure itself is best described as iterative, for it is necessary to return to each window as more is learned about the problem. Emphasizing the iterative nature of the model to students, however, is likely to be unhelpful, for they are novices being exposed to the model for the first time. Accordingly, students should be scaffolded into the framework, beginning with the linear approach then gradually letting go of the linearity of the model and, if real skill in deploying the model is developed, the model itself. This is akin to the old adage in language instruction—teach the rule before the exception—and is supported anew by good work on scaffolded instruction (e.g., Brown, 1996; Wertsch, 1991).

Like any model, this is an ideal-type framework. No argument is made that it is sufficient, let alone complete or omniscient. It is not a description of reality. It does not replace observation or insight. It certainly does not replace the good or bad judgment of its users. It is a tool, and its purpose is to help citizens participate more competently in democratic life by identifying, clarifying, and acting on shared problems. *Its claim to helpfulness is that it directs users' attention to a broad array of phenomena (i.e., problem dimensions) and perspectives (i.e., subject positions) that otherwise may be ignored or slighted. Furthermore, it helps clarify a problem space that otherwise may seem such a tangled mess as to be unworkable—unsolvable because unfathomable.* The tool's purpose is to disentangle the problem somewhat while affording a degree of analytic power and clarity missing without it. More fundamentally, its purpose is to combat idiocy by educating for its opposite: citizenship.

The model needs to be grounded in real public problems, of course, for dealing with real problems is the purpose here. Therefore, by way of illustration, I thread through my description of the model six problems: domestic abuse, sexual harassment, and urban homelessness; and, in more depth, racism, racial inequality, and citizen apathy.

Part I. Identify and explain a public problem

1. Identify a public problem. This initial phase of the model has students imagine a better world and clarify just where, how, and at whose expense we are coming up short. This is likely to involve negatively valued "social indicators" (increased number of hate crimes or sexual harassment reports, disproportionate number of arrests of African American males, increasing number of school shootings) and resulting complaints or protests to which elected officials feel some pressure to respond.

Determining the suitability of a problem for public policy analysis and action is a slippery problem. Nancy Fraser (1997) addressed it in her analysis of the Clarence Thomas/Anita Hill hearings before Congress. She examines the social construction of the boundary between "public" and "private" problems. She writes, "There are no naturally given, a priori boundaries" (p. 86) between publicity and privacy. Rather, "what will count as a matter of common concern will be decided through discursive contestation. It follows that no topics should be ruled off limits in advance of such contestation. Democratic publicity requires positive guarantees of opportunities for minorities to convince others that what in the past was not 'public' in the sense of being a matter of common concern should now become so." Domestic abuse and workplace sexual harassment are illustrative cases today. Both once were viewed as "private" problems unsuitable for public deliberation; today both are viewed as public problems.

An innovative high school program called "Student Voices" (Annenberg Public Policy Center, 2001), centered at the University of Pennsylvania and implemented in Seattle, Los Angeles, Detroit, and San Antonio, is worth noting at this point. The program has students track the local mayoral campaign in relation to city problems they themselves identify as important and intriguing. Rather than rushing into problem identification, students survey their neighbors in order to identify problems they might have overlooked themselves. Doing so helps them hear, and perhaps recognize, what they might not have been able even to imagine from within the confines of their own social positions as teenagers, urbanites, or suburbanites: what elderly residents worry about, for example; as well as the concerns of young children, affluent and poor neighbors, gay and straight people, Latino and Asian people, and so on. The issues that emerge from these interviews are brought together on a common class list, and from this universe of problems the students deliberate a prioritized handful of three to five problems. These are the bases for conversations with mayoral candidates later and for concerted study and, perhaps, action by students before and after the election.

2. Explain the problem. "Explain" means "to lay flat or lay bare." To explain a public problem, such as racial profiling by police departments and other hot points of racial inequality, students have to observe and analyze it thoroughly—certainly more than is necessary when all that is required of them is to defend opinions that have been formed before studying the problem.

A good way to focus student work at this step of the analysis is to ask students to hypothesize causes of the problem and eventually to develop an explanation and the beginnings of a causal theory. This explanation shapes the work done at each subsequent step, as we will see. It tells the story of the problem's rise and persistence and, perhaps, foreshadows its fall or resolution. When developing alternatives to resolve the problem, those alternatives will be relevant and attractive to the extent they "make sense" within the explanation developed at this step. For example, if students cling to "racism" as the single cause of racial inequality in the United States, they are not likely to generate wealth redistribution programs (e.g., full employment; progressive taxation) or social welfare programs (e.g., full health care and equal opportunity for education) as policy alternatives later at step five. Recall that King (1967b) discovered that desegregation was a more popular policy alternative in the 1960s, with both Blacks and Whites, than mounting a "poor people's campaign." Desegregate the schools and the lunch counters, Americans then seemed to be saying, but leave social class alone. Americans are notorious for leaving social class alone—leaving it out of their explanations of social problems. The American dream, after all, promises that it can be overcome (Hochschild & Scovronick, 2002).

Even if students singularly trumpet racism as the cause of racial inequality, they need to be encouraged to explain it. What is racism and what causes it? Is it a mental illness? Is it more a psychological problem than a sociological or economic one? Is it equivalent to anti-Semitism, sexism, and homophobia, or is it unique? Is racism a uniquely American problem or is it worldwide? Why does it persist?[7]

3. Map stakeholders and their perspectives. A further dimension of explaining a problem is learning how the various parties to it perceive and feel about it. Now competing interests and perspectives are brought under the analytic lens. Students survey the social landscape to determine who has a stake in the problem or its resolution. It is necessary here for students to map (locate and connect) stakeholders' interests, their definitions of the problem (including how these definitions arose), their prior positions and likely future positions on the problem and possible solutions to it, and their power and resources and willingness to use them.

Stakeholder analysis also involves sizing up the arenas in which important decisions actually will be made (the city council, the state legislature, blue-ribbon commissions, the courts, etc.) and assessing how and where diverse stakeholders will likely seek to make their influence felt. The research at this step needs also to be directed toward assessing how different decision-making arenas might favor certain groups. Citizens occupying different status positions in society are not equally comfortable in council chambers, Rotary luncheons, or public hearings.

As I write this, racial profiling by police is a heated issue in Seattle and drawing a good deal of media attention. An African American man was shot and killed recently by a White police officer in the city's central African American neighborhood. Several street protests were sponsored at the scene by an African American church located in the area. Its pastor called for a boycott of the Starbucks coffee shop located in that neighborhood. It was this latter tactic—the boycott—that drew media attention and a flurry of questions directed at the pastor. "Why boycott Starbucks?", he was asked on the evening television news. "To get your attention," he replied.

Another example: Lack of intelligent citizen participation in politics and public affairs is a crucial problem in a society struggling to be a democracy and one that school policy can and should do something about. Work at step two on this problem may point to multiple causes: government corruption ("Why participate when officials will do as they please?"), rational choice ("The system is entrenched, and my participation will make no difference."), materialism, religion, television, gender, and family income. Students who attempt to survey the social landscape of this problem and identify the stakeholders may begin with the simplistic "politicians" versus "taxpayers" map currently popular in political campaign ads and talk radio shows. The concept of "citizen" may not be part of their mental toolbox even, ironically, in a government course. (Such confusion can be learned from televised political ads where "viewers" are addressed as "taxpayers" and the concept of *citizen* is curiously avoided.) With coaching and hard work, students may develop a more textured representation of the stakeholder scene that is related to the hypothesized causes of the problem at step two.

Whether the problem is racial profiling or citizen apathy, if the "map" at step three lacks complexity and nuance, often a return to step two for another try at explaining the problem can be helpful. Some students may, as a result, hypothesize that despair and hopelessness drive citizen apathy. Others may look at methods to raise civic consciousness among the working poor, in which case "the working poor" (and with them the issue of wealth distribution) enter the stakeholders map. This is an important modification of the map, for once social class has been recognized, "the rich" may be mapped as another stakeholder group. This iteration of steps two and three should develop the map nicely.

Part II. Develop and Analyze Policy Alternatives

4. Formulate policy goals. Students are now in a position to formulate goals for policy. Of course, the basic goal usually is to solve the problem: to reduce police killings of African American males or increase the political participation of citizens. This is not usually as simple as it sounds, for there are multiple dimensions of the problem (e.g., new state policy disallowing affirmative action; entrenched politicians who need high levels of citizen apathy; amoral familism) and there are multiple stakeholders with differing priorities among the different goals.

Values analysis is part of every step of the model. At this goal-setting step, it needs to become more explicit. There are some general values goals that usually apply to the consideration of any policy action: equity, respect for democratic processes, preservation of individual liberty, and staying within legal and budgetary limitations. These values goals make analysis more complex and so, to simplify, they often are treated as *constraints*: widely held public values constrain policy alternatives that would surely get results. Communities seeking greater citizen participation typically do not force people to vote or to volunteer time at a police precinct or welfare agency. Either would violate a widely held public value: liberty. In this way, goals (problem solution) and constraints (public values) interact in policy deliberation in order to shape policy that achieves results without violating widely held social preferences.

Sometimes, policy goals and widely held public values are dead set against one another, and this is the classic circumstance for the growth of a social movement. The abolitionist and women's suffrage movements of the 19th century, the Civil Rights movement of the 1960s and 70s, and the gay and lesbian rights movement of today are examples. Within sociology, the field of collective behavior (e.g., Smelser, 1962; Tarrow, 1998) has much to say about the causes and conditions of social movements. On the origins of the Civil Rights movement, for example, see Morris (1984). It was Morris's description of social movements that informed my description in Chapter 3 of the Black church's role as a "movement center."

5. Develop policy alternatives. Policy alternatives are the potential actions that are available for addressing the policy problem and achieving the goals. Logically, these should derive from previous steps—problem explanation, stakeholder mapping, and goal formulation—but when it is time to proceed to developing concrete details of various alternatives, probably most relevant among the earlier steps is problem explanation. If this step has led to a broad and workable understanding of the causes of the problem, then it should also lead to ideas for actions that could solve or ameliorate the problem without violating deeply held values (unless such a violation is precisely what is needed).

Consider the problem of urban homelessness. Students' work at step two may have produced the finding that three important classes of homeless individuals are substance abusers, women and children fleeing environments plagued by domestic violence, and teenagers who have left home for a variety of reasons. On this diagnosis, policy interventions might well include strategically located treatment centers for the first group of individuals and specialized shelters and family intervention programs for the latter two. This example also points to the fact that the focus in policy analysis is necessarily on those variables in the problem space that policy can influence rather than on variables that are beyond policy control. Increased homelessness caused by a national recession, for example, would clearly be beyond a *city's* control. If students' work at step two suggested that this was the primary cause, then they might well conclude that the problem was not a useful one for further analysis at the city level (except perhaps to gauge the need for purely reactive services: shelters, counseling, and the like).

An array of promising alternatives is the desired outcome at this step of the model. While the array should build mainly on work done at preceding steps, additional research may be needed. This usually means interviewing stakeholders in order to discover their positions, reasons, and perspectives. Being close to the problem and to earlier efforts to ameliorate it, they may have helpful ideas. They may also have vested interests that skew their vision. Looking back at the three alternatives provided in the NIF booklet on racial inequality, we can see one array of alternatives:

- Choice 1: Civil Rights Strategy: Prohibiting Discrimination, Enforcing the Laws.
- Choice 2: Affirmative Action Strategy: Taking Race into Consideration.
- Choice 3: Ladder Out of Poverty: Helping the Poor, Closing the Racial Gap.

Other arrays could be generated, of course, and particular alternatives are missing (psychotherapy, for example). But these three alternatives, in my experience, have helpfully broadened students' thinking on the problem (beyond waiting for the older generation to die off!).

6. Assess consequences of alternatives and evaluate trade-offs. The idea at this step is to use the most powerful inquiry methods available, within time and resource constraints, to evaluate each alternative against each policy goal and one another. When time and resource limitations preclude this, as they almost always do in schools, students can use other means: searching the literature for results of similar policy approaches already tried elsewhere and interviewing experts, public officials, and stakeholders. An unintended consequence of the Starbucks boycott in Seattle's predominantly African American neighborhood—a boycott intended to bring a different kind of media attention to police actions in that community— might be to dissuade other prominent businesses from locating in this neighborhood, thereby stalling the economic revival there.

Students' responsibility does not end with assessing the consequences of policy alternatives. They have to think about trade-offs: how different valuations of particular goals relative to other goals might affect the choice among alternatives. Taking citizen participation as our sample case again, consider that increased voter turnout (whether the result of paying voters, requiring voting, or easing registration difficulties) can backfire: Citizens may participate more, but the upshot of that participation may be to reject governance altogether. Term limits and other simplistic ballot initiatives do indicate increased participation, but also indicate a retreat from governing. At least this is the view of stakeholders who, like Jefferson, Madison, and King, argue against majoritarian domination. They argue for citizen participation, yes, but enlightened, deliberative participation. A good deal of the current participation debate turns on this distinction (e.g., Fishkin, 1991).

Recall that Vivian Paley (1992) proposes a rule to her kindergartners and engages them in an ongoing inquiry lasting for months. The inquiry focuses on two questions: Will the rule work? Is it fair? These are compelling moral-practical questions for the children. Often in policy deliberation, one alternative performs better on one criteria (e.g., efficiency—will the alternative work?) while another does better on another criteria (e.g., justice—is the alternative fair?). Rigorous analysis of trade-offs is therefore a necessary contribution to wise decision making.

Part III. Decide

7. Selection. The idea here is to choose from the alternatives. Organizational politics will usually play a role in selection as powerful interests push their favorite alternatives. Politics will also play a role in policy choices made by broader groups, such as blue ribbon commissions (e.g., those that have produced curriculum standards for civics and history) and interagency groups in government (e.g., those that deliberate urban homelessness and racial inequality). The stakeholder map at step three can be helpful in predicting the contours of this political struggle, which takes us to step eight.

8. Political analysis. Students are helped in this phase of the model to infuse creative thinking about politics *per se* into the design and selection of policy alternatives. I use the terms "politics" and "political" in the usual way: power struggle among stakeholders, conflict over alternatives, the actual on-the-ground activity of self-government when something that will be binding on all must be decided.

Politics generally avoids metaphysics and political theory because the stakeholders cannot agree on them, at least not as regards the real problem at hand. (Value conflicts are real and sometimes incommensurable, especially when diversity is taken seriously.) Political struggle starts where philosophy leaves off. Democratic government—constitutional democracy—is itself an example. Politics pervade the entire deliberative model I am proposing, for politics deals with the domain of *necessary public action*, not armchair problems but actual ones on which some decision is needed and in a timely fashion. Politics deals with the question, "What shall we do when something has to be done that will affect us all, and we wish to be reasonable yet we disagree on means and ends and are without independent grounds by which we might arbitrate our differences . . . ?" (Barber, 1988, p. 206)

One often useful approach in this phase of policy analysis is to evaluate the political feasibility of an otherwise attractive policy option. Once the option's likely political hurdles are identified, these can be used to modify the option, enhancing its feasibility while doing as little damage as possible to its promise. In this way, understanding of the political environment ("democratic enlightenment," as it was called in Chapter 3) is used to frame analytically desirable alternatives in ways that move them toward selection ("engagement"). Beyond modifying the alternative to make it more feasible, practical understanding of politics is also helpful in devising political strategies to move desirable alternatives toward selection. This must have been on King's mind in August 1967 when, in the *Where Do We Go from Here?* speech delivered in Atlanta, he asked: "Why are there forty million poor people in America?" (1967b, p. 8). His political analysis suggested to him that all that could be done on this matter, at this time and place, was to raise the question:

> And when you begin to ask that question, you are raising a question about the economic system, about a broader distribution of wealth. When you ask that question, you begin to question the capitalistic economy. (*Yes*) And I'm simply saying that more and more, we've got to begin to ask questions about the whole society. We are called upon to help the discouraged beggars in life's marketplace. (*Yes*) But one day we must come to see that an edifice which produces beggars needs restructuring. (*All right*) It means that questions must be raised. (pp. 8–9)

Imagine a group of students who have been analyzing the problem of citizen apathy. Perhaps they decided from the alternatives they had generated in Part II to propose to the school board that students turning 18 years of age be required to register to vote as a condition for receiving the diploma at the end of the year. Considering the political environment, particularly a locally active chapter of the American Civil Liberties Union, the students then decide to retreat somewhat, working to secure the school's main office as a site for voluntary voter registration of 18-year-olds, but not requiring registration. Planning ahead, they figure that once the main office has become a smooth-running registration site, then they will take on the matter of requiring registration as a condition for graduation.

But should the teacher encourage them not to retreat? Should she encourage them not to cave in to political realities and to reject incrementalism for radical action? The answer will likely depend on whether the teacher agrees with their position and reasons and the teacher's pedagogical beliefs about teacher self-disclosure in the context of a classroom deliberation on a public issue.

REFLECTING ON THE MODEL

Let me summarize the model and its rationale, then I will make several suggestions. A public problem is tackled. Attention is given to the problem. An intellectual framework is brought to bear and wielded, toollike, to open a sequence of windows on the problem and spread deliberators' attention across multiple dimensions of the problem space and the multiple perspectives of stakeholders. The framework presented here is an authentic one, widely taught and used in the policy analysis field. It is a linear model in one sense (good work at earlier steps pays off at later steps), yet recursive in another (as a new view of the problem is achieved at a later step, earlier steps must be reworked). It is a political model, too, hence its interest in positionality (mapping the stakeholders) and its presumptions of disagreement and struggle—politics.

Why add the study and use of this model to an already crowded high school curriculum? Because there can be no democracy without democrats, and democrats are made, not born. James Baldwin (1988) warned that if children are not educated to live democratically, then they may well become far worse than apathetic: They could become the next generation of people to sponsor a Holocaust. "The boys and girls who were born during the era of the Third Reich," Baldwin said, "when educated to the purposes of the Third Reich, became barbarians" (p. 4). To think otherwise is to ignore history. Students need to be educated to participate substantively in democratic civic discourse—to talk about shared problems with people who are different from themselves, and to labor together to build and maintain a hopeful, imaginative, and just public square.

Content selection needs to proceed on at least two fronts. In terms of the multiple objectives discussed earlier, these are deciding which problems students should deliberate and which intellectual framework should shape their deliberations. In other words: What should students be asked to think about? And, what mental tools should they be taught to use? Suggestions were made for both. For the problems themselves, the 1916 Problems of Democracy course had two selection criteria: immediate interest to the class and vital importance to society. Later programs developed other criteria. For the intellectual framework, I turned to the field of public policy analysis and presented in some detail a three-part model.

There are issues on both fronts. Let me now venture some suggestions. I begin with criteria for problem selection, then I simplify the intellectual framework.

Problem Selection

As for selecting the problems, the two criteria given for the 1916 POD course strike me as necessary but insufficient. "Immediate interest to students" is important, but problematic. One can imagine problems in which students are interested but probably shouldn't be, and problems they should be interested in but are not, simply because they lack the information and experiences that could breed enthusiasm. And "vital importance to society" is too blunt, for there will be too many problems that meet this criterion. I recommend, therefore, modifying the first of these and replacing the second with four criteria that are more specific. Then, I add a sixth that increases the implementation feasibility of the whole effort.[8]

1. *Interest*: select problems in which students are or are likely (with coaching, knowledge, and experience) to become interested.
2. *Authenticity*: select genuine public problems, ones that an identifiable public (locally, nationally, internationally) is actually facing.
3. *Value conflict*: select problems in which value conflicts are vivid so as to encourage values analysis throughout the model (i.e., the needed policy choice requires students to examine alternatives that express diverse and competing values).
4. *Pluralism*: select problems in which the pluralistic nature of American society is evident (i.e., there are multiple and competing cultural and political perspectives on the issue and, therefore, the opportunity to adjudicate competing perspectives).
5. *Perenniality*: select problems for which analogous cases are available so as to encourage cross-case comparison. The immediate policy question should be an instance of an enduring public problem that publics across time and place have had to face.
6. *Curriculum materials*: select problems for which thoughtfully prepared instructional resources are already available.

Intellectual Framework

As for the intellectual framework brought to these problems, I presented a model used by professional policy analysts. Its advantages are artifice and authenticity. The artifice of models—by which I mean their refusal to entirely mimic reality by, for example, blurring boundaries or admitting exceptions—is their helpfully sharp edge when they are employed as mental tools to examine actual problems (see Vygotsky, 1978). As mental tools, they artificially clarify boundaries and skirt exceptions. It is a model's artifice that structures a problem in a particular way and, thereby, directs students' attention toward particular aspects of the problem space that otherwise might be ignored (e.g., political analysis) or rushed (thinking deeply about a broad array of stakeholders). On the other hand, the authenticity of the model affords an issues deliberation framework actually used by practitioners in the policy field to consider real problems faced by real publics. These practitioners are not working in utopias, but in actually existing democracies where political struggle is the norm. If the level of detail in the eight-step model strikes the reader as unwieldy, however, students can be presented simply with the three-part model, and the teacher can coach them on the details as he or she deems necessary:

     I. Identify and explain a public problem
     II. Develop and analyze policy alternatives
     III. Decide

The Course

Finally, a brief comment about course design. Something along the lines of the NIF approach mentioned earlier strikes me as sensible and most likely effective, but there needs to be serious attention to communicating across difference. A preparatory unit should introduce students to the concept of public controversy and to a select set of communication skills—from epistemic privilege, caution, and humility to the art of challenging ideas but avoiding personal attack. The class can then be helped to identify three or four problems for study and deliberation, and these are problems on which study material is readily available, such as the NIF booklets. The problems are studied and deliberated for 2 or 3 weeks each. Interviews and other research methods will be necessary to find and map the stakeholders and perspectives on each. The culminating activity of each unit is a deliberative forum in which class members try to decide which alternative to enact themselves or to recommend to officials. Finally, students should be ready to select and frame a problem themselves, and then deliberate it.

CONCLUSION

A curriculum proposal is a unique social text. It is at once a pedagogical theory, a moral argument, a political claim, a problem frame, and an action plan. It is itself a policy alternative on a central educational problem: What should students learn at school that will help them become citizens capable of self-government in a diverse society?

The PPD model I am proposing here is just one piece of the larger project to cultivate democrats and is not by itself adequate. It does not replace moral education, for example (though it incorporates it), nor does it replace a caring school environment, an open classroom climate, or government and history courses. PPD is one tool and only one part of the puzzle.

Still, it is at least this, and it is directly relevant to the practices of democratic citizenship in a diverse society. Teaching it to students in high school makes good sense. All citizens in a society struggling to be just and democratic are in principle obliged to participate, not just a tiny few. It makes no sense to offer policy study only to graduate students who elect it as a career track. With greater citizen involvement—with more people being on the governing end of the system rather than always on the receiving end of others' governing—democratic practice is made more democratic, more voices are included in the mix, fewer people are disenfranchised, and the stakeholder array is broadened. This last ingredient—a diverse array of views—is key. As we saw in Chapter 5, diversity is a deliberative asset. It helps to improve the fairness of social life, the wisdom of policy decisions, and it increases democratic solidarity—that in-between sense of "we-ness" needed to bind citizens together alongside their cultural and individual differences.

Learning to Lead Discussions

Moral education centers upon this conception of the school as a mode of social life, that the best and deepest moral training is precisely that which one gets through having to enter into proper relations with others.

—John Dewey (1897, pp. 8–9)

Student-teacher A: I like the part where King says that an act of civil disobedience must be done "openly and lovingly."

Student-teacher B: What do you mean?

Student-teacher A: What do I mean or what does King mean?

Student-teacher B: Both.

Student-teacher A: I'm not sure. I think it makes this kind of law-breaking really different—um, religious.

Student-teacher C: Religious?

Student-teacher D: Different from what?

This is an excerpt from a discussion of Martin Luther King Jr.'s "Letter from Birmingham Jail" (1963a), which I was attempting to facilitate in my curriculum and instruction class in the teacher education program at the university where I teach. My purpose in leading the discussion—a seminar—was to deepen these student-teachers' understanding of the issues, values, and ideas raised by the letter. I also wanted to teach them to facilitate such discussions with their students. They are my students, but they are in turn the teachers of other students. This is the layered, iterative world of teacher education where one pedagogic exchange is always conducted with an eye toward another that involves these students shifting to the role of teacher with their own students.

As the excerpt reveals, the discussion is going rather well. In just a few turns, students are expressing themselves, listening, challenging one another's statements, seeking clarity, and giving reasons. But are my students learning to lead discussions with their students?

I will share some of my recent efforts to teach future teachers and other adults to lead deliberations and another kind of discussion: the seminar.

The "other adults" are community activists, public health workers, college professors, service club members, book club enthusiasts, and leaders of scripture study groups at churches and temples. In these various roles, they are regularly trying to lead discussions of one sort or another and have enrolled in a summer institute on discussion facilitation that I conduct with colleagues called "Can We Talk?" Classroom teachers are enrolled in that institute as well, and together all study and practice the work of planning and leading discussions.

This work, both in the preservice teacher education course as well as the summer institute, requires me first to demonstrate purposeful discussion leadership, as best I can, and open these demonstrations to criticisms. It requires me also to help participants distinguish among *kinds* of discussion. For this reason I developed a typology of discussion. The typology was needed, I figured, because participants' knowledge of discussion was limited. Their critiques of my demonstrations often lacked nuance and missed the big picture—the discussion's purpose and whether or not it was achieved. For many participants, discussion tends to be both monolithic and invisible: monolithic because they have only a general and singular conception of discussion, and invisible because, while they no doubt had been involved in at least some purposeful discussions in their clubs, faith communities, school experiences, and elsewhere, they often could not describe their distinguishing characteristics well enough to appropriate discussion as a tool. It was as though they hadn't quite seen the discussions in which they had participated. They had memories of them being "interesting," but not much more. Emotionally, some had memories of shyness, others of topics, others of disbelief at what classmates were saying. These spotty recollections made it difficult for them to plan and lead disciplined (purposeful, meaningful, respectful) and lively (social, provocative, exciting) discussions of challenging texts or controversial public problems.

Here, I will focus on my work with preservice teachers enrolled in the aforementioned teacher education course and draw examples from that setting, as I suspect that will be relevant to many, if not all, readers of these pages. This is a two-quarter social studies curriculum and instruction course for future teachers of middle and high school students. It begins with a unit on teaching and learning with inquiry, which is framed by John Dewey's "double movement of reflection" (1910/1985b, p. 242; Fenton, 1967; Parker, 2001b), followed by a unit on concept development that relies on the work of Hilda Taba (et al. 1971; Fraenkel, 1980; Parker, 2001b). After these comes the seminar unit, which completes the first quarter of 10 weeks. The second half of the course (the second quarter) begins with a deliberation unit and proceeds to a unit called "History Workshop," which lasts the rest of the second quarter. This final unit is dedicated to teaching and learning with instructional methods that help students "do history" themselves rather than only "absorbing" the histories done by others (Levstik & Barton, 2001; Parker, 2001b)—for example, conducting oral histories of a family member or neighborhood leader, or writing original interpretations of journals and diaries. It includes teaching students to puzzle through document sets (sometimes asking students to lead seminars on key documents), compose and evaluate original historical narratives, and collectively decide on (deliberate) sensible standards for historical reasoning and scoring rubrics for historical compositions, whether cause-effect essays, museum exhibits, or original biographies. Seminar and deliberation facilitation are central units in the course, and both are featured in the culminating unit as a way to review them and put them to work.

The typology I developed distinguishes two discussions: seminars and deliberations. Seminars are discussions aimed at enlarging students' understandings of powerful texts. "Powerful texts" here are insightful printed documents, such as some primary and secondary sources in history and social science, some works of historical fiction, and some transcribed speeches. Texts also are works of film and photography, painting and theater, social happenings and performances, and so forth. A text worthy of a seminar is potentially mind-altering: one that gives rise to powerful issues, ideas, and values. A deliberation, as we have seen, is a discussion aimed at making decisions about what a *we* should *do*. Deliberation helps participants weigh policy alternatives on a public issue on which action is required. "Is it fair?" "Will it work?" With questions like these, participants in a deliberation look together at the problem, framing and reframing it, searching for an array of alternatives, then weighing them and eventually choosing a course of action. The social problem itself is now the "text" along with the alternative courses of action that might be taken to address and solve it. As we have seen, this may be a classroom issue (e.g., a kindergarten teacher asks students to decide whether a new rule is needed to remedy a classroom problem; a high school teacher asks students to decide whether tardiness should affect course grades), a school issue (e.g., student council members deliberate dress code policies), or a community issue (e.g., students decide what stand they will take, as a group, on a non-school public issue such as one of those featured in Chapter 6—domestic abuse, homelessness, citizen apathy, and so forth). Whenever a "we" is deciding what to do, and the decision is binding on all, then arguably a better decision will emerge when the parties to it have at least sought out one another's views and listened to and talked seriously with one another. In summary, seminars deepen our understanding of the world while deliberations help us decide, together, what to change and how.

One without the other is not desirable. The two kinds of discussion cover lots of ground and, for this reason alone, are widely useful instructional models in social studies and literature classrooms. The ground they cover includes both the content of the discussions—the text or controversial issue at hand—as well as the social and civic outcomes of being involved with one another in these two modes of face-to-face communication. Students may be discussing material that requires them to deepen their understanding of democracy in a diverse society, in a text such as King's "Letter" (1963a) or a public issue such as whether it is right to disenfranchise ex-convicts, a disproportionate number of whom are African American males. These subject matters are themselves clearly related to the education of democratic citizens in a diverse society, as is the method by which they are being considered: discussion. It is in discussion that listening and speaking function to enlarge our understanding of problems and one another's perspectives on them, and it is in discussion that power differences among participants appear and can be addressed. Let me turn now to teaching the two forms of discussion, seminar and deliberation, to future teachers.

DISCUSSION

The distinctive and peculiar contribution which discussion has to play in the development of one's knowledge or understanding . . . is to set alongside one perception of the matter under discussion the several perceptions of other participants . . . challenging our own view of things with those of others. (Bridges, 1979, p. 50)

David Bridges's description points to the basic *circumstance* of discussion—that it is a shared situation with a purpose—and to the *potential* of that circumstance to encourage participants to consider others' interpretations of things and, in that broadened horizon, to reconsider their own interpretations of things, thereby widening and deepening their own understanding. By being challenged, we might see through our taken-for-granted responses and stances. We might see the world differently and shift our place in it a little. The picture might widen; a window could open. We could imagine ourselves in jail with King or Socrates or Gandhi. We could grasp both the resentment and the empowerment of the women who met at Seneca Falls and delight in the brilliant rhetoric of their *Declaration*. We might wonder seriously, maybe for the first time, about the silence of the framers of the Constitution on the institution of slavery while appreciating the rights-based legal system they launched which, after a long time, was deployed against slavery itself and then Jim Crow.

Discussion is a kind of shared inquiry the desired outcomes of which rely on the expression and consideration of diverse views. This in turn requires discussants to do something difficult and existential: to switch loyalties from justifying positions and defending ground to listening intently, seeking understanding, and expressing ideas that are undeveloped and "in progress." This is to switch from a defensive stance to an inquisitive stance, and this makes for an "occasion" (Oliver, Newmann, & Singleton, 1992, p. 103; Burbules, 1993). The occasion is both a situation and a method, and these have consequences. Discussion results in what could be called shared understanding: Discussion widens the scope of each participant's understanding of the object of discussion by building into that understanding the interpretations and life experiences of other discussants. In Joseph Schwab's (1978) terms, discussion is "a species of activity" (p. 126) by which shared understanding can be achieved: "[D]iscussion is not merely a device, one of several possible means by which a mind may be brought to understanding of a worthy object. It is also the *experience* of moving toward and possessing understanding . . ." (p. 105).

To *lead* a discussion is not so difficult when the leader has lower standards. If a leader does not aim for full participation, for serious thinking together on powerful questions, for genuine exchange and perspective taking, for close reading and close listening, then leading a discussion requires nothing special of anyone involved, leader or discussants.

Seminars and Deliberations

Seminars and deliberations represent the distinction between the world-revealing and the world-changing functions of conversation. When we seek understanding together, we work to develop and clarify meanings. When we forge a decision together, we weigh alternatives and decide which action to take. One is akin to a liberal arts education where broadening one's horizons, expanding one's mind and senses, is the central aim. The other is more directly a civic education, where creating better futures is the aim. Of course, these overlap. Decision making requires understanding, but understanding is not its aim. Its aim is action. Meanwhile, understanding is always more or less related to action (humans are continually taking action), yet seminars are not driven by the desire to get anything done. Think of a political action committee meeting, then think of a poetry reading. With this distinction, we can see why a social studies (or literature or science) classroom should not be issue-centered—that is, deliberation-centered—any more than it should be centered on achieving enlarged understandings (seminar-centered). Given the aims of anti-idiocy education, courses routinely must try to do both in tandem. The horizon-widening and knowledge-deepening function of seminars helps to provide an enlightened platform for public decision making and action, and vice versa. To decide solutions to public problems without the advantage of historical and cultural knowledge or of knowing what one another thinks is like trying to rearrange furniture in a dark room. Understanding and decision making are functionally inseparable, like the two wings of an airplane. I cannot imagine serious work on one without the advantage provided by serious work on the other.

Here, then, is the typology (see Table 7.1). It may clarify the distinction between the two kinds of discussion I am describing and, thereby, help us participate in, lead, and teach discussion facilitation to others. A typology is a classification scheme, and any classification scheme should be handled gingerly. Typologies should not be believed, because they are not descriptions of reality. But they can be used; they are mental tools created to aid thinking and doing. They delineate things—all sorts of things, from poetry (haiku, free verse) to governments (autocracy, democracy). They are helpful because they idealize distinctions, making boundaries artificially clear and, thereby, providing analytic power and precision. A typology is adequate, according to Aristotle, "if it has as much clearness as the subject matter admits of" but no more (in Eisner, 1985, p. 192).

Table 7.1. A Typology Distinguishing Seminar and Deliberation

Dimension	*Seminar*	*Deliberation*
Purpose	1. Reach an enlarged understanding of a powerful text.	1. Reach a decision about what a "we" should do about a shared problem.
	2. Improve discussants' powers of understanding.	2. Improve discussants' powers of understanding.
Subject Matter	Ideas, issues, and values in a print or film selection, artwork, performance, political cartoon, or other text.	Alternative courses of action related to a public (shared; common) problem.
Opening Question	What does this mean?	What should we do?
Exemplar	Socratic Seminar	Structured Academic Controversy

The typology permits a rough comparison of seminars and deliberations on four dimensions: (1) the aim or purpose, (2) the subject matter under question, (3) the opening question, and (4) exemplars. Let me unpack it some by clarifying five of the central terms: deliberation, seminar, powers of understanding, opening question, and exemplar. Following that, I will outline my units on seminar and deliberation in the social studies curriculum and instruction course.

Deliberation

Deliberations are discussions aimed at deciding on a plan of action that will resolve a shared problem. The central activity of deliberation is together clarifying the problem and weighing alternatives. Deliberating public issues is the most basic citizen behavior in democracies because without it citizens exercise power (e.g., voting; direct action) without having thought together about how to exercise it. The opening question is usually some version of, "What should we do about this?"

Seminar

Seminars are discussions aimed at developing, exposing, and exploring meanings. A seminar's purpose is an enlarged understanding of the ideas, issues, and values in or prompted by the text. The text may be an historical novel, a primary document, an essay, a photo, film, play, or painting. A seminar is not planning for action. There may be deliberative moments within seminars, but the seminar's primary purpose is not to repair the world so much as to reveal it with greater clarity. Seminars enrich deliberation, to be sure, and for social studies teachers they go hand in hand by widening students' knowledge and deepening their understanding of issues. Seminars and deliberations overlap, but their emphases and teaching/learning purposes are distinct.

Powers of Understanding

Improving discussants' powers of understanding is a secondary aim of both seminars and deliberations. Sometimes termed "habits of mind" (Meier, 1995), these are the ancient arts of interpretation, also called critical thinking or higher-order reasoning. We can think of them as the inquiry skills and dispositions needed to apprehend the world (the purpose of a seminar) and those needed to help us decide what changes should be made (the purpose of a deliberation).

Opening Question

The opening question begins the discussion and is aimed at the purpose of the discussion—toward a decision or an enlarged understanding of a text. When it is effective, the opening question helps the group get to the heart of the matter, whether directly or along a meandering route. And the opening question is *genuine*. A question is genuine when the facilitator has not made up his or her mind as to the answer. The teacher doesn't have the answer, but infects students with the same sense of perplexity he or she feels. (Socrates provides the classic role model; see Plato's *Meno*, in *Protagoras and Meno*, 1956.) The genuineness of their questions helps discussion facilitators to be actually curious about and want, therefore, to listen to participants' responses because they themselves are grappling with them.

Exemplar

The purpose of any exemplar is to display vividly the critical attributes of the concept it represents. The typology gives one pedagogical exemplar for each of the two kinds of discussion: Socratic Seminar for seminar and Structured Academic Controversy for deliberation. Each will be detailed in the sections that follow.

SEMINAR

The Socratic Seminar is the product of a number of interests and forces, but for present purposes we can trace it to the Paideia Group and its publication, *The Paideia Proposal* (Adler, 1982), which advocated "the same course of study for all" (p. 21) and delineated three modes of teaching and learning: recitation and lectures for the acquisition of organized knowledge, coaching and practice in project work for the development of intellectual skills, and discussion of texts (books, art, letters, etc.) for "enlarged understanding of ideas and values" (p. 23). The National Paideia Center supports a network of "Paideia schools" (Roberts et al., 1998). The Great Books Foundation in Chicago, with which Adler was connected, also has done much to popularize the seminar mode of discussion, conducting teacher trainings across the nation and publishing collections of seminar texts, such as *Introduction to Great Books* (Great Books Foundation, 1990), a series of texts (with leaders' guides) that range from Tocqueville's *Democracy in America* to Virginia Woolf's *A Room of One's Own* and Freud's *On War*. Sophie Haroutunian-Gordon (1991) provides a comparative analysis of seminar-centered teaching and learning in urban and suburban high schools, and in a skillful analytic essay (1988) she asks whether Socrates was himself a "socratic" teacher. The seminar is used in higher education as well: Undergraduates at St. John's College in Annapolis, Maryland and Santa Fe, New Mexico experience seminars as an instructional staple across the undergraduate curriculum—from science and math to theology and history.

This pedagogical model has been associated with privileged students in the upper-middle and upper classes, and it has privileged a particular set of authors and artists—mainly White, mainly male, mainly European or European-American. But the seminar is increasingly being appropriated for use with students who occupy less privileged social positions and with newly privileged authors.[1]

Dennis Gray, who was a member of the Paideia Group, has helped immensely to popularize the Socratic Seminar in the past 15 years by conducting teacher trainings and writing a popular article in *American Educator* (1989). Gray writes:

> Seminars demand rigorous thinking by all the participants, not mere mastery of information. They require no predetermined notion of what particular understandings will be enlarged or what routes to greater understanding will be followed. The conversation moves along in accordance with what is said by the participants, rather than deference to a hard and fast lesson plan. Seminars are inhospitable to competition for right answers, particularly given the principal aim in engaging students in critical thinking about complex, multisided matters. Instead, they join participants in a collaborative quest for understanding, in mutual testing of each other's responses to the text. (p. 18)

In my preservice course, I begin the seminar unit with an overview that informs students that I will demonstrate a "Socratic Seminar" after which they will have two opportunities to plan and lead a seminar themselves. Those seminars will be "microseminars," that is, short seminars in small groups with each participant taking the facilitator role in turn, each with a different, short text. Each microseminar will last about 20 minutes, including 5 minutes for participants to read the text on which the seminar will be conducted. Prior to the microseminars, students who will be leading a discussion of the same text but in different groups will get together, Jigsaw style (Aronson et al., 1978), to discuss that text and prepare an opening question. Following the microseminars, they will go back to these planning groups to compare experiences and make facilitator notes. After they have each led two seminars, I tell them, I will lead one more and ask them to critique my facilitation based on what they have learned from their own experiences as a participant and facilitator up to that point.

Knowing all this in advance has advantages, of course. Students have the big picture in mind and they are motivated to pay close attention to the facilitator role in the first seminar, the one I lead, rather than focusing only on the text and on one another. They know they will be taking that role subsequently.

Debriefings play an important role, too; one follows each seminar and microseminar. A debriefing keeps everyone's attention on what just happened while at the same time extending the "occasion," providing a reflective opportunity to scrutinize what happened and why, and to hone one's understanding of the facilitator and participant roles. Students reflect on the seminar model itself and address the many problems that come to mind—how to frame an effective opening question; what to do with students whom they worry (rightly) will not do the reading and students who would if they could but cannot; what to do with students who are uncomfortable participating and students who dominate and will not listen; how to articulate the seminar model across students' cultural styles. Also, I provide direct instruction on a number of points:

- selecting a powerful text
- preparing to lead a seminar
- articulating the purpose of the seminar
- stating and/or eliciting norms and standards
- keeping a discussion going and on focus
- debriefing a seminar
- follow-up skills instruction (e.g., paraphrasing, privileging, caution, humility)
- follow-up writing assignments
- working with reading comprehension problems
- tolerating failed seminars and trying again

By placing this instruction in the debriefing context, light is shed on the just-completed seminar or microseminar and the information is brought back to concrete experience. This is reflection, from *reflectere:* bending backward to understand what happened and forward to imaginatively create one's behavior in the next seminar (see Valli, 1997). This is also the inductive/deductive "double movement of reflection" (Dewey, 1910/1985b, p. 242): students move from experience to creating a working hypothesis about that experience, and back to experience again to test the working hypothesis, then back to revise the hypothesis, and so forth, creating a practical "working theory" of discussion facilitation.

Incorporated in these debriefings is the viewing of videotapes showing classroom teachers and students engaged in seminars. A number are available, but let me provide a glimpse of the two I use currently. One is a 15-minute instructional video called *How to Conduct Successful Socratic Seminars* (Association for Supervision and Curriculum Development, 1999), featuring Colorado teacher John Zola and his high school students. While Mr. Zola instructs viewers on various elements of seminar planning and facilitation, he is shown leading a seminar with his students on a Supreme Court decision dealing with sexual harassment in the workplace (*Harris v. Forklift, 1993*). Here the seminar is focused on a primary document that deals with a controversial public issue on which the Court is rendering an opinion. The other video is one of a collection of videos that accompanies a teaching manual called *Preparing Citizens: Linking Authentic Assessment and Instruction in Civic/Law-Related Education* (Miller & Singleton, 1997; also available in condensed form[2]). The segment I use shows another Colorado teacher, Judy Still, and her middle school students having a seminar on Howard Fast's novel about the opening days of the American Revolution, *April Morning* (1961). Here the seminar is focused on historical fiction, and the students are working to understand how its main character and the new nation both are developing.

Let me attend now to several of the bulleted points above.

Selecting a Powerful Text

Powerful texts can call out to us in any medium—print (e.g., King's "Letter"; a Supreme Court opinion), visual (the Vietnam memorial; Jacob Lawrence's 60–panel series, *The Migration of the Negro*, depicting the great migration), auditory (a workers' song or national anthem), or theatrical (a scene from a play or musical). What makes them "powerful" is that they contain or arouse in participants challenging and perhaps liberating ideas, issues, and values. These are potentially mind-altering texts that raise persistent or surprising human questions and lend themselves to conflicting interpretations. The exchange and clarification of interpretations should arouse the discussants both intellectually and morally and, thanks to the diversity of participants and disagreements among them, broaden their horizons. The ideas, issues, and values carried along by these texts deal intimately with who we are and how we live together, how and who we are going to be, why we hate and love, why we suffer and hope, what we do and don't try to build. At least, this is the aim. Of course, not every text does this. At one point in Anglo-American history, such texts were listed and collected and called *the* "Great Books of the Western World" (Hutchins, 1952). With the broadening of the canon in recent decades, thankfully, the collection of texts that deserve to be called "great" has been sharply contested, demystified, and opened up significantly. Of course, this does not mean that all texts are equally powerful, as any teacher and any reader knows, and the chief task for a seminar facilitator is to select the most powerful text for the purposes and students at hand.

In Socratic Seminars, we typically deal with text *excerpts*. This flies in the face of conventional literature practice, but it has benefits that can outweigh the costs. Mainly, the class can concentrate more intently on, and dig more deeply into, a brief (one- to four-page) passage than an entire work. And, given the myriad reading ability problems in middle and high schools, the brevity of the passage lends itself to intensive work on a small area and, therefore, the experience of heightened comprehension.

In my social studies methods course, I try to select powerful texts that deal centrally with problems and principles of democracy in a diverse society. Of the two demonstration seminars I lead myself, recall that one comes at the beginning of the unit, the other after students have each facilitated two seminars and participated as discussants in six to eight more in microseminars. For these demonstrations, I often choose King's "Letter" for the first, which I have excerpted down to 4 pages from the 20-page version that appears as a chapter in King's book, *Why We Can't Wait* (1963c); and, for the second, Plato's *Crito* (1992b), which is an account of Socrates' time in jail prior to his drinking the hemlock. These make an unforgettable pair of seminars. I facilitate the first with the whole class; in the second I demonstrate a "fishbowl"-style seminar, with an inner and outer circle of students who trade places midway through the seminar. Students may speak only when in the inner circle.

I choose an additional eight to ten texts for the two rounds of microseminars. (Two microseminars with four participants each requires eight texts; if groups are of five students, then ten texts are required.) These texts must be very brief, as students in the microseminars are given only 5 minutes to read the text prior to the seminar. Typically these are not more than one page long and are often only one paragraph. My selections often include the following: James Baldwin's "A Talk to Teachers" (1988), Machiavelli's *The Prince* (1947), the Melian dialogue in Thucydides' *History of the Peloponnesian War* (1972), Toni Morrison's *Playing in the Dark* (1992), Jane Addams's "Why Women Should Vote" (1913), Tocqueville's *Democracy in America* (1848/1969), John Kenneth Galbraith's *The Affluent Society* (1998), John Dewey's *Democracy and Education* (1916/1985a), and public documents such as *The Declaration of Independence*, the *Seneca Falls Declaration*, *Federalist No. 10*, and *The Pledge of Allegiance*.

The Addams (1913) text excerpt concerning women who live in a "crowded city quarter" was provided in its entirety in Chapter 1 as an exemplar of non-idiotic reasoning. Below, I provide the Tocqueville and Morrison excerpts. Later in this chapter, I provide the opening questions I use for each of these three.

Alexis de Tocqueville: *There is, indeed, a most dangerous passage in the history of a democratic people. When the taste for physical gratifications among them has grown more rapidly than their education and their experience of free institutions, the time will come when men are carried away and lose all self-restraint at the sight of the new possessions they are about to obtain. In their intense and exclusive anxiety to make a fortune, they lose sight of the close connection that exists between the private fortune of each and the prosperity of all. It is not necessary to do violence to such a people in order to strip them of the rights they enjoy; they themselves willingly loosen their hold. The discharge of political duties appears to them to be a troublesome impediment which diverts them from their occupations and business. If they are required to elect representatives, to support the government by personal service, to meet on public business, they think they have no time, they cannot waste their precious hours in useless engagements; such idle amusements are unsuited to serious men who are engaged with the important interests of life. These people think they are following the principle of self-interest, but the idea they entertain of that principle is a very crude one; and the better to look after what they call their own business, they neglect their chief business, which is to remain their own masters. (1848/ 1969, p. 540)*

Toni Morrison: *My interest in Ernest Hemingway becomes heightened when I consider how much apart his work is from African-Americans. That is, he has no need, desire, or awareness of them either as readers of his work or as people existing anywhere other than in his imaginative (and imaginatively lived) world. I find, therefore, his use of African-Americans much more artless and unselfconscious than Poe's, for example, where social unease required the servile black bodies in his work. (1992, p. 68)*

Certainly a comment is needed about my rationale for choosing the texts I choose. My selection is inevitably limited to the extent of my own knowledge and interests, which result from a combination of my social position, education, and individual dispositions. Generally, I try to choose texts that force my student teachers and myself to grapple with how we want to live together; that is, with the arrangement of private and public life, the force of economic conditions, unequal relations in power hierarchies, and the pervasive threat of idiocy. I choose the Tocqueville and Addams texts because they go to a key issue in educating for democratic living: the tension between individual freedom and the common good (or independence and community; negative and positive liberty). Moreover, Tocqueville connects this tension to the problem of affluence, as does Galbraith, and Addams provides the singular contribution of blurring the boundaries between domestic life and public life. I choose the "Letter" and *Crito* because both feature great moral philosophers who are in jail, and who were there on purpose—for reasons of conscience, love of justice, and respect for community. Together, they provide a dramatic comparison. I choose the two "Declarations," *The Prince*, and the "Melian Dialogue" because they deal centrally with equality and inequality and the accompanying tension between right and might—that is, between justice and power. Madison's *Federalist No. 10*, Morrison's *Playing in the Dark*, and Baldwin's "A Talk to Teachers" each deals with diversity: Madison with the need to limit majority power, Morrison and Baldwin with the depth, persistence, and consequences of racism and prejudice. A good seminar on the *Pledge* spurs some participants for the first time to contemplate the idea of allegiance to a way of living together (a republic) rather than to a person (e.g., the prince) or a place (e.g., a "fatherland").

Preparing to Lead a Seminar

Preparing to lead a whole-class or fishbowl seminar, or a micro-seminar, involves numerous decisions and serious consideration of the text to be discussed. How will the class be arranged for seminar? (One large circle? Two concentric circles for alternating "fishbowl" discussions? Small groups?) Will participation be required? How will power differences among students be addressed? Will the seminar be evaluated? How will homework reading, if assigned, be checked prior to the seminar? Will students who haven't done the reading be allowed to participate? How will the seminar purpose be stated and communicated? What norms will be posted (or proposed or elicited from the group)? What question will open the seminar? Here, I deal with the last three questions concerning purpose, norms, and the opening question.

As for purpose and norms, I ask student teachers to prepare a poster that can be taped to the wall each time a seminar is held:

Purpose—

> *To enlarge your understanding of the ideas, issues, and values in this text.*

Norms—

> *1. Don't raise hands.*
> *2. Address one another, not the discussion leader.*
> *3. Use the text to support opinions.*

Communicating with students about the purpose and norms requires knowledge of the students, their discussion experience in and out of school, and the norms by which they usually interact with one another. Obviously, this takes time. The adolescents I have worked with often do not have language for challenging or clarifying one another's statements easily or courteously; accordingly, we teach them phrases such as these: "I have a different opinion" (then state it); or, "I disagree. Let me explain." And, for clarification: "I think I understand, but let me be sure" (then rephrase); or "What do you mean by . . . ?" But even with such language for interacting seriously with one another, power asymmetries will interfere with free and open discourse. That the teacher may have created a stifling classroom climate is one well-researched problem (Hahn, 1998); that boys out-talk girls is another (Sadker & Sadker, 1994); that dialect differences are stigmatized is another (Perry & Delpit, 1998); ethnocentrism another (Asante, 1998); racism and race-consciousness another (Gay, 2000; Hollins, King, & Hayman, 1994).

My general direction to student teachers is that they assess their students' behavior related to the second norm on the poster: address one another, not the discussion leader. Then, during the debriefing that follows the seminar, the teacher can ask students if they believe there was unequal expression or any domination during the discussion, share his or her observations, and forthrightly address problems and plan ahead for the next seminar. If, for example, students or the teacher observe that outsiders denied insiders' experiences and responses—with regards to whatever kind of group membership (race, gender, school cliques, whatever)—the teacher can share the idea of epistemic privilege (see Chapter 5); not using that label, of course, but conveying the strategy and asking students to try it in the next discussion.

In the videotape of Judy Still's middle school seminar on *April Morning*, we see her posting the following norms for her middle school students. Her students already know from prior seminar experience to address one another, and they no longer need that norm to be posted. However, they sometimes raise their hands, which forces the teacher into the moderator role. Accordingly, a related norm is posted. The second and third norms encourage students to listen carefully, to relate their own comments to those of others, and to draw one another into the discussion. The fourth and fifth specify additional expectations.

Norms—

1. *Don't raise hands.*
2. *Listen to and build on one another's comments.*
3. *Invite others into the discussion.*
4. *Support opinions by referring to passages in the book.*
5. *Tie what you know about the history of the revolution into your interpretation of* April Morning.

Preparing the opening question for a seminar is the most important aspect of seminar facilitation, without which the purposes and norms have nothing in particular to realize. The key here is advanced study of the text the students will be reading (viewing) and discussing. I indicated earlier that my student teachers participate in two rounds of microseminars, facilitating once in each round. Prior to this, they prepare, Jigsaw style, in planning groups with others who will lead a microseminar on the same text. This is an enormously important planning session, for here they discuss the ideas, issues, and values in the text, and then frame several opening questions and decide on one to try out. (This decision is actually a deliberation, since group members are weighing the suggested questions and deciding on one that all will use to open their seminars—that is, they are reaching a decision that will be binding on all.)

Opening questions should be interpretive, rather than factual or evaluative. An interpretive question concerns the meaning of the ideas, issues, and values in a text. It has no single correct answer as does a factual question, so the discussion will be text-based as students *use* the text to marshal evidence for and against particular interpretations. Of course, there will be disagreement. An evaluative question also has no single correct answer, but it is less about interpreting the text and more a matter of making value judgments about something in the text or related to it. (This distinction among question types is given concisely in the discussion leader's handbook of the Great Books Foundation [1999].) Here are some examples. First, I give opening questions I have used with the three texts printed earlier by Tocqueville, Addams, and Morrison. Each is interpretive.

- What does Tocqueville mean in the last sentence of the paragraph, where he writes, *but the idea they entertain of that principle (the principle of self-interest) is a very crude one*?
- What would be a good title for this paragraph, one that captures Addams's key concerns?
- Is Morrison approving of Hemingway's literary treatment of African Americans?

Here are opening questions I have used with "Letter" and *Crito*. I provide an interpretive, then an evaluative question for each.

- How does King distinguish between just and unjust laws?
- Should teachers urge their students to follow King's example?
- Why didn't Socrates escape when he had the chance?
- Would you have tried to escape if you were in Socrates's place?

Debriefing a Seminar

A common approach to debriefing a seminar, which I model for students in the demonstration seminars on "Letter" and *Crito*, is to go around the circle of participants and ask, "Did we achieve the purpose? Was your understanding enlarged?" And/or ask each participant to make an observation about the seminar: "What is one thing you noticed about the seminar we had today?" Both are good assessment opportunities for both facilitator and participants, and either should suggest problems that can be addressed immediately or in the next seminar. If students are avoiding a problem, then the teacher should encourage them to address it.

DELIBERATION

As the reader well understands by now, deliberation is discussion with an eye toward deciding what a "we" should do. This "we" is a community that shares a problem. Deliberation is a community-building enterprise because it brings people together around a problem they share and creates a particular kind of democratic culture among them: listening as well as talking, forging decisions together rather than only defending positions taken earlier, and coming to an agreement or disagreement.

Selecting a pedagogical exemplar for deliberation is more difficult than for a seminar because there are more possibilities. The public policy deliberation model (PPD) outlined in the prior chapter has the advantage of thoroughness and authenticity. It is the model of choice in public affairs departments at universities and used, more or less, by practicing policy agents working in government. The public issues model (Evans & Saxe, 1996; Hess, 2002; Oliver & Shaver, 1974; Oliver et al., 1992; Patrick, Vontz, & Nixon, 2002), however, is probably the most venerated in the elementary and secondary school fields, and for good reason: Students are engaged in large- and small-group discussions of an enduring public issue; they study the issue in depth, including its instanciation across analogous cases; they learn to distinguish between *kinds* of issues (those involving value conflicts as opposed to definitional disputes or disagreements over the facts); they are taught numerous skills of civic discourse, such as clarification, stipulation, and drawing analogies; and classroom assessment schemes have been developed (Harris, 2002). However, for the unique pedagogical circumstance of teaching new teachers to lead deliberations I have come to appreciate Structured Academic Controversy (SAC) as developed by the cooperative learning researchers, David Johnson and Roger Johnson

(1985, 1988). I believe it provides a working platform—a scaffold—from which PPD or the public issues model can be explored later. (*Note:* In chapter 5, "SAC" referred to the student advisory councils—Big SAC and Little SAC—at Cottage Lane Elementary School. Here, "SAC" means Structured Academic Controversy.)

This "unique pedagogical circumstance" involves novices, not experienced teachers, whose own 16-year "apprenticeship of observation" (Lortie, 1975, p. 61) has taught them a great deal about the IRE (initiate-respond-evaluate) pattern of teacher-student recitation but little about orchestrating purposeful student-student discussions of controversial issues, and who worry, understandably, about the their performance as student teachers in relation to their students, peers, cooperating teachers, and university supervisors. This is no ordinary circumstance. My attempts at teaching new teachers to lead deliberative discussions have taught me that structured academic controversy is the better place to begin the journey, while the public issues model and PPD allow plenty of room for growth later. In other words, SAC scaffolds student teachers successfully into controversial issues deliberations, after which they are welcome to work with more ambitious models.

Johnson and Johnson (1988) call the strategy structured academic controversy in order to emphasize, first, the structured or scaffolded nature of the discussion and, second, the academic or subject-matter controversies (as opposed to nonacademic or interpersonal controversies) that are at issue. Briefly, here is the SAC procedure as I've adapted it.[3]

Students read, in small groups of four, background material (e.g., historical narrative; journalism) on the issue at hand (e.g., Should states be permitted to disenfranchise ex-felons? Was World War II the second half of World War I? Why was slavery abolished so late in U.S. history? Should physician-assisted suicide be permitted in our state?). Then, each group breaks into two pairs. Each pair is assigned a different position on the issue, affirmative and negative, and given a set of primary and secondary sources in order to study the position and its supporting arguments. This period of text-based study can take anywhere from 20 minutes to several hours or days, depending on the amount and depth of material involved. (Hence, SAC can be adapted to a single lesson or a whole unit.) Following study, each pair plans a presentation of its position and arguments, then presents to the other pair. Next, the pairs reverse perspectives: Each pair feeds back the other pair's position and reasoning until each is satisfied that its case has been heard and understood. All this discussion, recall, is occurring within the relatively safe settings of, first, a pair of students, and then two pairs together in a small group of four students. Following the presentation of the affirmative and negative cases and the subsequent reciprocity, the pairs are asked to dissolve themselves so that the group of four can become one deliberative body. The pairs are asked to drop the positions to which they were assigned. Individuals are encouraged now to be genuine, drawing not only on the readings but also on their life experiences and emotions. "See if you can forge a position, together. Feel free to change your mind." The small group's task now is to reason together in the direction of a consensus on the question; or if not consensus, then to "come to disagreement," clarifying the nature of the disagreement.

This small-group discussion is the culminating activity of SAC and the source of the discussion excerpt, which follows. To speak of it as a culminating activity is to say, in linear terms, that it is the final activity setting in the sequence of activity settings that constitutes SAC. Students have been prepared for it not only by studying the issue but by discussing it with a partner, then (after planning) representing it to an audience (the opposing pair), then reversing perspectives, and then exploring it again—now through small-group discussion, setting one perspective alongside others, "challenging our own view of things with those of others" (Bridges, 1979, p. 50).

The SAC procedure may strike some readers as too structured, yet in the culminating discussion students typically change their minds as they see fit, not necessarily clinging to initially assigned positions; they are listening to and challenging one another, and each of them is contributing. This is not magic. *It was the earlier work in the sequence that scaffolded students up to this culminating discussion.* The work done in pairs developed whatever students' initial understanding of the issue might have been, and students were able to broaden that knowledge thanks to the dynamics of presenting and reversing positions and then discussing the issue in the group of four. The scaffold, in other words, has the desired consequences. When we recall the stubborn persistence of recitation in classrooms through the grade levels, this is no small feat. Walking around the classroom, listening to the discussions in each group of four, is routinely a satisfying moment.

A brief excerpt from a SAC discussion should be helpful. Here students are in groups of four each, and they are discussing a controversy concerning crime, race, and citizenship. At issue is whether ex-felons should be disenfranchised. Value conflicts and disagreements over facts arise in only a few turns.

> *Terrell:* You're absolutely right, ex-cons should be allowed to vote. They paid their time didn't they? If you don't let them vote you're saying they haven't paid their time.
> *Sara:* But shouldn't we have more respect for the ballot box?

Terrell: Now what does that mean?

Sara: It means, show a little respect for the victims why don't you.

Angie: Wait. You switched reasons. Let's get back to the ballot box. I think you're right there. Most states don't let ex-cons vote once they're let out of prison because the felons disqualified themselves from citizenship when they violated community norms. It's like they broke the social contract. Sorry, Terrell, but that makes sense to me. You can't treat citizenship as cheap.

Sara: Some states, I think. Not most states.

Byron: Do you know who most of those felons are? Maybe not most, but lots? Black. Its says right here (pointing to article) that thirteen percent of all Black men can't vote today because of current or prior felon convictions. Now what do you really think this issue is about? Crime? Race?

Sara: Now I know why Democrats want the voting restrictions lifted and Republicans don't.

There are at least two good reasons for teaching the SAC method to preservice teachers of social studies, literature, and science courses. First, it encourages them to uncover and feature the controversies that suffuse the subject matter they are planning to teach, and doing so improves the quality of their curriculum swiftly and surely. Scholars are in continual disagreement about the nature of their fields and the claims they are advancing. Scholarship, in fact, is defined by one's participation in these disagreements: A scholar's grasp of the questions and conflicts that mark her field, combined with her willingness to subject her understandings to the criticism of peers, in large measure constitutes her as a scholar. Historians disagree fundamentally about why Rome fell, why the tyrannies of Hitler and Mussolini arose in democracies, why women were executed as witches in Salem, why slavery in North America wasn't abolished sooner, and which of these questions is worth pursuing further. None are settled matters, especially not among the people who know a great deal about them. Competing accounts are adjudicated differently, evidence is evaluated differently, and arguments are made, interpreted, and deployed differently.

Second, along with this uncovering function, SAC sponsors a unique kind of classroom discourse. It involves students in what should be safe and focused discussions with one another during which competing ideas and values are set alongside one another. And, it does it in a way that, in my experience at least, is feasible for the novice teacher who is worried about the commonplaces of student teaching: classroom management, relating with students, teaching subject matter, and appearing competent before supervisors.

The discussion excerpt above is, all things considered, quite good. It is a small-group discussion. Students are expressing positions, challenging positions, seeking clarity, giving reasons, and following the reasoning (Angie noted Sara's "switch"). Moreover, they are addressing one another, and each student contributes. These objectives are not easily achieved, as any teacher knows. It is important to note that the discussion occurred with no explicit instruction on how to have such a discussion; instead, careful prompts were given in a particular sequence, which is what earns SAC the word "structured" in its name. In this way, SAC scaffolds students into impressively demanding discussions which otherwise may be beyond their reach.

But my objective here is to teach these preservice teachers to facilitate SAC deliberations with *their* students, which requires more than their engagement in this one demonstration lesson. If I did only this, much of the pedagogy would remain invisible and, therefore, unusable. To appropriate it as a tool in their own teaching, they need not only to be involved in it while their attention and intellectual effort is focused on the issue being deliberated; they need also to place their attention and intellectual effort on the pedagogy itself. What to do? Following the strategy described earlier for seminars, I could move from the SAC demonstration lesson, as with seminars, to "microSACs," in which students would take turns in the leader role. That would not be feasible, however, because of the large amount of study time needed for the pairs to prepare for their presentations. Instead, I require each student to develop a full SAC lesson plan, and to append the affirmative and negative readings their students will study at the outset. I am under no illusion that this prepares them adequately to conduct a SAC with their students, but it is sufficient to prompt most of them to at least attempt SAC during their internships.

As with seminar, a good deal of the direct instruction on SAC occurs during the debriefing of the demonstration lesson, but a significant portion of it also occurs during the question-and-answer portion of class sessions, in which students are sharing their work on their own SAC plans. The array of problems and considerations needing attention is similar to those for seminar:

- Selecting a powerful issue
- Articulating to students the purpose of the deliberation
- Stating and/or eliciting norms and standards for the deliberation
- Deciding whether to reveal one's own position on the issue
- Keeping the discussions going and on focus (in pairs; in small groups)
- Debriefing a SAC
- Follow-up writing assignments

- Follow-up skills instruction (e.g., paraphrasing, privileging, caution, humility)
- Working with reading comprehension problems
- Tolerating failed deliberations and trying again

Each is important, but I will touch upon just the first four.

Selecting a Powerful Issue

The SAC plan my students develop includes a written rationale for the selected issue, which requires them to wrestle with the selection of subject matter, as they must with seminars. I stipulate that to be powerful, the selected issue should be central—not peripheral—to the course of study at hand (e.g., in a history course, central to the historical era or unit theme). Additionally, it should feature one or more value conflicts and represent one or more larger, perennial issues. A perennial issue, as we saw in Chapter 6, is an enduring issue. It arises again and again in human affairs, across time and place. The issue of felon disenfranchisement, for example, is to me central to a civics or government course that deals with voting rights, voter behavior, and such values as liberty, justice, and equality. It represents a number of enduring issues about crime and deviance in any society, especially a society where justice, equality, one-person-one-vote, and the rights *and* responsibilities of citizens are espoused ideals. And in a racially mixed classroom, it encourages students to talk directly about race and racism. Similarly, a SAC deliberation on the causes of the American Revolution and whether its instigators were "traitors" or "patriots" is central to a U.S. history course. Here, a perennial issue might be: When is rebellion justified?[4]

Articulating the Purpose of a SAC Deliberation

At this point in debriefing the demonstration lesson on ex-felon voting rights, I introduce the typology presented earlier in this chapter (see Table 7.1). In order to perceive the purpose of deliberation and use it appropriately as a tool in their own classrooms, teachers need a differentiated (rather than monolithic) understanding of discussion. Then, they (and we) can distinguish among different purposes, tailoring the discussion to different kinds of subject matter. Do students need to deepen and broaden their understanding of the ideas, issues, and values in a particular text? Or do they need to reach a decision? I have found that the typology is not helpful until after the second discussion framework, deliberation, is introduced. At that point, the problem of distinguishing between the two arises.

Norms

Because SAC discussions are conducted within small groups, it is unnecessary to establish the hand-raising and address-one-another norms of the seminar. Needed instead are norms related to reaching decisions on controversial issues through civilized disagreement and deep exploration of the issue itself. A videotape I show at this point displays a high school class in Denver deliberating the issue of physician-assisted suicide.[5] We see the discussion leader elicit from students and write on the chalkboard the following norms:

Norms—

1. *Hear all sides equally.*
2. *Listen well enough to respond to and build upon each other's ideas.*
3. *Talking loudly is no substitute for reasoning.*
4. *Back up opinions with clear reasons.*
5. *Speak one at a time.*

The Teacher's Role

The question my student teachers wrestle with more than any other, once they begin to facilitate deliberations on actual controversies (or imagine themselves doing so), is this: What should I do with my own position and reasons on the issue? Should I disclose them? When the question is raised, I ask a student to facilitate a brief deliberation. The opening prompt: "See if you can come to a consensus on this issue, or at least clarify the disagreement." Listening to this discussion is invariably a useful informal assessment of students' reasoning on the issue and their background assumptions about the politics of teaching. I follow up by distributing a brief article by Thomas Kelly (1989). It suggests reasons why disclosure should be avoided (the teacher's power gives status to her argument that it may not deserve, and doing so undermines students' own critical work on the issue) as well as reasons why disclosure can have positive consequences: by thinking aloud, the teacher models for students at least one way to come to a reasoned position on the issue at hand. Also, nondisclosure can be interpreted by students as a cowardly retreat from taking a stand or "a presumptuous underestimation of students' independence of mind" (p. 370). Kelly concludes that, if teachers decide to disclose, they can minimize negative consequences by employing four practices:

1. Publicly engage in self-critique.
2. Actively encourage students to critique their own positions, too.

3. Sincerely praise competing viewpoints.
4. Honestly critique views that merely parrot those of the teacher. (p. 370)

Kelly's article makes a good text for a seminar discussion with these preservice teachers. An opening interpretive question might be, "Is Kelly recommending disclosure?" The evaluative question could more directly draw out students' own views on the question: "Do you intend to be a disclosing teacher or not?"

CONCLUSION

Seminars are discussions aimed at enlarging students' understandings of select texts, while deliberations are discussions aimed at making decisions about what a community should do. Deliberation is the basic labor of democratic life, and it requires not only a "we" with a problem but a "we" with knowledge. A classroom, therefore, should not be deliberation-centered any more that it should be seminar-centered. Classrooms routinely should try to do both in tandem. The depth of understanding promised by the seminar helps provide an enlightened platform for public action. The reverse is true, as well. While taking bold social action without the advantage of social understanding reeks of action for its own sake, a mindless outburst; to possess understanding but take no action is an "academic" form of social irresponsibility, cruel inaction in the face of cruel circumstances.

Pedagogical tools—scaffolds—tailored to the two emphases are needed. Seminar and deliberation are two such tools. Each is worth honing by new and experienced teachers alike. This entails something more than *participating* in them as discussants. It requires also developing *reflective knowledge* of both, the sort of knowledge that results from planning (with others) to lead them, reflecting (with others) on discussions in which they have participated or led, and studying (with others) the distinctions among different kinds of discussion.

In a society that is trying to achieve democracy, all adults are called upon to be its stewards. Teachers have a special responsibility, however, for they are planning and implementing curriculum and instruction, both formal and informal, that are designed intentionally toward this end. "Teaching in a democracy is not at all the same thing as teaching in a dictatorship," Roger Soder writes (1996, p. 246). Teachers are political and moral agents, not clerks. They contribute no less than to the conscious formation of selves—of subjectivities—and they must be mindful that this is what they are doing. No one is simply a math teacher or a history teacher or a music teacher. This is why James Baldwin in his "talk to teachers" (1988; Chapter 6, this volume) cautioned them against creating the next generation of barbarians and to strive, instead, to cultivate democrats. But aside from their ability to foster and lead discussions in their classrooms with their students, teachers have a special obligation to be able to engage in seminars and deliberations themselves, for in this way their own understandings can be enlarged and their own public problems—curriculum choices, assessment decisions, and other school policies—can be resolved through deliberation.

8

Access to a Non-Idiotic Education

> Education is important to all citizens; it is absolutely essential to those
> who must go on to face continued obstacles of racism, classism,
> and sexism, to those who have been distanced and disenfranchised
> from the U.S. mainstream culture, and to those who have suffered
> lifetimes of oppression and marginalization.
> —Vivyan C. Adair, 2001, p. 219

The campaign for democratic education needs to be carried forward on multiple fronts. Programs are needed both inside and outside schools, as we saw earlier in this book, and not only with students but, as we saw in the previous chapter, with their teachers. On each front the access problem looms large. By access, I mean admittance to a reasonably high-quality education for democratic living in a diverse society. In this concluding chapter I concentrate on two often overlooked aspects of the access problem: first, its economic root, and the role racism plays in compounding it; second, the importance of assuring access to democratic education not only for groups typically excluded (e.g., the poor) but to privileged groups as well (we must not assume they are getting it). Finally, I ask, "Access to *what*?" It does no good to argue for inclusion without specifying the kinds of democratic education in which inclusion is sought.

ASPIRATION AND DENIAL

The access problem is complex. When we factor in underlying economic conditions, then combine these with racial prejudice, equal access to democratic education becomes a steep uphill climb indeed. A central dilemma in liberal capitalist democracies is the contradiction between the conventional ideology of equal opportunity for vertical mobility—the "American dream" in the United States—and the limited number of actual opportunities in the upper reaches of organizational hierarchies. For sociologists, this is not news. Burton Clark (1960) wrote:

> Democracy asks individuals to act as if social mobility were universally possible; status is to be won by individual effort, and rewards are to accrue to those who try. But democratic societies also need selective training institutions, and hierarchical work organizations permit increasingly fewer persons to succeed at ascending levels. Situations of opportunity are also situations of denial and failure. (p. 569)

While the belief in equal opportunity encourages individual aspirations to make it to the top, or at least to move up a rung or two on the socioeconomic ladder, numerical realities in occupational hierarchies render upward mobility an impossibility for everyone. Consequently, such a society has the dual challenge of motivating achievement through effort while simultaneously denying access to many. The American dream is promoted as though it could be granted to all even though, clearly, it cannot. Sociologists like Clark point to the "dissociation between culturally instilled goals and institutionally provided means of realization" (p. 563) and argue that this is a structural source of individual failure, alienation and, potentially, rebellion (Merton, 1968).

This discrepancy becomes more apparent as industrial democracies move toward a "postindustrial" model in which natural resources and economic growth are seen to have limits. As recognized limits to further waste and growth put a more visible ceiling on the promise of vertical mobility for all, the gap between individual aspirations and their achievement is underscored, especially for those of whom Adair (2001) speaks in this chapter's opening quotation, for whom education is made all the more important *and*, simultaneously, all the more difficult because of "lifetimes of oppression and marginalization."

Schools have long been expected to help manage this discrepancy between aspiration and denial. Willard Waller pointed this out in his splendid *The Sociology of Teaching* (1932). They accomplish it, he explained, by means of a "sorting process" in which a few students "are carried by the express elevators of prep schools which do not stop below the college level" (p. 20); meanwhile, a good percentage drops out of school early and is allocated to the lowest status ranks in the occupational hierarchy: the unemployed and underemployed. (Fifty-three percent of adults living in extreme poverty in the United States do not graduate from high school [Kasarda, 1993]). The remainder—the working and middle classes—are sorted and segregated within and among schools through devices such as low and unequal funding of education, curriculum tracking, and the substitution of accountability (e.g., high-stakes testing) for opportunities to learn (adequate school buildings, teachers, curriculum, materials). Were the sorting done transparently, anger or rebellion would seem inevitable. At least a lively debate should ensue. That neither occurs is testimony, I believe, to the lack of transparency of the "sorting machine" (Spring, 1989) and to the resilience of the American dream.

To understand the lack of transparency, we would have to return to the discussion of *ideology* in Chapter 4 and the difficulty of "cutting through conventional wisdom." As for the strength of the American dream, suffice it to note that all manner of surveys, opinion polls, campaign platforms, and other indicators of popular culture show that it has broad and deep support in American society (Hochschild, 1995). We can characterize it as follows:

> The American dream is the promise that all residents of the United States have a reasonable chance to achieve success as they define it (material or otherwise) through their own efforts and resources, and to attain virtue and fulfillment through that success. . . . Equality of opportunity to become legitimately unequal is an essential part, though not the whole, of the American dream. From this perspective, publicly provided education is intended to enable individuals to succeed. (Hochschild & Scovronick, 2002, p. 4)

But how is the emotional impact of denial dealt with? How is adaptation to failure accomplished? Erving Goffman (1952) worked with this idea under the title "Cooling Out the Mark." The concept of *cooling out* is borrowed from the classic *con game*. In a con game, the "mark" is the person who is "conned" (fooled and robbed) by a con artist and then "cooled out" by a "cooler," who is a confederate of the con artist. If effectively cooled out, the mark does not report the con game to authorities. Cooling out the mark, therefore, is critical to the game. The cooler's job is to befriend the mark and keep him or her from calling the police or in some other way blowing the whistle on the game. By analogy, those who are denied their aspirations in school must be artfully mollified so as to adapt them to failure while the structural inevitability of their failure is concealed from them. Their disappointment is reduced through the provision of alternatives and consolation. Above all, the less successful have "to be made to feel that their failure to attain was a personal failure and not the failure of the system" (Geis, Hilton, & Plitt, 1976, p. 249). This reduces their inclination to inveigh against a system that intentionally raised their aspirations and then shut the door.

Burton Clark's (1960) analysis of junior college students provides a vivid empirical case of the adaptation-to-failure process. Clark explored the system (the game) by which transfer students, who aspire to enter a 4-year college following a successful 2-year stint at a junior college are cooled into terminal students whose higher education will end after, if not before, the 2-year junior college program. Guidance counselors play the role of coolers by "assisting" students to evaluate their own "abilities, interests, and aptitudes" and, thereby, redirecting their vocational choices (p. 572).

Comparing the status-allocating function of schools to a con game may seem extreme to some, but the structural similarities are rather plainly seen. It is unlikely that schools will soon forfeit their control over this process, and perhaps (all things considered) it is done most fairly by the school. Consider the alternatives. If one's position in the social hierarchy is not to be "earned" by achievement—albeit in a system riddled with inequalities of opportunity (e.g., school funding; curriculum tracking)—then on what other platform should it be decided? Should it be assigned by some form of ascription—birth, family, race, ethnicity, and other characteristics of one's thrownness? Should a lottery system be used to decide who will land on one of the relatively few rungs at the upper end of the ladder?

Yet the *present* system is rigged too much toward ascription, against achievement. Being thrown into a White, English-speaking, upper-middle-class family positions a child very well for completion of K-12 and post-secondary education, then movement into a "white collar" occupation (likely to be a job in which one is manipulating information and supervising other workers) and then, perhaps, into a legislative body or board room. Nothing is guaranteed either way, but being placed in an impoverished minority setting positions a child for something entirely different.

A Newark, New Jersey inner-city school described by Jean Anyon [1997]) provides a cogent example. This is a K-8 school, located in central Newark. The student population is 71% African American and 27% Hispanic, and all but three of the 500 students are eligible for free lunch. Most live in nearby housing projects. The principal was formerly a shop teacher at a Newark high school and had probably landed this position as part of the political patronage system plaguing the Newark schools. A state investigator reported that "most of the problems seem to stem from a complete lack of competence on the part of the administrative staff" (p. 157). Teachers' attitudes toward students at this school is best portrayed by quoting them:

- You're disgusting; you remind me of children I would see in a jail or something. (African American teacher to her class of African American and Hispanic first graders)
- Shut up and push those pencils. Push those pencils—you border-line people. (African American teacher to his class of African American and Hispanic sixth graders)
- If I had a gun I'd kill you. You're all hoodlums. (White fifth-grade teacher)

- Don't you have *any* attention span? You have the attention span of cheerios! (White principal trying to quiet a class of African American and Hispanic fourth graders) (Anyon, p. 30)

None of this is accidental. Anyon reports that by 1961 Newark's schools were filled mainly with poor African American students, which is when state funding plummeted and legislators began courting the sensibilities of suburban taxpayers. In a prior era, when Newark was a prosperous industrial city and many White affluent children attended the schools, the Newark system was well funded and was studied as a model for other systems.

How does the systematic production of inequality happen? I have been addressing so far what is primarily an economic explanation, but that explanation is entangled with racism. In the last book King wrote, *Where Do We Go From Here: Chaos or Community?* (1967c), he concluded that racism had become a "faith" (p. 69) that emerged from the basic tenets of colonialism. Initially racism was not a faith, only a justification of the power differential that colonialism required. This justification eventually turned into a sort of religious dogma—a belief about hereditary inferiority and superiority. Not all Whites are believers, King maintained, nor is racism the only avenue to the systemic production of inequality. King himself believed the more basic route was economic:

> It is important to understand that the basis for the birth, growth and development of slavery in America was primarily economic. . . . [T]he colonies had to provide an abundance of rice, sugar, cotton and tobacco. In the first few years of the various settlements along the East Coast, so-called indentured servants, mostly white, were employed on plantations. But within a generation the plantation operators were demanding outright and lifetime slavery for the Africans they imported. As a function of this new economic policy, Africans were reduced to the status of property by law, and this status was enforced by the most rigid and brutal police power of the existing governments. By 1650 slavery had been legally established as a national institution . . . (and) had a profound impact in shaping the social-political-legal structure. (1967c, p. 72)

An extension of this political economy today is the fully legal, yet fully inequitable and inadequate, education funding that is available to children in impoverished city centers specifically and urban school districts generally. The cause mainly is the localization of school funding in the United States, exemplified in Anyon's account of Newark. Most states, like New Jersey, rely to a significant extent on local property taxes for education funding; consequently, wealthy school districts generate more funds than poor, and children of color disproportionately suffer the consequences. School districts and municipalities are both creations of state governments, and for this reason we see occasionally court rulings that direct state legislatures to address the funding inequity. But, in an idiotic era where "taxpayers" have largely replaced "citizens," little has actually been done.

In an appendix to this last book, King devotes a short section to education. He summarizes the whole phenomenon, including the con and the cooling:

> American society has emphasized education more than European society. The purpose is to use education to make a break between the occupation of the parents and those of their children. The schools have been the historic routes of social mobility. But when Negroes and others of the underclass now ask that schools play the same function for them, many within and outside the school system answer that the schools cannot do the job. They would impose on the family the whole task of preparing and leading youngsters into educational advance. And this reluctance to engage with the great issue of our day—the full emancipation and equality of Negroes and the poor—comes at a time when education is more than ever the passport to decent economic positions. (1967c, p. 193)

On King's account, "cooling out the mark" is attempted by blaming the lack of "educational advance" on the victims themselves, particularly their families. But he blows the whistle: "Whatever pathology may exist in Negro families is far exceeded by the social pathology in the school system that refuses to accept a responsibility that no one else can bear and then scapegoats Negro families for failing to do the job" (p. 193).

ACCESS FOR WHOM?

As Vivyan Adair states in the quote that opens this chapter, "education is important to all citizens; it is absolutely essential to those who . . . have suffered lifetimes of oppression and marginalization" (p. 219). Adair is only half right. It is "absolutely essential" that we increase access to quality education for members of historically privileged groups, too. The reason is straightforward: They hold the reigns of power and, therefore, whether politically, economically, or culturally, can do the most harm or good.

It is important that this not be confused with privileging an already privileged group with still more education. We must attend to the moral development of everyone, and this certainly includes those who (presently) possess the power to direct public policy. This is a *both-and* argument. It is an argument that invokes King's message in his "Beyond Vietnam" address (1967a): "[W]e shall surely be dragged down the long, dark, and shameful corridors of time reserved for those who possess power without compassion, might without morality, and strength without sight" (p. 11).

While the United States's record in the developing world provides ample examples of "might without morality," and while the recent Rwandan genocide of 1994 adds yet another example of extraordinary force (Mamdani, 2001), there is another, from antiquity, that has served for centuries as the paradigm case. In Thucydides' (1972) history of the Peloponnesian War, we learn that at one point the Athenians were preparing to lay siege to the small and relatively powerless island community of Melos. About 30 Athenian ships with 3,000 warriors surrounded the island and awaited the order to attack and plunder. There was no doubting on either side who had the might (the Athenians). But who was *right*? The Athenians, before doing any harm, sent representatives to win a surrender. They said to the Melian representatives, in effect, let us have a proper discussion. According to Thucydides' account of the dialogue that followed, the Melian representatives quickly pointed out the power differential:

> No one can object (to the Athenian proposal) of each of us putting forward our own views in a calm atmosphere. That is perfectly reasonable. What is scarcely consistent with such a proposal is the present threat, indeed the certainty, of your making war on us. We see that you have come prepared to judge the argument yourselves, and that the likely end of it all will be either war, if we prove that we are in the right, and so refuse to surrender, or else slavery. (p. 401)

Members of the dominant group within any society have the power to oppress members of other groups in numerous ways, formally and informally. Accordingly, "their minds must be improved to a certain degree" as Thomas Jefferson (1787/1954, p. 148) said or "developed" as Piaget and Kohlberg said. The access argument sometimes is one-sided as though only marginalized populations needed a good education and as though members of the dominant groups were getting one. This is true only in a gross comparative sense. It leaves aside the question, Who is looking after the moral education of dominant group members? One could argue that those who *most* need democratic enlightenment, especially a highly developed sense of justice, are those who occupy the board rooms, legislatures, court chambers, and faculty positions at prestigious universities. We are led back again, then, to the conclusion that *all* children, if they are to walk the democratic path with diverse others, require a high-quality education for freedom, justice, and equality. This applies equally to the powerless and the powerful.

Turning from Melos to Birmingham, recall that King's "Letter from Birmingham Jail" was written not to the dispossessed but to the affluent White clergy of Alabama who had published a statement to which he was then responding. He began the letter, "While confined here in the Birmingham city jail . . ." I came across your recent statement calling my present activities 'unwise and untimely.' . . . Since I feel that you are men of genuine good will and that your criticisms are sincerely set forth, I want to try to answer your statements in what I hope will be patient and reasonable terms" (1963a, p. 76). The "Letter," then, is an attempt to educate whom? These privileged readers. On what? On the matter of justice and injustice and the "inescapable network of mutuality" in which we are all "caught" (p. 77).

ACCESS TO WHAT?

Amid the struggle to win access to a quality school experience for students now excluded from it altogether, such as those in the Newark school, but also the mass of students in the mediocre "middle track" of the nation's schools, educators need to clarify and justify the particular kind of subject matter and experience to which access is desired. It does little good to argue for inclusion in a vacuum—that is, inclusion for its own sake. Needed also is concern for the kind of education to which inclusion is sought. Access *for whom* and *to what* need to work in tandem. I will turn to the second of these now, and outline a rudimentary anti-idiocy education. This should summarize much of this book.

The general idea is that a diverse society that is hoping to realize democratic ideals faces a challenging question: *How can we live together justly, in ways that are mutually satisfying, and which leave our differences, both individual and group, intact and our multiple identities recognized?* Such a society should assure all students, in culturally and developmentally appropriate ways, access to serious work on this question. This is an education that aims for enlightened political engagement—for entry into a state of mind and conduct suitable for public life, for democratic living. The ever-present opposite is idiocy: a state of self- or family-centered absorption and withdrawal from the public square. Idiocy is the formidable opponent against which a high-quality curriculum is wielded, and the campaign against it is the compelling reason why access to an education for democracy is morally required regardless of one's eventual position in social hierarchies.

Access to what, specifically? Just one aspect of enlightened political engagement is toleration for beliefs and behaviors of which one disapproves. The tolerant stance, writes Patricia Avery (2002, p. 114), "is neither one of approval nor indifference—it is an acknowledgement of everyone's right to basic civil liberties in a democracy." Granted, we hope for more than toleration. We hope for the ambitious moral development of a King, Hanh, Gandhi, or Jane Addams, to name four visionaries, especially given their ability to cut through conventional wisdom when needed and push it, opening and lovingly, toward justice. While hoping for more, educators should recognize that tolerance is no small achievement and is absolutely essential to democratic living. Those who forget history often forget this and then take tolerance for granted. When history is remembered, all the slaughter especially, we come to understand that, as Michael Walzer (1997) writes, toleration is sufficiently rare that "even the most grudging forms (of it) and precarious arrangements (for it) are very good things" (p. xi).

Walzer makes an additional point about the subjectivity and objectivity of toleration. "As an American Jew," he says, he grew up thinking of himself not as someone morally obliged to tolerate others but as an *object* of others' toleration. Thrown into a group that was often the object of intolerance, he dared not expect tolerance from others but certainly hoped for it, and he hoped for it in its simplest form: live and let live; peaceful coexistence. But, what of his moral and political obligation to tolerate others? Surely no one in a diverse society is let off that hook. "It was only much later," he continues, "that I recognized myself as a subject too, an agent called upon to tolerate others . . ." (1997, p. xi). (Reflecting on Walzer's story, I realize that I have never thought of myself as an object of toleration. I have regarded myself only as its agent. Here is one advantage of being a member of this society's most advantaged group: I do not even hope to be tolerated myself. There is simply no need for it.)

Tolerance is only one aspect of the educational aim, however. That aim can be divided into two general emphases dubbed "democratic enlightenment" and "political engagement" by Nie and his colleagues (1996). The first emphasis contains moral-cognitive attributes that enable—perhaps "require" is the better term—citizens to steer their engagement toward democratic ideals. Included here are knowledge of those ideals (e.g., toleration, liberty, equality, justice) as well as knowledge of current political facts, political attentiveness, and a well-developed sense of justice. The second emphasis, political engagement, contains attributes that enable citizens to actually participate in popular sovereignty—to engage in politics and influence public policy. Included are paying attention to political affairs (e.g., reading newspapers), voting, and participation in more difficult political activities, such as contacting political officials and attending political meetings. A citizen who does these things is better positioned to influence public policy than the citizen whose engagement begins and ends with watching political spectacles on television and/or voting.

Another way to characterize the prize is with reference to broad, sweeping aspects of the democratic citizen's life: participation, path, and pluralism. One concerns the kind of participation for which citizens need to be educated. Here is the tension between direct involvement in public life, on the one hand (through voting, organizing, campaigning, direct action, and so forth), and detached apathy or civic voyeurism on the other. A second concerns the citizen's outlook on democracy. Here is the tension between viewing democracy as a closed accomplishment needing mainly protection and an open path that people try to walk together in community service, deliberation, and political action. A third is coming to grips with pluralism. Here is the tension between diversity and assimilation. Contested is whether the "little publics" threaten or invigorate the "big public"—the overarching political community. The "advanced" idea of democracy is that *e pluribus unum* means the political one alongside (not instead of) the cultural many. With this meaning, difference is not a threat to but a necessary condition for a deeply democratic political community. For this reason diversity should be fostered, not merely tolerated.

Access to participation, path, and pluralism can be approached both outside and inside schools. Outside, young people need access to a variety of voluntary associations (temples, choirs, clubs, teams, etc.) and thereby access to other young people and responsible adults who are likely to be more diverse than one's family members. One's own perspective becomes one of several in the reflective mirror afforded by pluralism, and difference becomes a palpable feature of one's own life. Furthermore, one engages public problems—"public" because they stretch beyond one's own and one's family's problems—and thereby one might sense the "inescapable network of mutuality" (King, 1963a, p. 77) or "interbeing" (Hanh, 1988, p. 3). Additionally, one is exposed to norms of deliberating across difference; that is, one gains access to civility—mannerly conduct that allows conflict in a diverse group without threatening the group's existence. For these three reasons, government should support out-of-school youth associations, through grants and tax relief.

Inside schools, meanwhile, students should have access to curricular and extracurricular programs that aim for both sides of the citizenship coin: democratic enlightenment and democratic engagement. Students need access, that is, to coursework and participatory experiences in which democracy is studied and practiced in all its variety and in both its actual and ideal forms. Seminars and deliberations were the instructional approaches featured in this book for these two emphases. Enlarged understandings of powerful ideas, issues, and values is the aim of seminar; deciding on right action is the aim of deliberation. Several models of the latter were detailed: public policy deliberation (PPD) and structured academic controversy

(SAC) on the curricular front, and classroom meetings (Paley, 1992), student advisory councils (Shaheen, 1989), and Just Community school meetings (Power, Higgins, & Kohlberg, 1989) on the extracurricular front.

Access to deliberation, as we have seen, means access to well-led forums in which candid talk and serious listening across difference are encouraged. Difference is not only a social fact but a political fact, because power is involved. The plurality of ethnic, racial, class, and other social groups in a society is arrayed across a power hierarchy, and this challenges everyone's ability and willingness to listen. This is true especially for persons who were thrown into the more powerful positions, for members of these groups often are the most likely to deny the existence of a power hierarchy or, if acknowledged, to attribute it to achieved (e.g., hard work) rather than ascribed (e.g., race; gender) characteristics. Accordingly, strategies are needed especially for helping outsiders (e.g., Whites; middle-class people; Christians; men) listen to insiders (e.g., people of color; the poor; Hindus; women). Three were singled out here: epistemic privilege, humility, and caution. Each promises to give the more privileged discussants access to the vantage points, beliefs, and experiences of the more vulnerable discussants by combating the arrogance that, through the ages, has accompanied power. Doing so amounts not only to treating one another decently, allowing one another to be genuine. It also results in better ways of living together. This is because diversity is an asset in deliberation: It motivates citizens to justify their proposals with appeals to fairness, it enlarges their understanding of the problem at hand and the perspectives of different stakeholders, and it makes it more likely that one's own views will be subjected to challenge, thus stimulating moral development and affording enlarged understandings.

Schools are ideal places to educate citizens for democratic living in a diverse society. They are places where diverse children are congregated in a buzzing variety that does not exist in many other places, certainly not in private places like our homes. Schools are places where people from numerous private worlds and social positions come together in face-to-face contact around matters that are central to the problems of actually living together on common ground. When aimed at democratic ends and supported by the proper democratic circumstances, this interaction in schools can help children develop the habits of thinking and caring necessary for public life—the courtesies, tolerance, respect, sense of justice, and knack for forging public policy with others whether one likes them or not. If students are fortunate—if the right conditions, both social and psychological, are present and well used—they may even give birth to critical, postconventional consciousness and, thereby, to better futures.

CONCLUSION

Better futures. There is the point. Education represents "not only the development of children and youth," Dewey wrote (1985a, p. 85), "but also of the future society of which they will be the constituents." They achieve puberty, if they are fortunate, not only to fashion their own lives as they choose but to help achieve the kind of public life that secures the liberty to do just that, and in a way that allows others to do the same. Idiocy fights against this realization. It denies the interdependence of diversity and unity, of freedom and community, as though the former (diversity, liberty) was possible somehow without the latter (unity, community) and vice versa. Education for democracy has this realization as its central goal. It is to this that access for all should be assured.

Notes

Chapter 1: From Idiocy to Citizenship

1. Much has been written recently on the decline of community. See Bellah et al. (1985), DuBois (1903/1990), Kemmis (1995), Putnam (2000). Bender (1978) rejects the "decline" argument.

2. On mutuality, in addition to King see Hannah Arendt's *vita activa*, (1958), John Dewey's "conjoint living" (1916/1985a), Mohandas Gandhi's "satyagraha" (1951), and the Buddhist literature on interdependence (e.g., Trungpa, 1991).

3. Thich Naht Hanh here is commenting on *The Prajnaparamita Heart Sutra*, a collection of the Buddha's teachings that have been at the core of the monastic curriculum in Mahayana Buddhist countries (e.g., India, Tibet) for 2,000 years. Some version of the *Heart Sutra* is recited in virtually all Mahayana Buddhist sects.

4. See any publication of Plato's *Crito* (e.g., 1992b).

Chapter 2: Democracy and Difference

1. My thanks to Gloria Ladson-Billings (cf., 1995) for pointing me toward Vincent Harding's (1990) work.

2. See John Gray's (1992) devastating critique of the communitarian position. It prompted numerous responses in *Social Research* (fall 1994, *61* [3]).

3. Portions of this and the next section draw on themes developed in "Curriculum for Democracy" (Parker, 1996b), and the entire chapter is based on Parker (1996a).

4. I am referring especially to recent analyses of race relations and racial formation (Anzaldua [1987], Code [1991], hooks [1989], Omi & Winant [1986], Said [1978], and West [1993b]) and feminist critiques of the patriarchy that has suffused liberalism and Marxism alike (Collins [1990], Dietz [1992], Fraser [1997], and Fraser & Nicholson [1988]). This line of work is not brand new, of course. T. H. Marshall's great work on citizenship in 1964, *Class, Citizenship, and Social Development*, argued that "citizenship has itself become, in certain respects, the architect of social inequality" (p. 70).

5. While other democratic experiments have failed for other reasons (e.g., warfare, economic collapse, demagoguery), the American democracy could for this reason—our collective inability to work with both *unum* and *pluribus*.

Chapter 3: Toward Enlightened Political Engagement

1. The term is from Nie, Junn, and Stehlik-Barry (1996).
2. Among the best: Torney-Purta, Schwille, and Amadeo (1999) and Torney-Purta, Lehmann, Oswald, and Schulz (2001) gathered case studies of civic education in 28 nations and compared the civic knowledge and engagement of 14-year-olds in those nations; Niemi and Junn (1998) analyzed the effects of civics courses using data from the 1988 NAEP civics assessment; Hahn (1998) compared student political attitudes and school civics curriculum and instruction across five established democracies; Avery et al. (1992) explored adolescents' political tolerance; Kohlberg and his colleagues created and studied "just communities" in schools (Power, Higgins, & Kohlberg, 1989); Cogan and Derricott (1998) compared civic education policy in nine nations. Also, see the reviews by Avery (2002), Patrick (1999), Patrick & Hoge (1991), Hahn (1996), and Youniss, McLellan, and Yates (1997).
3. See the analyses of justice and caring in Katz, Noddings, and Strike (1999). This volume tries, in some chapters, to venture beyond the justice/caring dualism. See also Callan (1997).
4. These are Chapters 6 and 9, respectively, in my collection of influential works in democratic education since Dewey (Parker, 1996c).

Chapter 4: Promoting Justice: Two Views

1. This version was retrieved October 7, 2001 from the Jewish Virtual Library on the World Wide Web: *http://www.stanford.edu/group/King/speeches/*.
2. This approach is elaborated in Chapter 7.
3. *Crito* is included in Plato's *The Trial and Death of Socrates: Four Dialogues* (New York, Dover, 1992b).
4. Both Marx and Kohlberg are children of the Enlightenment—"moderns" and "universalists." A whole range of postmodern critics will challenge them on this basis alone. See Walzer (1983) on Marx, and Gilligan (1982) on Kohlberg.
5. See also Power, Higgins, and Kohlberg (1989), Gardner (1993), and Vygotsky (1978).
6. Related concepts and strategies are discussed in Chapter 5.
7. On the problem of inequity in discussion, much will be said later in this volume. See the following section on "reversibility" and, in the next chapter, the section called "Striving for Inclusion and Genuine Exchange." A good sampling of work on the matter, from different perspectives, would include Rawls (1971), Benhabib (1996), Gilligan (1982), Burbules (1993), Narayan (1988), Young (1990), and Delpit (1988).

Chapter 5: Can We Talk?

1. See Elisabeth Young-Bruehl's *The Anatomy of Prejudices* (1996). Her phenomenology of prejudice pluralizes Gordon Allport's earlier work on that sub-

ject (*The Nature of Prejudice*, 1954), which saw it as a general attitude. Young-Bruehl finds four prejudices: racism, anti-Semitism, sexism, and homophobia.

2. Excellent treatments of this point are found in Radencich and McKay (1995) and Cohen (1994).

3. The concept of discussion as an "occasion" is elaborated in Chapter 7. See Parker, Ninomiya, and Cogan (1999) for a multinational curriculum that centers on deliberation.

4. The literature on this point often centers on the work of Hannah Arendt (1958). See also Dewey (1927), Habermas (1989), and Mathews (1994).

5. These distinctions are from Dillon (1994). See also Gutmann and Thompson (1996).

6. See Gary Howard's (1999) insightful discussion of the "inner work" of teaching in multiracial schools.

7. There is the question, however, as to whether this liberal ideal of individual choice requires the presence of cultural diversity (e.g., Muslim children going to school with Baptist children) or, more simply, the range of differences contained within a single cultural group (e.g., diversity of individuals, all of whom are Muslim or all of whom are Baptist, such as differences among jobs and professions, political beliefs, friends, and marriage partners). See Walzer (1997), and Raz (1994).

Chapter 6: Making Publics, Finding Problems, Imagining Solutions

1. *National Issues Forum in the Classroom*, a program of the Kettering Foundation, is available from Kendall-Hunt, Dubuque, Iowa.

2. Washington State, for example, has a "Contemporary World Problems" course, and New York has a "Participation in Government" course. NIF materials have been used in both. In Seattle, NIF materials have been used in one way or another in each of the city's high schools.

3. *Choices* is available from Brown University, Providence, RI (http://www.choices.edu).

4. See also Oliver and Newmann (1967) and Oliver and Shaver (1974).

5. This section draws on Parker and Zumeta (1999).

6. See Stone (1997) and Wildavsky (1979).

7. See Wilson (1978).

8. Readers may wish to compare these criteria to those in Massialas (1996) and Oliver (1957).

Chapter 7: Learning to Lead Discussions

1. See, for example, Roberts et al. (1998) and Giroux (1993).

2. Social Science Education Consortium (2001), Boulder, CO.

3. This description of Structured Academic Controversy draws from Parker and Hess (2001).

4. The U.S. history booklets published as the *Public Issues Series* by the Social Science Education Consortium in Boulder, Colorado carefully tie case issues to enduring issues.

5. This video is available from the same source as the *April Morning* seminar discussed earlier (Social Science Education Consortium, 2001). See my analysis in Parker, 2001a.

References

Adair, V. C. (2001). Poverty and the (broken) promise of higher education. *Harvard Educational Review, 71*, 217–239.

Addams, J. (1913). Why women should vote. In F. Maule (Ed.), *Woman suffrage: History, arguments, and results* (pp. 1–12). New York: National American Woman Suffrage Association.

Adler, M. J. (1982). *The paideia proposal.* New York: Macmillan.

Al-Hibri, A. Y. (1999). Is western patriarchal feminism good for third world/minority women? In J. Cohen, M. Howard, & M. C. Nussbaum (Eds.), *Is multiculturalism bad for women? (Susan Moller Okin with respondents)* (pp. 41–46). Princeton, NJ: Princeton University Press.

Allport, G. W. (1954). *The nature of prejudice.* Cambridge, MA: Addison-Wesley.

Althusser, L. (1984). *Essays on ideology.* London: Verso.

American Association of University Women. (1992). *How schools shortchange girls.* Washington, DC: Author.

Annenberg Public Policy Center, University of Pennsylvania. (2001). *Student voices.* Philadelphia: Author.

Anyon, J. (1997). *Ghetto schooling: A political economy of urban educational reform.* New York: Teachers College Press.

Anzaldua, G. (1987). *Borderlands: La Frontera: The new mestiza.* San Francisco: Spinsters/Aunt Lute.

Apple, M. W. (1975). The hidden curriculum and the nature of conflict. In W. Pinar (Ed.), *Curriculum theorizing: The reconceptualists* (pp. 95–119). Berkeley, CA: McCutchan.

Arendt, H. (1958). *The human condition.* Chicago: University of Chicago Press.

Aristotle. (1958). *The politics of Aristotle* (E. Barker, Trans.). New York: Oxford University Press.

Aristotle. (1985). *Nicomachean ethics* (I. Irwin, Trans.). Indianapolis: Hackett.

Aronson, E., Blaney, N. T., Stephan, C., Sikes, J., & Snapp, M. (1978). *The Jigsaw classroom.* Beverly Hills, CA: Sage.

Asante, M. K. (1998). *The Afrocentric idea* (revised and expanded edition). Philadelphia: Temple University Press.

Association for Supervision and Curriculum Development. (1999). *How to conduct successful Socratic seminars* (videotape). Alexandria, VA: Author.

Avery, P. G. (2002). Political tolerance, democracy, and adolescents. In W. C. Parker (Ed.), *Education for democracy: Contexts, curricula, and assessments* (pp. 113–130). Greenwich, CT: Information Age.

168 References

Avery, P. G., Bird, K., Johnstone, S., Sullivan, J. L., & Thalhammer, K. (1992). Exploring political tolerance with adolescents. *Theory and Research in Social Education, 20,* 386–420.

Bahmueller, C. F. (Ed.). (1991). *Civitas: A framework for civic education.* Calabasas, CA: Center for Civic Education & National Council for the Social Studies.

Baldwin, J. A.(1963). *The fire next time.* New York: Dell.

Baldwin, J. A. (1988). A talk to teachers. In R. Simonson & S. Walker (Eds.), *Multicultural literacy* (pp. 1–15). St. Paul, MN: Graywolf Press.

Banfield, E. C. (1958). *The moral basis of a backward society.* New York: Free Press.

Banks, J. A. (1996). Foreword. In W. C. Parker (Ed.), *Educating the democratic mind* (pp. xi–xiii). Albany: State University of New York Press.

Banks, J. A. (1997). *Educating citizens in a multicultural society.* New York: Teachers College Press.

Banks, J. A. (2002). Teaching for diversity and unity in a democratic multicultural society. In W. C. Parker (Ed.), *Education for democracy: Contexts, curricula, assessments* (pp. 131–150). Greenwich, CT: Information Age.

Banks, J. A., Cookson, P., Gay, G., Hawley, W. D., Irvine, J. J., Nieto, S., Schofield, J. W., & Stephan, W. G. (2001). *Diversity within unity: Essential principles for teaching and learning in a multicultural society.* Seattle: Center for Multicultural Education, University of Washington.

Barber, B. R. (1988). *The conquest of politics.* Princeton, NJ: Princeton University Press.

Barr, R., Barth, J., & Shermis, S. (1977). *Defining the social studies.* Washington, DC: National Council for the Social Studies.

Beauvoir, S. de (1948). *The ethics of ambiguity.* New York: Citadel.

Beiner, R. S. (1984). *Political judgement.* Chicago: University of Chicago Press.

Bellah, R. N., Madsen, R., Sullivan, W. M., Swidler, A., & Tipton, S. M. (1985). *Habits of the heart: Individualism and commitment in American life.* Berkeley: University of California Press.

Bender, T. (1978). *Community and social change in America.* Baltimore: Johns Hopkins University Press.

Benhabib, S. (Ed.). (1996). *Democracy and difference: Contesting the boundaries of the political.* Princeton, NJ: Princeton University Press.

Berkowitz, M. (1981). A critical appraisal of the educational and psychological perspectives on moral discussion. *Journal of Educational Thought, 15,* 20–33.

Berlin, I. (1998). *The proper study of mankind.* New York: Farrar, Straus & Giroux.

Berman, P. (2001, October 22). Terror and liberalism. *The American Prospect, 12,* 18–23.

Berry, C. J. (1989). *The idea of a democratic community.* New York: St. Martin's Press.

Bickmore, K. (1993). Learning inclusion/inclusion in learning: Citizenship education for a pluralistic society. *Theory and Research in Social Education, 21,* 341–384.

Blankenship, G. (1990). Classroom climate, global knowledge, global attitudes, political attitudes. *Theory and Research in Social Education, 18,* 363–386.

Blatt, M., & Kohlberg, L. (1975). The effects of classroom moral discussion upon children's moral judgment. *Journal of Moral Education, 4,* 129–161.

Bohm, D. (1996). *On dialogue*. London: Routledge.

Boyte, H. (1994). Review of the book: *Civitas: A framework for civic education. Teachers College Record, 95*, 414–418.

Bridges, D. (1979). *Education, democracy and discussion*. Atlantic Highlands, NJ: Humanities Press.

Brown, A. (1996). Design experiments: Theoretical and methodological challenges in creating complex interventions in classroom settings. *Journal of the Learning Sciences, 2*, 141–178.

Burbules, N. C. (1993). *Dialogue in teaching*. New York: Teachers College Press.

Butts, R. F. (1980). *The revival of civic learning*. Bloomington, IN: Phi Delta Kappa Educational Foundation.

Callan, E. (1997). *Creating citizens*. Oxford, UK: Clarendon.

Carson, C., & Shepard, K. (Eds.). (2001). *A call to conscience: The landmark speeches of Dr. Martin Luther King, Jr.* New York: Warner Books.

Center for Civic Education. (1994). *National standards for civics and government*. Calabasas, CA: Author.

Cherryholmes, C. H. (1980). Social knowledge and citizenship education: Two views of truth and criticism. *Curriculum Inquiry, 10*, 115–151.

Clark, B. R. (1960). The "cooling-out" function in higher education. *American Journal of Sociology, 65*, 569–576.

Clark, S. (1984). Interview of November 17, 1978, conducted by and reported in A. D. Morris, *The origins of the civil rights movement*. New York: Free Press.

Code, L. (1991). *What can she know? Feminist theory and the construction of knowledge*. Ithaca, NY: Cornell University Press.

Cogan, J., & Derricott, R. (Eds.). (1998). *Citizenship for the 21st century: An international perspective on education*. London: Kogan-Page.

Cohen, E. G. (1994). *Designing groupwork: Strategies for the heterogeneous classroom* (2nd ed.). New York: Teachers College Press.

Collier, A. (1981). Scientific socialism and the question of socialist values. In K. Nielsen & S. C. Patten (Eds.), *Marx and morality* (pp. 121–154). Guelph, Canada: Canadian Association for Publishing in Philosophy.

Collins, P. H. (1990). *Black feminist thought*. New York: Routledge.

Commission on the Reorganization of Secondary Education of the National Education Association, Committee on Social Studies. (1916). *The social studies in secondary education* (Bureau of Education Bulletin No. 28). Washington, DC: U.S. Government Printing Office.

Converse, P. E. (1972). Change in the American electorate. In A. Campbell & P. E. Converse (Eds.), *The human meaning of social change* (pp. 263–337). New York: Russell Sage Foundation.

Cormack, M. J. (1992). *Ideology*. Ann Arbor: University of Michigan Press.

Delli Carpini, M. X. D., & Keeter, S. (1996). *What Americans know about politics and why it matters*. Chicago: University of Chicago Press.

Delpit, L. D. (1988). The silenced dialogue: Power and pedagogy in educating other people's children. *Harvard Educational Review, 58*, 280–298.

Delpit, L. D. (1995). *Other people's children: Cultural conflict in the classroom*. New York: The New Press.

Dewey, J. (1897). *My pedagogic creed.* New York: E. L. Kellogg & Co.

Dewey, J. (1927). *The public and its problems.* Chicago: Swallow.

Dewey, J. (1985a). *Democracy and education* (Vol. 9). In J. A. Boydston (Ed.), *John Dewey, the middle works, 1899–1924.* Carbondale: Southern Illinois University Press. (Original work published 1916)

Dewey, J. (1985b). *How we think, and selected essays* (Vol. 6). In J. A. Boydston (Ed.), *John Dewey, the middle works, 1899–1924.* Carbondale: Southern Illinois University press. (Original work published 1910)

Dietz, M. G. (1992). Feminism and theories of citizenship. In C. Mouffe (Ed.), *Dimensions of radical democracy: Pluralism, citizenship, community* (pp. 63–85). London: Verso.

Dillon, J. T. (Ed.). (1994). *Deliberation in education and society.* Norwood, NJ: Ablex.

Doble, J. (1996). *The story of NIF: The effects of deliberation.* Dayton, OH: Kettering Foundation.

DuBois, W. E. B. (1990). *The souls of black folk.* New York: Vintage. (Original work published 1903)

Dyson, M. E. (2001). *I may not get there with you.* New York: Touchstone.

Ehman, L. H. (1970). Normative discourse and attitude change in the social studies classroom. *The High School Journal, 54,* 76–83.

Eisner, E. W. (1985). *The educational imagination.* New York: Macmillan.

Engle, S. H. (1960). Decision making: The heart of social studies instruction. *Social Education, 24,* 301–304, 306.

Engle, S. H., & Ochoa, A. S. (1988). *Education for democratic citizenship.* New York: Teachers College Press.

Etzioni, A. (1993). *The spirit of community: Rights, responsibilities, and the communitarian agenda.* New York: Crown Publishers.

Evans, R. W., & Saxe, D. W. (Eds.). (1996). *Handbook on teaching social issues.* Washington, DC: National Council for the Social Studies.

Evans, S. M., & Boyte, H. C. (1992). *Free spaces: The sources of democratic change in America.* Chicago: University of Chicago Press.

Farkas, S., & Friedman, W. (1996). *The public's capacity for deliberation.* New York: Public Agenda.

Fast, H. (1961). *April Morning.* New York: Bantam.

Fenton, E. (1967). *The new social studies.* New York: Holt, Rinehart & Winston.

Fishkin, J. S. (1991). *Democracy and deliberation.* New Haven, CT: Yale University Press.

Foucault, M. (1977). *Discipline and punish* (A. Sheridan, Trans.). New York: Random House.

Fraenkel, J. R. (1980). *Helping students think and value: Strategies for teaching the social studies* (2nd ed.). Englewood Cliffs, NJ: Prentice Hall.

Fraser, N. (1995). Politics, culture, and the public space: Toward a post-modern conception. In L. Nicholson & S. Seidman (Eds.), *Social postmodernism: Beyond identity politics* (pp. 287–312). Cambridge, UK: Cambridge University Press.

Fraser, N. (1997). *Justice interruptus: Critical reflections on the "postsocialist" condition.* New York: Routledge.

Fraser, N., & Nicholson, L. (1988). Social criticism without philosophy: An encounter between feminism and postmodernism. In A. Ross (Ed.), *Universal abandon? The politics of postmodernism* (pp. 83–104). Minneapolis: University of Minnesota Press.

Frazier, E. F. (1963). *The Negro church in America*. New York: Schocken.

Freedom House. (2001). *Freedom in the world: The annual survey of political rights and civil liberties*. Washington, DC: Author.

Freire, P. (1970). *Pedagogy of the oppressed*. New York: Seabury.

Fukuyama, F. (1992). *The end of history and the last man*. New York: Macmillan.

Gadamer, H. G. (1984). *Truth and method*. New York: Crossroads.

Gagnon, P. (1987). *Democracy's untold story*. Washington, DC: American Federation of Teachers.

Gagnon, P. (1996). History's role in civic education. In W. C. Parker (Ed.), *Educating the democratic mind* (pp. 241–262). Albany: State University of New York Press.

Galbraith, J. K. (1998). *The affluent society* (40th anniversary edition). Boston: Houghton Mifflin.

Gandhi, M. K. (1951). *Non-violent resistance (satyagraha)*. New York: Schocken.

Garcia, E. E., & Gonzalez, R. (1995). Issues in systematic reform for culturally and linguistically diverse students. *Teachers College Record, 96*, 418–431.

Gardner, H. (1993). *Multiple intelligences: The theory in practice*. New York: Basic Books.

Gay, G. (2000). *Culturally responsive teaching*. New York: Teachers College Press.

Geis, S., Hilton, J., & Plitt, W. (1976). School reform: Catching tigers in red weather. *Educational Studies, 7*, 244–257.

Gibbs, J. C. (1979). Kohlberg's moral stage theory: A Piagetian revision. *Human Development, 22*, 89–112.

Gilligan, C. (1982). *In a different voice: Psychological theory and women's development*. Cambridge, MA: Harvard University Press.

Giroux, H. (1993). *Living dangerously: Multiculturalism and the politics of difference*. New York: Peter Lang.

Glendon, M. A. (1991). *Rights talk*. New York: Free Press.

Goffman, E. (1952). Cooling the mark out: Some aspects of adaptation to failure. *Psychiatry, 15*, 451–463.

Goldhaber, M. D. (2000, October 25). Cell-block voting bloc? Felons sue for suffrage. *The Recorder*, pp. 3–4. Retrieved October 30, 2000 from http://web/lexis-nexis.com/universe/document

Goodlad, J. I. (1984). *A place called school*. New York: McGraw-Hill.

Goodstein, L. (2001, September 15). Falwell's finger-pointing inappropriate, Bush says. *The New York Times on the web*. Retrieved September 16, 2001, from: http://www.nytimes.com.

Gould, C. C. (1996). Diversity and democracy: Representing differences. In S. Benhabib (Ed.), *Democracy and difference* (pp. 171–186). Princeton, NJ: Princeton University Press.

Gray, D. (1989). Putting minds to work. *American Educator, 13*(3), 16–23.

Gray, J. (July 3, 1992). Against the new liberalism. *London Times Literary Supplement*, pp. 13–15.

Great Books Foundation. (1990). *Introduction to great books*. Chicago: Author.

Great Books Foundation. (1999). *An introduction to shared inquiry: A handbook for Junior Great Books leaders* (4th ed.). Chicago: Author.

Greene, M. (1993). Diversity and inclusion: Toward a curriculum for human beings. *Teachers College Record, 95*, 211–221.

Greene, M. (1995). *Releasing the imagination: Essays on education, the arts, and social change*. San Francisco: Jossey-Bass.

Greene, M. (1996). Plurality, diversity, and the public space. In A. Odlenquist (Ed.), *Can democracy be taught?* (pp. 27–44). Bloomington, IN: Phi Delta Kappa.

Gutmann, A. (1999). *Democratic education* (2nd ed.) Princeton, NJ: Princeton University Press.

Gutmann, A., & Thompson, D. (1996). *Democracy and disagreement*. Cambridge, MA: Harvard University Press.

Habermas, J. (1971). *Knowledge and human interests* (J. J. Shapiro, Trans.). Boston: Beacon Press.

Habermas, J. (1989). *The structural transformation of the public sphere: An inquiry into a category of bourgeois society* (T. Burger & F. Lawrence, Trans.). Cambridge: MIT Press.

Habermas, J. (1990). *Moral consciousness and communicative action*. Cambridge: MIT Press.

Hahn, C. L. (1996). Research on issues-centered social studies. In R. W. Evans & D. W. Saxe (Eds.), *Handbook on teaching social issues* (pp. 25–41). Washington, DC: National Council for the Social Studies.

Hahn, C. L. (1998). *Becoming political*. Albany: State University of New York Press.

Hahn, C. L., & Tocci, C. M. (1990). Classroom climate and controversial issues discussions: A five nation study. *Theory and Research in Social Education, 18*, 344–362.

Halberstam, D. (1998). *The children*. New York: Random House.

Hampshire, S. (1977). Epilogue. In S. Hampshire & L. Kolakowski, *The socialist idea* (pp. 246–249). London: Quarter.

Hanh, T. N. (1988). *The heart of understanding*. Berkeley: Parallax.

Hanh, T. N. (2001, October). What I would say to Osama bin Laden. *Changemakers.Net Journal*. Retrieved October 14, 2001, from: http://www. changemakers.net.

Hanna, P. R. (1936). *Youth serves the community*. New York: D. Appleton-Century.

Harding, V. (1990). *Hope and history: Why we must share the story of the movement*. Maryknoll, NY: Orbis.

Haroutunian-Gordon, S. (1988). Was Socrates a "Socratic" teacher? *Educational Theory, 38*, 213–224.

Haroutunian-Gordon, S. (1991). *Turning the soul*. Chicago: University of Chicago Press.

Harrington, M. (1963). *The other America*. New York: Macmillan.

Harris, D. (2002). Classroom assessment of civic discourse. In W. C. Parker (Ed.), *Education for democracy: Contexts, curricula, and assessments* (pp. 211–232). Greenwich, CT: Information Age.

Harwood Group. (1993). *Meaningful chaos: How people form relationships with public concerns.* Dayton, OH: Kettering Foundation.

Heath, S. B., & McLaughlin, M. W. (Eds.). (1993). *Identity and inner-city youth.* New York: Teachers College Press.

Hess, D. (2002). Discussing controversial public issues in secondary social studies classrooms: Learning from skilled teachers. *Theory and Research in Social Education, 30,* 10–41.

Hess, K. (1979). *Community technology.* New York: Harper & Row.

Hill, P. T., Pierce, L. C., & Guthrie, J. W. (1997). *Reinventing public education.* Chicago: University of Chicago Press.

Hochschild, J. L. (1995). *Facing up to the American dream: Race, class, and the soul of the nation.* Princeton, NJ: Princeton University Press.

Hochschild, J. L., & Scovronick, N. (2002). Democratic education and the American Dream: One, some, and all. In W. C. Parker (Ed.), *Education for democracy: Contexts, curricula, and assessments* (pp. 3–26). Greenwich, CT: Information Age.

Hollins, E. R., King, J. E., & Hayman, W. C. (Eds.). (1994). *Teaching diverse populations.* Albany: State University of New York Press.

hooks, b. (1989). *Talking back.* Boston: South End Press.

hooks, b. (2000a). *All about love: New visions.* New York: William Morrow.

hooks, b. (2000b). *Where we stand: Class matters.* New York: Routledge.

Howard, G. R. (1999). *We can't teach what we don't know: White teachers, multiracial schools.* New York: Teachers College Press.

Hunt, M. P., & Metcalf, L. E. (1955). *Teaching high school social studies: Problems in reflective thinking and social understanding.* New York: Harper & Row.

Hutchins, R. M. (1952). *The great conversation: The substance of a liberal education.* Chicago: Encyclopaedia Britannica.

Jackson, P. W. (1968). *Life in the classroom.* New York: Holt, Rinehart & Winston.

Jacobs, J. (1961). *The death and life of great American cities.* New York: Vintage.

Jacoby, R. (1975). *Social amnesia.* Boston: Beacon Press.

James, W. (1958). *Talks to teachers.* New York: W. W. Norton. (Talks originally given in 1892)

Jay, J. (1937). Federalist No. 2. In J. Madison, A. Hamilton, & J. Jay (Eds.), *The Federalist* (pp. 7–12). New York: Modern Library. (Original work published 1787)

Jefferson, T. (1954). *Notes on the State of Virginia.* New York: W. W. Norton. (Original work published 1787)

Johnson, C. (1998). *Dreamer.* New York: Simon & Schuster.

Johnson, D. W., & Johnson, R. T. (1985). Classroom conflict: Controversy vs. debate in learning groups. *American Educational Research Journal, 22,* 237–256.

Johnson, D. W., & Johnson, R. T. (1988). Critical thinking through structured controversy. *Educational Leadership, 45*(8), 58–64.

Kasarda, J. D. (1993). Cities as places where people live and work: Urban change and neighborhood distress. In H. G. Cisneros (Ed.), *Interwoven destinies: Cities and the nation* (pp. 81–124). New York: W. W. Norton.

Katz, M. S., Noddings, N., & Strike, K. A. (Eds.). (1999). *Justice and caring: The search for common ground in education.* New York: Teachers College Press.

Kegan, R. (1982). *The evolving self.* Cambridge, MA: Harvard University Press.

Kelly, T. E. (1989). Leading class discussions of controversial issues. *Social Education, 53,* 368–370.

Kelsey, G. (1965). *Racism and the Christian understanding of man.* New York: Scribner.

Kemmis, D. (1995). *The good city and the good life.* Boston: Houghton Mifflin.

Kerr, D. (1997). Toward a democratic rhetoric of schooling. In J. I. Goodlad & T. J. McMannon (Eds.), *The public purpose of education and schooling* (pp. 73–83). San Francisco: Jossey-Bass.

Khyentse, D. (1993). *Enlightened courage.* Ithaca, NY: Snow Lion.

King, M. L., Jr. (1958). *Stride toward freedom.* New York: Harper & Row.

King, M. L., Jr. (1963a). Letter from Birmingham Jail. In *Why we can't wait* (pp. 76–95). New York: Mentor.

King, M. L., Jr. (1963b, August). *I have a dream* (address). The Martin Luther King, Jr. Papers Project at Stanford University. Retrieved October 27, 2000 from the World Wide Web. Available: http://www.stanford.edu/group/King/speeches/.

King, M. L., Jr. (1963c). *Why we can't wait.* New York: Montor.

King, M. L., Jr. (1964, December). *Address delivered in acceptance of the Nobel Peace Prize.* The Martin Luther King, Jr. Papers Project at Stanford University. Retrieved August 21, 2001 from the World Wide Web. Available: http://www.stanford.edu/group/King/speeches/.

King, M. L., Jr. (1967a, April). *Beyond Vietnam* (address). The Martin Luther King, Jr. Papers Project at Stanford University. Retrieved January 16, 2000 from the World Wide Web. Available: http://www.stanford.edu/group/King/speeches/.

King, M. L., Jr. (1967b, August). *Where do we go from here?* (address). The Martin Luther King, Jr. Papers Project at Stanford University. Retrieved January 16, 2000 from the World Wide Web. Available: http://www.stanford.edu/group/King/speeches/.

King, M. L., Jr. (1967c). *Where do we go from here: Chaos or community?* Boston: Beacon Press.

Kohlberg, L. (1971). From is to ought: How to commit the naturalistic fallacy and get away with it in the study of moral development. In T. Mischel (Ed.), *Cognitive development and epistemology* (pp. 151–235). New York: Academic Press.

Kohlberg, L. (1979). Justice as reversibility. In P. Laslett & J. Fishkin (Eds.), *Philosophy, politics and society* (pp. 257–272). New Haven, CT: Yale University Press.

Kohlberg, L., Levine, C., & Hewer, A. (1984a). The current formulation of the theory. In L. Kohlberg (Ed.), *Essays on moral development* (Vol. 11). *The psychology of moral development: The nature and validity of moral stages* (pp. 212–319). San Francisco: Harper & Row.

Kohlberg, L., Levine, C., & Hewer, A. (1984b). Synopses and detailed replies to critics. In L. Kohlberg (Ed.), *Essays on moral development* (Vol. 11). *The psychology of moral development: The nature and validity of moral states* (pp. 320–386). San Francisco: Harper & Row.

Kohlberg, L., & Mayer, R. (1972). Development as the aim of education. *Harvard Educational Review, 42,* 451–496.

Kozol, J. (1992). *Savage inequalities.* New York: HarperCollins.

Kurth-Schai, R. (1992). Ecology and equity: Toward the rational reenchantment of schools and society. *Educational Theory, 42*, 147–163.

Kymlicka, W. (1995). *Multicultural citizenship: A liberal theory of minority rights.* Oxford, UK: Clarendon.

Kymlicka, W. (1999). Education for citizenship. *The School Field, 20*(1/2), 9–35.

Ladson-Billings, G. (1995). Toward a theory of culturally relevant pedagogy. *American Educational Research Journal, 32*, 465–491.

Lapham, L. (2001, December). "Res Publica," *Harper's Magazine,* pp. 8–11.

Lazarsfeld, P., Berlson, B., & Gaudet, H. (1944). *The people's choice: How the voter makes up his mind in a presidential campaign.* New York: Columbia University Press.

Lee, G. C. (1965). *Education and democratic ideals.* New York: Harcourt, Brace & World.

Levin, M., Newmann, F. M., & Oliver, D. W. (1969). *A law and social science curriculum based on the analysis of public issues (final report)* (HS 058. Grant no. 310142). Washington, DC: U.S. Government Printing Office.

Levstik, L. S., & Barton, K. C. (2001). *Doing history: Investigating with children in elementary and middle schools* (2nd ed.). Mahwah, NJ: Erlbaum.

Lortie, D. C. (1975). *Schoolteacher.* Chicago: University of Chicago Press.

Lourde, A. (1984). *Sister outsider: Essays and speeches.* New York: Crossing Press.

Machiavelli, N. (1947). *The Prince* (T. G. Bergin, Trans.). New York: Appleton-Century-Crofts.

Madison, J. (1937). Federalist No. 10. In Madison, J., Hamilton, A., & Jay, J, *The Federalist* (pp. 53–62). New York: Modern Library. (Original work published 1787)

Mamdani, M. (2001). *When victims become killers.* Princeton: Princeton University Press.

Marshall, T. H. (1964). *Class, citizenship and social development.* New York: Doubleday.

Marx, K. (1990). *Capital* (B. Fowkes, Trans.). Vol. 1. New York: Penguin Classics. (Original work published 1867).

Massialas, B. G. (1996). Criteria for issues-centered content selection. In R. W. Evans & D. W. Saxe (Eds.), *Handbook on teaching social issues* (pp. 44–50). Washington, DC: National Council for the Social Studies.

Massialas, B. G., & Cox, C. B. (1966). *Inquiry in social studies.* New York: McGraw-Hill.

Mathews, D. (1994). *Politics for people: Finding a responsible public voice.* Urbana: University of Illinois Press.

Matynia, E. (1994). Women after communism: A bitter freedom. *Social Research, 61*, 351–377.

McIntosh, P. (1997). White privilege: Unpacking the invisible knapsack. In V. Cyrus (Ed.), *Experiencing race, class, and gender in the United States* (pp. 194–198). New York: McGraw-Hill.

McNeil, L. (1988). *Contradictions of control.* New York: Routledge.

Meier, D. (1995). *The power of their ideas.* Boston: Beacon Press.

Merton, R. K. (1968). *Social theory and social structure.* New York: Free Press.

Miller, B., & Singleton, L. (1997). *Preparing citizens: Linking authentic assessment and instruction in civic/law-related education*. Boulder, CO: Social Science Education Consortium.

Morris, A. D. (1984). *The origins of the civil rights movement*. New York: Free Press.

Morrison, T. (1992). *Playing in the dark: Whiteness and the literary imagination*. Cambridge, MA: Harvard University Press.

Moses, G. (1997). *Revolution of conscience: Martin Luther King, Jr., and the philosophy of nonviolence*. New York: Guilford.

Mosher, R., Kenny, R. A., Jr., & Garrod, A. (1994). *Preparing for citizenship: Teaching youth to live democratically*. Westport, CT: Praeger.

Mouffe, C. (Ed.). (1992). *Dimensions of radical democracy*. London: Verso.

Narayan, U. (1988). Working together across difference: Some considerations on emotions and political practice. *Hypatia, 3*(2), 31–47.

National Assessment Governing Board. (1997). *NAEP Civics 1998*. Washington, DC: Author.

National Issues Forum. (1990). *Remedies for racial inequality: Why progress has stalled, what should be done*. Dubuque, IA: Kendall-Hunt.

Newmann, F. M. (1975). *Education for citizen action: Challenge for the secondary curriculum*. Berkeley: McCutchan.

Newmann, F. M. (1989). Reflective civic participation. *Social Education, 53*, 357–360, 366.

Newmann, F. M. & Associates. (1996). *Authentic achievement*. San Francisco: Jossey-Bass.

Nie, N. H., Junn, J., & Stehlik-Barry, K. (1996). *Education and democratic citizenship in America*. Chicago: University of Chicago Press.

Niemi, R. G., & Junn, J. (1998). *Civic education: What makes students learn*. New Haven, CT: Yale University Press.

Noddings, N. (1992). *The challenge to care in schools*. New York: Teachers College Press.

Oakeshott, M. (1967). *Rationalism in politics*. London: Methuen.

Okihiro, G. Y. (1994). *Margins and mainstream: Asians in American history and culture*. Seattle: University of Washington Press.

Okin, S. M. (1999). Is multiculturalism bad for women? In J. Cohen, M. Howard, & M. C. Nussbaum (Eds.), *Is multiculturalism bad for women? (Susan Moller Okin with respondents)* (pp. 9–24). Princeton, NJ: Princeton University Press.

Oliver, D. W. (1957). The selection of content in the social sciences. *Harvard Educational Review, 27*, 271–300.

Oliver, D. W., & Newmann, F. M. (1967). *Taking a stand: A guide to clear discussion of public issues*. Middletown, CT: Xerox Corporation/American Education Publications.

Oliver, D. W., Newmann, F. M., & Singleton, L. R. (1992). Teaching public issues in the secondary school classroom. *The Social Studies, 83*, 100–103.

Oliver, D. W., & Shaver, J. P. (1974). *Teaching public issues in the high school*. Logan: Utah State University Press. (Originally published by Houghton Mifflin, Boston, 1966)

Omi, M., & Winant, H. (1986). *Racial formation in the United States*. New York: Routledge.

Onosko, J. J. (1991). Barriers to the promotion of higher order thinking in social studies. *Theory and Research in Social Education, 19,* 341–366.

Osborne, K. (1995). Review of the book: *Democratic teacher education: Programs, processes, problems, and prospects. The Canadian Journal of Higher Education, 25,* 119–123.

Paley, V. G. (1992). *You can't say you can't play.* Cambridge, MA: Harvard University Press.

Pallas, A. M., Natriello, G., & McDill, E. L. (1989). The changing nature of the disadvantaged population: Current dimensions and future thrends. *Educational Researcher, 18,* 16–22.

Parker, W. C. (1996a). "Advanced" ideas about democracy: Toward a pluralist conception of citizen education. *Teachers College Record, 98,* 104–125.

Parker, W. C. (1996b). Curriculum for democracy. In R. Soder (Ed.), *Democracy, education, and the schools* (pp. 182–210). San Francisco: Jossey-Bass.

Parker, W. C. (Ed.). (1996c). *Educating the democratic mind.* Albany: State University of New York Press.

Parker, W. C. (2001a). Classroom discussion: Models for leading seminars and deliberations. *Social Education, 65,* 111–115.

Parker, W. C. (2001b). *Social studies in elementary education* (11th ed.). Upper Saddle River, NJ: Merrill/Prentice Hall.

Parker, W. C., & Hess, D. (2001). Teaching with and for discussion. *Teaching and Teacher Education, 17,* 273–289.

Parker, W. C., McDaniel, J. E., & Valencia, S. W. (1991). Helping students think about public issues. *Social Education, 55,* 41–44, 67.

Parker, W. C., Ninomiya, A., & Cogan, J. (1999). Educating "world citizens": Toward multinational curriculum development. *American Educational Research Journal, 36,* 117–145.

Parker, W. C., & Zumeta, W. (1999). Toward an aristocracy of everyone: Policy study in the high school curriculum. *Theory and Research in Social Education, 27,* 9–44.

Patrick, J. J. (1999). Education for constructive engagement of citizens in democratic civil society and government. In C. F. Bahmueller & J. J. Patrick (Eds.), *Principles and practices of education for democratic citizenship: International perspectives and projects* (pp. 41–60). Bloomington, IN: ERIC Clearinghouse for Social Studies/Social Science Education.

Patrick, J. J., & Hoge, J. D. (1991). Teaching government, civics, and law. In J. P. Shaver (Ed.), *Handbook of research on social studies teaching and learning* (pp. 427–436). New York: Macmillan.

Patrick, J. J., Vontz, T. S., & Nixon, W. A. (2002). Issue-centered education for democracy through *Project Citizen.* In W. C. Parker (Ed.), *Education for democracy: Contexts, curricula, assessments* (pp. 93–112). Greenwich, CT: Information Age.

Perry, T., & Delpit, L. (Eds.). (1998). *The real Ebonics debate: Power, language, and the education of African-American children.* Boston: Beacon Press.

Phillips, A. (1991). *Engendering democracy.* University Park: Pennsylvania State University Press.

Phillips, A. (1993). *Democracy and difference*. University Park: Pennsylvania State University Press.

Phillips, A. (1995). *The politics of presence: Issues in democracy and group representation*. Oxford, UK: Oxford University Press.

Piaget, J. (1965). *The moral judgement of the child*. New York: Free Press.

Plato. (1956). *Protagorás and Meno* (W. K. C. Guthrie, Trans.). New York: Penguin.

Plato (1992a). *The republic* (G.M.A. Grube, Trans.). Indianapolis: Hackett.

Plato. (1992b). Crito. In *The trial and death of Socrates: Four dialogues* (pp. 43–54). New York: Dover.

Power, F. C., Higgins, A., & Kohlberg, L. (1989). *Lawrence Kohlberg's approach to moral education*. New York: Columbia University Press.

Pratt, R. (Ed.). (2000). *The condition of education, 2000*. Washington, DC: U. S. Government Printing Office.

Pratte, R. (1988). *The civic imperative: Examining the need for civic education*. New York: Teachers College Press.

Putnam, R. D. (1994). *Making democracy work: Civic traditions in modern Italy*. Princeton, NJ: Princeton University Press.

Putnam, R. D. (2000). *Bowling alone: The collapse and revival of American community*. New York: Simon & Schuster.

Radencich, M. C., & McKay, L. J. (1995). *Flexible grouping for literacy in the elementary grades*. Boston: Allyn & Bacon.

Ravitch, D. (2000). *Left back: A century of failed school reforms*. New York: Simon & Schuster.

Rawls, J. (1971). *A theory of justice*. Cambridge, MA: Harvard University Press.

Raz, J. (1994, Winter). Multiculturalism: A liberal perspective. *Dissent*, 67–79.

Reiman, J. H. (1981). The possibility of a Marxian theory of justice. In K. Nielsen & S. C. Patten (Eds.), *Marx and morality* (pp. 307–322). Guelph, Canada: Canadian Association for Publishing in Philosophy.

Roberts, T., & the staff of the National Paideia Center. (1998). *The power of paideia schools*. Alexandria, VA: Association for Supervision and Curriculum Development.

Rorty, R. (1999). *Philosophy and social hope*. New York: Penguin.

Rosenblum, N. L. (1994). Civil societies: Liberalism and the moral uses of pluralism. *Social Research, 61*, 539–562.

Rossi, J. A. (1995). In-depth study in an issues-oriented social studies classroom. *Theory and Research in Social Education, 23*, 88–120.

Rugg, H. (Ed.) (1939). *Democracy and the curriculum*. New York: Appleton-Century.

Sadker, M. P., & Sadker, D. M. (1994). *Failing at fairness: How America's schools cheat girls*. New York: Scribner.

Said, E. (1978). *Orientalism*. New York: Pantheon.

Sartre, J.-P. (1948). *The wall* (L. Alexander, Trans.). New York: New Directions.

Schlesinger, A. M. Jr. (1992). *The disuniting of America: Reflections on a multicultural society*. New York: W. W. Norton.

Schumpeter, J. (1950). *Capitalism, socialism, and democracy* (3rd ed.). New York: Harper & Row.

Schwab, J. J. (1970). *The practical: A language for curriculum.* Washington, DC: National Education Association.

Schwab, J. (1978). Eros and education: A discussion of one aspect of discussion. In I. Westbury & N. Will (Eds.), *Science, curriculum, and liberal education: Selected essays* (pp. 105–132). Chicago: University of Chicago Press.

Sennett, R. (1974). *The fall of public man.* New York: W. W. Norton.

Shaheen, J. C. (1989). Participatory citizenship in the elementary grades. *Social Education, 53,* 361–363.

Shaver, J. P., Davis, O. L. Jr., & Helburn, S. W. (1979). The status of social studies education: Impressions from three NSF studies. *Social Education, 43,* 150–153.

Shulman, L. S. (1986). Those who understand: Knowledge growth in teaching. *Educational Researcher, 15,* 4–14.

Siegel, L. (1977). Children and adolescents' reactions to the assassination of Martin Luther King: A study of political socialization. *Developmental Psychology, 13,* 284–285.

Sizemore, B. (1972). Is there a case for separate schools? *Phi Delta Kappan,* 281–284.

Slavin, R. E. (1995). Cooperative learning and intergroup relations. In J. A. Banks & C. A. McGee Banks (Eds.), *Handbook of research on multicultural education* (pp. 628–634). New York: Macmillan.

Sleeter, C. E. (1992). *Keepers of the American dream.* London: Falmer.

Smelser, N. J. (1962). *Theory of collective behavior.* New York: Free Press.

Smith, L. (1994). *Killers of the dream.* New York: W. W. Norton. (Original work published 1949)

Social Science Education Consortium. (2001). *Preparing Citizens Video and Guide.* Boulder, CO: Author.

Soder, R. S. (1996). Teaching the teachers of the people. In R. S. Soder (Ed.), *Democracy, education, and the schools* (pp. 244–274). San Francisco: Jossey-Bass.

Spring, J. (1989). *The sorting machine revisited.* New York: Longman.

Stanley, W. B. (1992). *Curriculum for utopia.* Albany: State University of New York Press.

Stanley, W. B., & Nelson, J. L. (1994). The foundations of social education in historical context. In R. A. Martusewicz & W. M. Reynolds (Eds.), *Inside out: Contemporary critical perspectives in education* (pp. 265–284). New York: St. Martin's Press.

Stanley, W. B., & Whitson, J. A. (1992). Citizenship as practical competence: A response to the new reform movement in social education. *International Journal of Social Education, 7,* 57–66.

Stone, D. (1997). *Policy paradox: The art of political decision making.* New York: W. W. Norton.

Suskind, R. (1998). *A hope in the unseen: An American odyssey from the inner city to the Ivy League.* New York: Broadway Books.

Taba, H., Durkin, M. C., Fraenkel, J. R., & McNaughton, A. H. (1971). *A teacher's handbook to elementary social studies: An inductive approach.* Reading, MA: Addison-Wesley.

Takaki, R. (1993). *A different mirror*. Boston: Little, Brown.

Tapp, J. L., & Kohlberg, L. (1971). Developing senses of law and legal justice. *Journal of Social Issues, 27*, 65–71.

Tarrow, S. (1998). *Power in movement: Social movements and contentious politics*. Cambridge, UK: Cambridge University Press.

Taylor, C. (1994). The politics of recognition. In A. Gutmann (Ed.), *Multiculturalism: Examining the politics of recognition* (pp. 25–73). Princeton, NJ: Princeton University Press.

Taylor, C. (1998). The dynamics of democratic exclusion. *Journal of Democracy, 9*(4), 143–156.

Theobald, P. (1997). *Teaching the commons*. Boulder, CO: Westview.

Thucydides. (1972). *History of the Peloponnesian War* (R. Warner, Trans.). London: Penguin.

Tocqueville, A. de (1969). *Democracy in America* (J. P. Mayer, Ed.; G. Lawrence, Trans.). Garden City, NY: Doubleday. (Original work published 1848)

Torney-Purta, J., Lehmann, R., Oswald, H., & Schulz, W. (2001). *Citizenship and education in twenty-eight countries: Civic knowledge and engagement at age fourteen*. Amsterdam: International Association for the Evaluation of Educational Achievement.

Torney-Purta, J., Schwille, J., & Amadeo, J. (Eds.). (1999). *Civic education across countries: Twenty-four national case studies from the IEA civic education project*. Amsterdam: International Association for the Evaluation of Educational Achievement.

Trend, D. (1995). *The crisis of meaning: Contests of meaning in culture and education*. Minneapolis: University of Minneapolis Press.

Trungpa, C. (1991). *The heart of the Buddha*. Boulder, CO: Shambhala.

Tucker, R. (1969). *The Marxian revolutionary idea*. New York: W. W. Norton.

Valli, L. (1997). Listening to other voices: A description of teacher reflection in the United States. *Peabody Journal of Education, 72*, 67–88.

Verba, S., & Nie, N. H. (1972). *Participation in America: Political democracy and social equality*. New York: Harper & Row.

Vygotsky, L. S. (1978). *Mind in society*. Cambridge, MA: Harvard University Press.

Wade, R. C. (2000). Beyond charity: Service learning for social justice. *Social Studies and the Young Learner, 12*(4), 6–9.

Waller, W. (1932). *The sociology of teaching*. New York: Wiley.

Walzer, M. (1983). *Spheres of justice*. New York: Basic Books.

Walzer, M. (1992a). The civil society argument. In C. Mouffe (Ed.), *Dimensions of radical democracy* (pp. 89–107). London: Verso.

Walzer, M. (1992b). *What it means to be an American*. New York: Marsilio.

Walzer, M. (1997). *On toleration*. New Haven, CT: Yale University Press.

Wertsch, J. V. (1991). *Voices of the mind: A sociocultural approach to mediated action*. Cambridge, MA: Harvard University Press.

West, C. (1993a). The new cultural politics of difference. In C. McCarthy & W. Crichlow (Eds.), *Race, identity, and representation in education* (pp. 11–23). New York: Routledge.

West, C. (1993b). *Race matters*. Boston: Beacon Press.

West, C. (1999). The moral obligations of living in a democratic society. In D. Batstone & E. Mendieta (Eds.), *The good citizen* (pp. 5–12). New York: Routledge.

Wildavsky, A. (1979). *Speaking truth to power: The art and craft of policy analysis*. Boston: Little, Brown.

Williams, M. S. (2000). The uneasy alliance of group representation and deliberative democracy. In W. Kymlicka & W. Norman (Eds.), *Citizenship in diverse societies* (pp. 124–152). Oxford, UK: Oxford University Press.

Wilson, W. J. (1978). *The declining significance of race: Blacks and changing American institutions*. Chicago: University of Chicago Press.

Wineburg, S., & Wilson, S. M. (1988). Models of wisdom in the teaching of history. *Phi Delta Kappan, 70*, 50–58.

Wolff, R. P. (1965). Beyond tolerance. In R. P. Wolff, B. J. Moore, & H. Marcuse (Eds.), *A critique of pure tolerance* (pp. 3–52). Boston: Beacon Press.

Wood, A. (1972–1973). The Marxian critique of justice. *Philosophy and Public Affairs, 1*, 244–282.

Young, I. M. (1990). *Justice and the politics of difference*. Princeton, NJ: Princeton University Press.

Young, I. M. (1997). Difference as a resource for democratic communication. In J. Bohman & W. Rehg (Eds.), *Deliberative democracy: Essays on reason and politics* (pp. 383–406). Cambridge, MA: MIT Press.

Young, A. (2001). Introduction. In C. Carson & K. Shepard (Eds.), *A call to conscience: The landmark speeches of Dr. Martin Luther King, Jr.* (pp. vii–xi). New York: Warner Books.

Young-Bruehl, E. (1996). *The anatomy of prejudices*. Cambridge, MA: Harvard University Press.

Youniss, J., McLellan, J. A., & Yates, M. (1997). What we know about engendering civic identity. *American Behavioral Scientist, 40*, 620–631.

Index

About the Author

Walter C. Parker is Professor of Education and Adjunct Professor of Political Science at the University of Washington, Seattle, where he chairs the Social Studies Education program. His work centers on kindergarten through high school social studies education generally and education for democracy specifically, and has appeared in such journals as *Teachers College Record, American Educational Research Journal, Teaching and Teacher Education*, and *Theory and Research in Social Education*. He is the research editor for the journal *Social Education*. His books include *Education for Democracy: Contexts, Curricula, and Assessments* (Information Age, 2002), *Social Studies in Elementary Education* (Merrill, 2001), *Educating the Democratic Mind* (State University of New York Press, 1996), and *Renewing the Social Studies Curriculum* (Association for Supervision and Curriculum Development, 1991).